∾ Hermanitos Comanchitos ∾

Pasó Por Aquí

Series on the Nuevomexicano Literary Heritage

Edited by
GENARO M. PADILLA,
ERLINDA GONZALES-BERRY,
& A. GABRIEL MELÉNDEZ

Hermanitos Comanchitos

INDO-HISPANO RITUALS of captivity and redemption

ENRIQUE R. Lamadrid

WITH PHOTOGRAPHS BY MIGUEL A. GANDERT

University of New Mexico Press   Albuquerque

Library of Congress Cataloging-in-Publication Data

Lamadrid, Enrique R.
    Hermanitos comanchitos : Indo-Hispano rituals of captivity
and redemption / Enrique R. Lamadrid ; with photographs by
Miguel A. Gandert.— 1st ed.
        p. cm. — (Pasó por aquí)
Includes bibliographical references and index.
    ISBN 0-8263-2877-6 (cloth : alk. paper) — ISBN 0-8263-2878-4
(pbk. : alk. paper)
    1. Comanche Indians—New Mexico—Rites and ceremonies.
2. Comanche Indians—Cultural assimilation—New Mexico.
3. Hispanic Americans—New Mexico—Rites and ceremonies.
4. Hispanic Americans—Cultural assimilation—New Mexico—
Cultural assimilation. 5. Festivals—New Mexico—History.
6. Fasts and feasts—New Mexico—History.   7. Hybridity
(Social sciences)—New Mexico—History.   8. New Mexico—
History—To 1848.   9. New Mexico—History—1848–
10. New Mexico—Social life and customs.   I. Title.   II. Series.
    E99.C85 L35 2003
    305.8'059745720680789—dc22
                        2003018068

Design: Melissa Tandysh

Para Carlota y toda la familia

Contents

Note from the Series Editors

A widely held view among cultural historians working today is that the best predictor of a people's vitality is the ability of the group to transform itself and adapt its cultural forms to prevailing social, economic and political forces. A second truism that holds wide currency among researchers, is that aims to preserve a people's culture as one would specimens in a jar, no matter how well-intentioned the motive, is often ruinous, and nearly always antithetical to the ways cultures choose to represent themselves at any given time in their history and development. It is with these ideas in mind that *Pasó Por Aquí* hails the publication of Enrique Lamadrid's *Hermanitos Comanchitos,* a study mindful of the contexts—historical, political and religious—that continue to shape the multiple tributes *Nuevomexicanos* pay in ritual and performance to their experiences as Indo-Hispanos.

The starting point for this work is the Spanish colonial folk play, *Los comanches,* a matter of special interest to the Pasó *Por Aquí Series* which works to disseminate scholarship and knowledge of the Nuevomexicano Literary Heritage. While Lamadrid's treatment of *Los comanches* as a work of literature is exhaustive, his conclusions are not tedious, rather they point, in provocative ways, to expanded notions of literary discourse. Lamadrid's unique approach is to see this colonial text as present and alive in a set of interrelated cultural practices that can be witnessed in New Mexico today. As he reminds us, "the text leads and can be followed off the page and into the realm of orality and festival behavior (12)". In exploring the ritual complex "Comanche," a set of mimetic tributes to a feared and admired adversary and ally in colonial New Mexico, the reader will readily come away with the sense that she/he is a participant in one of Enrique's now legendary field schools in the towns and villages of northern New Mexico, such are Lamadrid's skills of observation and documentation. By and by the reader will be brought back to the theoretical and descriptive explanations of mestizo discourses, hybrid identities and specific situations of transcultural exchange in the upper Río Grande basin, a major North American "contact zone," variously called throughout its history Comanchería, Apachería or simply, El Norte.

Moving far beyond the simple act of collecting folk material, several elements add to the dynamic presentation of this study. First, is the very novel act of recovering the *Los comanches* drama as both text and performance, a process informed by years of fieldwork, musical transcriptions, the superb photography of Miguel Gandert and by the field recordings found in the accompanying "Hermanitos Comanchitos" CD. And so it is with pleasure that we invite readers to take in, "off the page," the sights and sounds of this dance of intercultural exchange that Lamadrid describes so passionately. *Hermanitos Comanchitos'* array of war harangues, laments, lullabies, captivity tales and ballads provides a full measure of the awe, fascination and trepidation that "Comanche" inspired and continues to inspire in the upper Río Grande. Yes, we believe that New Mexico, indeed the nation, is ready to understand the complex cultural diversity of its peoples.

For the Series Editors
Gabriel Meléndez
Albuquerque, New Mexico, Summer 2003

List of Illustrations

Preface

The cultural work to identify, define, and represent the mestizo cultures of New Mexico is fraught with intellectual challenges and institutional hazards. Since categories of racial and cultural hybridity in the United States have no legal status beyond basic citizenship and little social prestige, they are generally avoided if possible. Before acknowledging allies, benefactors, and colleagues in this work, some clarification is necessary.

For half of Mexico to become a region of the United States, it had to be naturalized, its history obscured, its people subordinated. From the first decades of American commerce after independence from Spain in 1821, a cultural dichotomy was hewn between Indians and Hispanos to construct a persistent new paradigm of Indianism (idealization of Indian culture) and Hispanophobia (denigration of Hispano culture) that has lasted to the present day. This operation effectively compromised an Indo-Hispano political, social, and economic alliance that evolved in the era between the great Pueblo Revolt of 1680 and the American Occupation of 1846.

The wedge was set early by Anglo-American traders, soldiers, and travelers on the Santa Fe Trail, who expressed admiration for the exotic Pueblos and unmitigated disdain for the *Nuevo Mexicanos*. Of all the imagined character flaws of the *Mexicanos,* miscegenation was, and still is, the most primal and most indelible. In an often-quoted passage, George Brewerton, a longtime associate of Kit Carson, captured the American conception of *mestizaje* when he wrote that the mixed bloods of New Mexico possess "the cunning and deceit of the Indian, the politeness and the spirit of revenge of the Spaniard, and the imaginative temperament and fiery impulses of the Moor" (quoted in Pettit 1980:11). *Mestizos,* or mixed bloods, are despised precisely because they bridge the gap between Indian and Spanish.

The military annexation of New Mexico was consolidated practically overnight, but its psychological annexation to the American imagination is still in progress. As the land was resurveyed to map the new American ownership, so the indigenous peoples' cultures were confined within the parameters of a new social order. American novels, historical treatises, ethnic humor, movies, fine art, and photography are not merely entertainments constructed around Indian and Mexican cultural others. Rather, they are components in a massive process that shifted the axis of cultural orientation and representation a full ninety degrees: "*El Norte*" was fast becoming "the Great Southwest."

To the south, the Mexican Revolution and its aftermath created a cultural agenda that honored the hybrid cultures of Mesoamerica and its peoples. In the northlands, the deeper mestizo story of "*Nuevo México Profundo*" would have to wait until the late twentieth century to be told and represented (Gandert and Lamadrid 2000).

For a quixotic few, concerned with caste and the *castizo* privilege of pallor, the cultural history of New Mexico is exemplified by the image of imperial Spain. In multiethnic Iberia, the prolonged wars of Reconquest had spawned notions of *limpieza de sangre* (blood purity) which racialized Christianity through bloodline and complexion. Across the Americas, the pale *castizos,* with the most honorable and unsullied names and lineages, were put forward in royal petitions for grants of land. Place names and family names became a bulwark of cultural pride in New Mexico. But by the end of the seventeenth century, castizo aspirations were immersed in the hybrid, mestizo realities of life and society in New Spain and Mexico. Even the leaders of the new colony were already calling themselves *españoles mexicanos,* "Spanish Mexicans," already becoming indigenous to the region.

Conflict has indeed preserved cultural differences, but it has also created a deep and complex mestizo tradition that serves as a fascinating register of cultural and historical relations. In *Nuevo México,* Indo-Hispano identity is not the result of reflection or contemplation. It is vigorously enacted in ritual settings, not for the tourist gaze (for there are virtually no tourists at these celebrations), but rather to celebrate the historic survival of a community and its *querencia,* or deeply rooted sense of place.

My indefatigable partner in this fieldwork is Miguel Gandert, who has generously taught me to see through his lens. Through his images, Indo-Hispano culture has quite a bit to say about itself. Besides photography, the other key cultural documentation of this tradition is music. Everything I know about field recording is due to the generosity of Jack Loeffler, who has retuned my ear to understand, contextualize, and capture these hybrid sounds. His Peregrine Sound Archive not only mastered the "Hermanitos Comanchitos" CD, but contributed five pieces to the mix and began the process of musical transcriptions.

In terms of ideas, my thinking has developed in dialogue with colleagues and *camaradas,* including Erlinda Gonzales-Berry, Gabriel Meléndez, Charles Briggs,

Brenda Romero, Peter García, Sylvia Rodríguez, Tom Kavanagh, Joseph Sánchez, Bernardo Gallegos, Ramón Gutiérrez, Michael A. Thomas, Thomas Steele S.J., Diana Rebolledo, Tomás Atencio, Tobías Durán, Felipe Gonzales, Ted Jojola, Francisco Lomelí, E. A. Mares, Jerry Gurulé, the late Alfonso Ortiz, Genaro Padilla, Arturo Madrid, Donald Cutter, María Williams, Steve Loza, and Ed Wapp. Hopefully, each will find a bit of themselves herein, a first installment on a debt of intellectual gratitude.

Besides the Domínguez and Chávez families of Taos, I received my earliest guidance and encouragement for this project from Donald Cutter and the late John D. Robb, whose Archive has contributed an early recording to the CD. Another accolade is due my collaborators in the other great forum for public education, the museum, including Olivia Cadaval, Helen Lucero, Thomas Chávez, Jim Moore, MariLynn Salvador, Reeve Love, Tey Marianna Nunn, and Cynthia Vidaurri. Special thanks to student fieldworkers, including Maya Gonzales Berry, Félix Torres, Bárbara Gonzales, Heidi McKinnon, Molly Timko, Ivan Valerio, Jr., Deidre Maestas, and most significantly, David F. García, who provided the majority of the musical transcriptions. His violin and devotion to *la cultura* are the link to a new generation.

The primary facilitators and generous supporters of this work include the Smithsonian Center for Folklife and Cultural Heritage (Rockefeller Humanities Fellowship), UNM's Center for Regional Studies (Research Grant), and the Recovering the U.S. Literary Heritage Project (Research Grant), the John D. Robb Musical Trust (CD production grant), and UNM's Arts of the Americas Institute (musical transcriptions). UNM's Southwest Hispanic Research Institute and my own Department of Spanish and Portuguese have always been the forum in which my work reaches colleagues and students. The UNM Colleges of Arts and Science and Fine Arts and former deans Michael Fischer and Tom Dodson have also done their part in supporting and promoting this work and UNM's 1998 Cuartocentenario Festival. Thanks also to the dedicated and resourceful staff at UNM's Center for Southwest Research in Zimmerman Library, as well as to the helpful archivists of the Photo Archives of the Museum of New Mexico, the Taos Historic Museums, and the Spanish Colonial Research Center, National Parks Service. For their patience and forbearance, the editorial and design team at UNM Press deserves special recognition including David Holtby, Evelyn Schlatter, Melissa Tandysh, and David Margolin.

This book was written quite literally "from the margins" at La Orilla ("the other shore"), the Washington, D.C., cultural center, sanctuary, and refuge of Olivia Cadaval and David Bosserman, who created the space in which it was accomplished, and the daily dialog that sustains it.

My gracious collaborators in the community, from whom I have learned so much, include community scholars, cultural activists, and many more (north to south): Larry Torres (Taos); the late Nestor Gonzales and his son Francisco "El Comanche" and extended family (Ranchos de Taos); the late Luis Girón (Ranchos de Taos); Jerry Padilla (Taos); Noberto Ledoux (Ranchos de Taos); Ivan Valerio

(Talpa); Cipriano Vigil (El Rito); the late Juan and Leo Sánchez, Galento Martínez, and the late Dr. Roberto Villalpando (Alcalde); Andy García (San Juan); Liz and Tomás Sánchez (Española); Josie and Percy Luján (Chimayó); Michael Vigil (Tesuque); Charlie Carrillo and Felipe Mirabal (Santa Fe); Arnold Herrera (Cochití); Harold Littlebird (Laguna/Santo Domingo); Charles Aguilar (Bernalillo); Eduardo Chávez and his late wife Priscilla (Los Ranchos de Albuquerque); Rose García (Alameda); Maclovia Zamora (Albuquerque); María Baca (Albuquerque); Ray Pérez (San José); Dorela and Roberto Perea (San Antonito); Abe Peña and Margaret Johnson (Grants); Herman Bustamante (Gallup); Pablita Chávez Bent (Atarque); Rafaelita Salazar Baca, Eufemia Salazar Trujillo, Vangie Salazar Armijo, and Ida Salazar Segura (San Mateo); and Alfonso R. Sánchez (Las Cruces). I especially honor the memories of Priscilla Chávez, Dr. Villalpando, Nelson Gonzales, and two of the finest horsemen of the Española Valley, Juan and Leo Sánchez.

This project was quite literally assigned to me by my New Mexican family, the Domínguezes of Chamisal and Taos and the Chávezes of Ranchos de Taos. The legacy of cultural pride of Fermilia "Phil" Domínguez Wood, Dr. José Amado Domínguez, and Anita and Bernabé Chávez are remembered and honored here. Thanks to Anita Clark Domínguez for her guidance and her daughter, Carlota. Thanks to Barbara McPherson for her encouragement and support, as well as to John and Charisse DeFlice and Carmela Domínguez. This work is dedicated especially to the education of a new generation of Nuevo Mexicanos—Carlos, Gianna, Armando, Mario, Dominic, and Yasmín, and all their primos, *coyotitos todos.*

Dispensen lo mal trovado.
ya está seca mi garganta.
será que no he tomado
de esa agüita que ataranta. c/s

La Orilla, Washington, D.C.
Los Gallegos, New Mexico

Prologue

festival, *familia*, and intercultural relations

Nuevo México querido,
no hagas caso al mitote,
entre indios y americanos
toditos semos coyotes.

New Mexico beloved,
pay no attention to rumor,
among Indians and Americans
we are all coyotes [mixed bloods].

—*Verso popular, San Antonio del Embudo, N.Mex.*

Village and urban festivals are part of living and coming of age in New Mexico, from the multitudinous State Fair and Santa Fe Fiestas, to the small-town rodeos and cook-offs, sports events, and the *Funciones,* or patron saint's day feasts, in *Hispano* and *Mexicano*[1] barrios, towns, and Indian pueblos.[2] At a fiesta, in celebration mode, a community and its contradictions are on full display. Culture and identity are enacted and negotiated in the plaza, both formally and informally (Grimes 1992, Rodríguez 1994). The ritual music, drama, and dance to be seen on the plaza are deeply invested with meaning (Turner 1974).

In Native communities, the remarkable sights and sounds of Pueblo Corn, Buffalo, Deer, and Eagle dances animate a millennial spirit and primordial sense of place (Sweet 1983, 1985, 1999). The symbolism of conquest, resistance, and reconciliation is registered in the graceful arabesques of the Matachines dancers.

These enigmatic maneuvers between cultures are performed in both Hispano and Pueblo communities across the region. Each local performance tradition generates meanings specific to its community and articulates both Indo-Hispano identity and intercultural relations (Rodríguez 1996, Sklar 2001).

A lesser-known but equally widespread Indo-Hispano celebration honors another historical confrontation that profoundly affected all of New Mexico— the encounter with the Comanche, or Numunuh, culture of the southern Plains (Lamadrid 1992a, 1992b).

CHAPTER ONE

2

1.1.   (opposite, top) La Luz de Malinche (Bernalillo). Like the Virgin Mary, la Malinche represents goodness and purity. She portrays the first Christian convert and is considered the daughter or bride of Moctezuma, the monarch.

1.2.   (opposite, bottom) La Sombra del Toro (San Luis). Totem of Spain and symbol of the darker forces, the bull stalks Malinche and the Monarca (or Moctezuma). The bull's death and castration by the abuelos is especially significant.

1.3.   (above) La Reverencia (San Luis). The Bernalillo Matachines pay reverence to San Luis Gonzaga on his feast day in San Luis, New Mexico. Their patron saint is San Lorenzo, the first Spanish-born saint.

Before the burgeoning popularity of powwows, and with the exception of their yearly visits to Taos Pueblo, the only glimpse of those many-feathered "other Indians" from across the mountains was at Pueblo "Comanche" dances; but everyone knew they were just local people "dressing up." The sheer spectacle of the colorful costumes and spirited dancing was exotic and exciting anyway. Much more than a victory celebration, the dances emulate and share in the spirit of another people. Cross-cultural mimesis enacted in the ritual arenas of Indo-Hispano cultures has a resonance and complexity far beyond what Philip Deloria has disparaged as "playing Indian" (Deloria 1998). What is negotiated on the feast day plazas of New Mexico is not New Age cultural appropriation but a much more ancient dialogue across cultures about history, heritage, and identity. But just who were all these "Comanches," and why were so many traditional communities celebrating them?

There are few ready-made answers in scholarship for questions of identity and cultural relations. However, much can be learned directly from family, friends, and neighbors. Although different ethnic groups observe their social boundaries, both self-drawn and ascribed (Barth 1969, Spicer 1972:54–64), a tradition of reciprocal visitation during festivals existed well before cultural tourism came into play in New Mexico. Cross-cultural hospitality and neighborly curiosity accommodate a process of personal discovery that becomes the basis of more formal scholarly and ethnographic inquiry. As a bilingual New Mexico-born Latino from an intercultural, urban, middle-class background and Chicano education, my "coyote" (Hispanic/Anglo) status gives me insight into and a natural attraction for the dilemmas of identity, mestizaje, hybridity, cultural liminality, and the rites, attractions, and dangers of crossing cultural

1.4. Comanches de San Ildefonso (San Ildefonso Pueblo). Tewa "Comanches" dance at the San Ildefonso Pueblo feast on January 23. Winter is the season for enemy and animal dances. Photo courtesy of author.

boundaries. As a literary folklorist, my approach to discourse and inscription draws equally from cultural and literary theory and ethnography. Some of my best opportunities and insights have come about *de chiripada,* that is to say by serendipity, coincidence, and good fortune.

Until the spring of 1973, when my wife Carlota Domínguez's aunt Fermilia "tía Phil" Domínguez Wood rearranged her office at the New Mexico State Records and Archives Center, I had never heard of Hispano "Comanches." Knowing of my penchant for poetry, she gave me the photocopy of a well-worn manuscript dated 1863 and signed J. J. Vigil, with various sections of verse titled "Cuerno Verde," "Don Carlos Fernández," "Cabeza Negra," and "Don José de la Peña." Although it lacked stage directions, I immediately recognized it as some sort of dramatic poem. The first verses caught my eye:

Del Oriente al Poniente	*From East to West*
del Sur al Norte frío,	*from South to frozen North,*
suenen brillantes clarines	*let brilliant trumpets sound*
y brille el acero mío.	*and my steel shine.*

My recovery project began at this instant.[3] As a student of Hispanic literature, I was reminded of the heroic boasts of El Cid Campeador and his enemies, but Cuerno Verde was obviously an Indian, specifically a Comanche. The Native American invocation to the four directions is not associated with Iberian heroes. But the blaring trumpets and shining steel certainly are. As in the classic epics and martial chronicles, from Homer to Julius Caesar and Thucydides, the indigenous adversary is portrayed in the most noble of terms possible, to enhance the warrior status of his antagonist. In his *arengas,* or harangues, Cuerno Verde speaks with as much rhetorical virtuosity as the Spanish soldiers who oppose him. His mastery of the Spanish language is complete, and his ambitions as a leader of his nation are every bit as lofty and ambitious as those of the captains and governors who oppose him. As I would later learn, the title of the drama was *Los comanches,* only one of numerous and diverse Hispano Comanche celebrations of the same name across northern New Mexico.

The only reference point in the Americas that I could recall was *La Araucana,* the great epic poem of the conquest of Chile by Alonso de Ercilla (1590). The life-and-death struggle of the indomitable and undefeated Araucanian Indians was punctuated by the stirring speeches of Lautaro and Caupolicán, indigenous heroes still revered in Latin America for their heroic resistance to the Spanish Crown and its armies. Since Ercilla had already been assigned a foundational place in the Latin American literary canon, there was little chance in the 1970s of studying texts as remotely regional as New Mexico's own Renaissance epic *Historia de la conquista de la Nueva México,* by Gaspar Pérez de Villagrá (1610), let alone anything as anonymously folkloric as *Los comanches.* But what the New Mexican poem may have lacked in literary stature was well compensated for in raw poetic power. I was determined to delve into this conundrum, no matter how long it took. By the time I discovered that my J. J. Vigil manuscript was the same one on which Aurelio M. Espinosa had based his "critical edition" of 1907, I had found quite a different version of it alive and well in the community.

In the meantime my most immediate answers would be forthcoming from history. Professor Donald Cutter directed me to Alfred Barnaby Thomas's *Forgotten Frontiers,* where to my surprise a quick check of the index turned up most of the characters as actual people of the late eighteenth century. It became clear that the battles of this dramatic poem had taken place in the plains and mountains of New Mexico. The trail was warmer than I thought.

At the next Domínguez family gathering, tía Phil asked me if I had made any progress toward publishing the poem. By then the topic of Comanches emerged, and I was astonished to find that both my father-in-law and my wife's uncle could not only recite Cuerno Verde's invocation, they had memories of seeing the play itself! Dr. José Amado Domínguez remembered the battles of Indians and Spanish soldiers on foot in the village plaza of Chamisal (Domínguez 1988).Bernabé Chávez remembered full-scale equestrian productions with as many as twenty mounted actors thundering around the fields of Ranchos de Taos (B. Chávez 1988). In this village there would be much more to see in coming years.

For the moment I was pleased I had recovered eyewitness accounts of actual productions of this two-hundred-year-old folk drama, which I had assumed was an artifact from another time. My next discovery emerged from my 1980 appointment to Northern New Mexico Community College in Española to teach Spanish. In my very first class, a Los Alamos fire fighter named José Márquez turned in a cultural report describing his participation in productions of *Los comanches* staged in Alcalde by a retired educator, Dr. Roberto Vialpando, and a group of the finest horsemen in the Española Valley. That year I met them on their December 27 feast day, on the plaza of Alcalde's new church, by the Taos highway. My colleague from the college, Liz Sánchez, introduced me to her husband Tomás and his brothers Leo and Juan. With astonishing energy, and terrifying black-and-white face paint, Tony "Galento" Martínez played Cuerno Verde that year, frightening children and adults alike with his threats and the charges and feints of his war pony.

As I would learn, the ambivalent and multilayered conversations of conquerors and conquered within the frame of ritual folk drama were taking place not only in New Mexico but also in every corner of Latin America. The texts I was studying quite literally ran off the page into the context of the larger social and cultural discourse of conquest and resistance, whose reverberations are felt as strongly today as they were in colonial times.

The next facet of Hispano Comanche culture also came to my attention through family connections. When my mother-in-law Anita Clark Domínguez learned of my interest in Comanches, she told me about several students of hers

1.5. Amenaza de Cuerno Verde (Alcalde). Played by Juan Sánchez, the feared Cuerno Verde was as well known for his boasts as for his distinctive green buffalo-horn headdress.

from the Gonzales clan of Ranchos de Taos who talked about their "Comanche dances" in class projects and presentations. I had seen these children in the annual Taos Fiesta parade, but assumed that they were generic powwow dancers who were there to add a bit of color to the image and campaigns of their father, local politician Francisco "el Comanche" Gonzales. After accepting the hospitality of this community at their feast of the Manueles on New Year's Day, I appreciated the dancing and singing in their full context.

Many communities in greater Mexico observe New Year's by recognizing those people named Manuel or Manuela, after its patron saint, Emmanuel, the name the Old Testament prophets used for the coming Christ. People gather in procession to the homes of these namesakes in the community to honor them with feasting and song. In Ranchos de Taos, the Manueles are celebrated "Comanche style," with songs that have been passed down through generations of elders. Although mostly composed of vocables or syllable singing, the Spanish lyrics of some of the songs astounded me. They referred to episodes of warfare and captivity in the eighteenth century. Fresh from my readings in the colonial history of New Mexico, I immediately recognized the political context of these lyrics:

The Apache and the Comanche
made a date for battle,
the Apache doesn't give up and
the Comanche bears down harder.
                    —*"Coplas comanches," Talpa, N.Mex.*

The Jicarilla Apaches of the northern mountains and plains of New Mexico were a peaceful people whose settlements were plundered and decimated by Comanche bands coming west off the Plains. After particularly fierce attacks in 1723 and 1724, in which two-thirds of their women and children were carried off into captivity, their leaders, including Chief Carlana, went in mourning to Santa Fe to plead with the governor to grant them military protection (Noyes 1993:20).

Aspects of the Ranchos de Taos celebrations resembled powwows in costume and choreography, but the historical memory in the songs was quite profound. Once more, in interviews the Hispano Comanches of Ranchos de Taos fully identified themselves with what they defined as *"nuestra cultura comanche"* (our Comanche culture). With no formal tribal affiliation, they also identified as Hispano and even Chicano, since Francisco Gonzales was one of the student

1.6.   El Comanche y su Tombé (Talpa). With the passing of his father, Nelson, Francisco Gonzales is the elder singer of the Gonzales clan of Talpa. The signature of Senator Ted Kennedy is on the drum.

leaders of the Chicano movement at the campus of Highlands University in Las Vegas, New Mexico. They trace their roots to "Comanche captives who were raised in the Ranchos de Taos community and the Hispano captives who grew up Comanche" (F. Gonzales 1992).

What immediately impressed me was the range of identity formations and the cross-cultural mimesis of the Comanche celebrations. Pueblo dancers dance and sing "like Comanches" in order to emulate and honor, but they never waiver in their identities as Pueblos. The Hispano actor with the role of Chief Cuerno Verde is convincing on the mock battlefield, but never ceases to be himself, despite his studied demeanor and impressive headdress. In contrast, the Ranchos de Taos dancers "are Comanches" even though they are also "Hispanos and Chicanos." The complexity and ambivalence of Comanche celebrations is perplexing. Why would so many people choose Comanches to emulate and mimic, rather than other regional groups such as Utes, Apaches, or Navajos?

When this inquiry began, postcolonial and cultural theory had not yet developed. Revisionist approaches to history and literary studies were in their infancy. There was theoretical writing on mestizaje, part of the cultural legacy of the Mexican Revolution, but it had not been applied to anything from New Mexico yet. With the notable exceptions of Edward Dozier, Edward Spicer, and Alfonso Ortiz, studies of Natives and Hispanos were being written in such essentialist terms that Spanish influence on Pueblo culture was considered as a kind of European contamination. Likewise, the Iberian legacy was discussed and valorized in purist terms. In their writings about warfare in colonial New Mexico, historians mentioned captives and slaves in passing, sympathizing with their plight without reflecting very deeply on their cultural transformations. Folklorists were interested in New Mexico as a kind of Spain on the banks of the Río Grande and tended to avoid mestizo topics. The entire world of mestizo social and cultural reality had been successfully erased from the public mind (M. García 1989). It was not acknowledged or represented anywhere beyond the traditional communities that celebrated it. Painters would not paint it, writers were silent, and photographers averted their gaze.

Now, in the postmodern age of the incipient twenty-first century, the realities of globalization make it clear that cultural hybridity in the future will be the rule rather than the exception. Cultural theory has opened a way to understand it, as well as performance and identity formation. Revisionist history enables a reconfiguration of the historical subjects and a deeper understanding of ethnogenesis, the emergence and configuration of new cultural groups. Postcolonial theory reveals the agency and resistance of subjugated peoples. And finally, ethnodocumentary photography, in the hands of Miguel Gandert, is finally turning a lens to illuminate the complex cultures that have been here all along (Gandert and Lamadrid 2000). New Mexico may finally be ready to understand the complex cultural diversity of her peoples.

2

Allí Vienen los Comanches

DANCING WITH THE ENEMY

Ay, nanita, allí vienen los cumanchis
Oh, Granma, here come the Comanches
—refrain from an Indita ballad (A. Espinosa 1907)

Nʉmʉnʉ kima
Here come the Comanches
—Comanche words in a Tewa Comanche song (Wapp 1998)

The waxing of the first autumn moon, New Mexico's "Comanche Moon," lights the beginning of a unique cycle of traditional feasts that unites the entire region in carnivalesque celebration of cultural otherness. The harvest was traditionally a peak time for visitors from the Great Plains, who came west with horses laden with goods, anxious to trade and celebrate the bounty of the season.

From the San Gerónimo Fiesta at Taos Pueblo on September 30 until Lent, Hispanos and Pueblo Indians dressed and singing as "Comanches" may be found somewhere along the Río Grande del Norte at every major feast, including Christmas and New Year's. Hispano and Pueblo communities alike come alive with colorful processions, heroic historical drama, religious morality plays, and boisterous ceremonial dancing (Hurt 1966; Campa 1941, 1979; Cavallo-Bosso 1956; Frisbie 1980; King 1979; Lamadrid 1992a, 1922b; Martínez 2001; Sweet 1985, 1999); all in mixed defiance and emulation of a much-admired former foe from the southern Plains—those Yamparicas, Jupes, and Kotsotecas known collectively to themselves as Numunuh, the People, and to their enemies and friends as los comanches.[1]

Comanche is a Spanish phonological adaptation of *komantcia,* a term the Utes used disparagingly against their enemies, who included not only the Numunuh, but also the Kiowas, Arapahos, and Cheyennes. Its approximate meaning is "someone who wants to fight me all the time," and was applied specifically to the Numunuh by the mid-eighteenth century (Wallace and Hoebel 1952). Likewise, the Spanish term also includes a range of meanings including and beyond the already broad cultural category of Numunuh, as will be seen in the usage of Hispano-Comanche groups all across northern New Mexico.

By the mid-eighteenth century, maps of the region designated the huge areas north and east of the Río Grande as "La Gran Comanchería," while "La Gran Apachería" was west and south. In these "contact zones," as Mary Louise Pratt has called them, the colonial encounter was marked by "conditions of coercion, radical inequality, and intractable conflict" (Pratt 1992:6). Along such an interface, the adaptations of language and culture "are commonly regarded as chaotic,

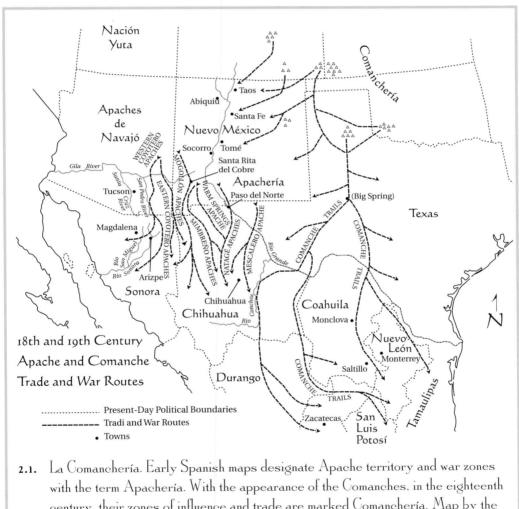

2.1. La Comanchería. Early Spanish maps designate Apache territory and war zones with the term Apachería. With the appearance of the Comanches, in the eighteenth century, their zones of influence and trade are marked Comanchería. Map by the University of New Mexico Press.

barbarous, lacking in structure," as are the societies that produce them. John G. Bourke, early folklorist and U.S. Army captain who came to New Mexico in 1869, was dismayed by the "Indian problem" in the territory. He saw the Río Grande as a kind of "Congo" of the Southwest and likened the Comanches and Apaches to the "wild tribes of Central Africa [that] kept the forces of civilization at bay" (Bourke 1894:591). After getting assigned to south Texas during a period of border unrest, he included the mestizo Mexicanos in this negative assessment of barbarism vs. civilization. But hybridity and transculturation, the cultural processes of the contact zone, are dynamic, complex, and compelling. People struggling with each other are profoundly and mutually transformed.

Exuberant and ambiguous, the cross-cultural image of the Comanches is unified under a sign of anarchic individualism, the explanation for legendary prowess as formidable warriors and prodigious traders. In the Indo-Hispano imagination, this compelling image of Comanches has animated a process of subjectification and transculturation that in New Mexico folk traditions encompasses all points on the scale from cultural self to Other. In some communities, performances are "about Comanches," with considerable subjective distancing; in others, performers "are Comanches," in ever-increasing degrees. This regional tradition of cross-cultural mimesis symbolically and metaphorically articulates Indo-Hispano cultural relations from three perspectives: Pueblo, Hispano, and "Comanche." A fourth perspective that interacts mimetically with all three is the Anglo-American, especially after the Spanish-American War (Márez 2002). An entire century earlier, well before the 1846 Mexican-American War, a typology of relations between cultural Others had already emerged in song, oral narrative, dance, and literature.[2]

☙ Mestizo Discourses: Hybridity and Transculturation

Because Comanche celebrations include ritual performance and cultural symbols, as well as literary text, a wide and eclectic frame of reference is necessary. In a performance tradition, texts as well as rituals evolve and change in relation to historical and social contexts (Bauman 1986). Since the point of entry of this study is a Spanish colonial folk play, the major point of critical departure is the replacement of privileged Eurocentric practices of writing and "literature" with an expanded notion of "discourse." The dominion of the word is thus opened to many previously unheard voices, engaging and contesting themselves in the "dialogized heteroglossia" that Mikhail Bakhtin has taught us to listen for (Bakhtin 1981, 1984). The conversation of symbols and choreography is also a dialogue that can be seen as well as heard from this perspective (Kapferer 1986).

Rolena Adorno initiates a new critical paradigm that pushes the focus beyond literary history "to the model of discourse in the colonial context as a study of synchronic, dialogic, relational, and interactive cultural practices" (1988:11). In this approach, the text leads and can be followed right off the page into the realm of orality and festival behavior and on into the culture and society that engendered and inscribed it. The Comanche texts I will consider here are highly embedded in ritual practice and a strong collective sense of history in the Indo-Hispano community.

Another useful literary model based on Latin American ethnic and mestizo writing was developed by Uruguayan critic Angel Rama (1982) and refined by the Peruvian Antonio Cornejo Polar, who proposes a critical typology of "heterogeneous, hybrid, transcultural, and diglossic" literatures of cultural otherness. The three nuclei of his analysis are discourse, subject, and representation (Cornejo Polar 1994:17). He traces the roots of mestizo discourse to the first and most rapacious era of the Spanish conquest, whose cultural program:

> [D]estroyed the subject and perverted all its relations (with the self, with peers, with the new lords, with the world, with the gods, with destiny, and with desire) which configured it. In more than one sense, the colonial condition consists precisely of negating the colonized an identity as a subject, in destroying all the links that conferred that identity and imposing others to disturb and disarticulate it, with special crudity at the moment of the conquest. (1994:19; my translation)

The most basic goal of mestizo texts, both written and recited, is thereby the reconstruction, reinscription, and reenactment of a new and self-defined subject. The dance of intercultural relations in enmity as well as amity is an intimate affair, complicated by violence, desire, and mimesis, as the complex Comanche traditions will reveal.

Since Indo-Hispano culture is hybrid by nature and design, an assessment of hybridity theory will help locate the particular cultural synthesis that most characterizes it. It is no longer enough to use the terms mestizo and mestizaje without careful definition, since in postrevolutionary Mexico they have designated both progressive and repressive public policies. Even though Mexico officially aggrandizes its indigenous heritage, in the name of the mestizo majority and its national interests, surviving native cultures are obscured and excoriated (Bartra 1993). Cultural difference is officially celebrated but actually treated as counter to the interests of the nation.

Much more precise than the sometimes indeterminate terms of mestizaje are Bakhtin's definitions of linguistic hybridization and how they apply to the realm of culture. He distinguishes unconscious, "organic" hybridity from conscious, or "intentional," hybridity (1981:358). Organic hybridity is a feature of the historical evolution of all languages and cultures. Despite the illusion of boundedness, cultures evolve historically through unreflective borrowings, mimetic appropriations, exchanges, and inventions. There is no culture in and of itself, because all cultures result from the synthesis of cross-fertilization. Since it is unconscious, organic hybridization does not disrupt the sense of order or continuity; new words, images, and objects are integrated into language or culture subliminally. Yet despite the fact, he says, that "organic hybrids remain mute and opaque, such unconscious hybrids . . . are pregnant with potential for new world views" (1981:360).

Organic hybridity creates the historical and psychological foundations on which intentional or aesthetic hybrids build to shock, change, and challenge. Deliberate mixing and crossing of cultural categories revitalizes or disrupts through crafted fusions of distinct social languages and images. Intentional hybrids create an iconic double consciousness, a "collision between differing points of views on the world" (Bakhtin 1981:360). Culturally mimetic traditions such as *Los comanches* conduct conversations across cultures in choreography and music. In Indo-Hispano songs, Spanish verses alternate with the syllabic chant of vocable choruses. Pueblo songs often include Numunuh words, even though the singers may not know what they mean. Hispanos and Pueblo Indians dress, sing, and dance as or about "Comanches," creating a dialogue that questions history as it challenges and affirms identity.

Since so many of the Comanche performances and celebrations are "off the page" of the text, in the allusive realm of ritual and symbol, some additional ethnographic framing is necessary to understand what is going on in the processions and plazas. Renato Rosaldo notes that in such spaces, which he calls "multiple border zones," previous notions of "homogenous community" are displaced. The "unified subjects" who once resided securely within their cultural boundaries and groups acquire "a multiple personal identity." (1989:16). Individuals belong to various communities whose borders cross and mix, confounding the dividing lines of group and culture.

After hybridity, transculturation is the other most emphatic cultural force in "La Gran Comanchería," especially as experienced by captives. The term was introduced by the sociologist Fernando Ortiz (1978), in his endeavor to recast the concept of Afro-Cuban culture and to replace the ethnocentric paradigm of acculturation and deculturation. As the most crucial personal experience of Hispano-Comanche relations, captivity is distinguished by the process of imposed transculturation. Captives are represented and remembered in all Comanche celebrations.

Intercultural conversations are inscribed in Comanche texts, but since they are also overheard on the plaza, basic ethnographic methodology is also necessary to pursue this inquiry. What the celebrations mean to the performers, and what they reveal about them, is only knowable within the context of each community, based on direct observation, conversation with participants, and analysis of how indigenous symbols operate. "Thick description," as defined in practice by Clifford Geertz (1973:9) is the objective of fieldwork and the most assured entry into the conversation.

✎ Pueblo and Spanish Rituals of Alterity and Integration: Enemy Dances and *Moros y Cristianos*

Before considering the models of alterity practiced in Iberian cultures, it is useful to explore the epistemological strategies of the indigenous peoples of the Upper Río

Grande who encountered the Spanish Mexicans and the Numunuh in New Mexico and how they perceived and construed their enemies and cultural Others.

In his survey of the mixed cultural landscapes of Mesoamerica, Edward Spicer (1962) proposes a typology of cultural assimilation and resistance in Mesoamerica. In areas such as central Mexico, which suffered the full impact of the Spanish imperial project, a forced assimilation drove indigenous people into a kind of cultural anomie, an in-between space, an apathetic no-man's-land of the spirit that earned the Nahuatl name of *nepantla.* In the northlands farther removed from the seats of power, a process of cultural "fusion" occurred, under the tutelage of Jesuits who supervised the grafting of the Christian story of sacrifice and redemption onto the theology of Cahitan groups and rituals such as the Yaqui Deer dance (Spicer 1954).

In his survey of acculturation patterns in the "greater Southwest," Spicer also defines patterns of "reorientation" among Athabascans (Apaches and Navajos). Like groups in central Mexico, the Piros, or Southern Pueblos, experienced "complete assimilation," while the Hopis, the westernmost Pueblo group, achieved "complete rejection" of Spanish culture and religion. The defining circumstance for the Eastern Pueblos of the upper Río Grande valley was historical: the great Pueblo Revolt of 1680 and its enduring cultural legacy. After the Reconquest of 1693 and the return of the Spanish-Mexican colonists, a new cultural militancy was born that took on a deceptively compliant face. The Pueblos nominally accepted Christian practices without compromising their native beliefs, keeping each insulated from the other in separate "compartments" (Spicer 1954).

Spicer (1954:663–78) and Edward Dozier (1961) speak directly to the unique case of New Mexico in their discussion of this "compartmentalization." Pueblos performed Spanish traditions and practices alongside and separate from their own, without replacing or compromising them. In her documentation of Tewa dance, Jill Sweet (1985) discusses the example of the separation of Catholic practice and kiva ritual. After the Pueblo Revolt of 1680 and the relaxation of restrictive Spanish policies toward native religion,

> [T]he Tewas began more freely to combine, recombine, and juxtapose the foreign with the native. Yet they continued to practice a cognitive form of compartmentalization by remaining aware of the origins of most borrowed elements. They are masters at discriminately selecting foreign objects and practices and interlacing them with existing Tewa traditions, all the while maintaining a clear distinction between what came from "us" and what came from "them." (1985:77)

The only exception to this cultural blending is expressed in the Matachines and Horse dances (Ellis 1954:678).

Aspects of the compartmentalization strategy may also be seen in relation to other Native cultures, both hostile and friendly. In Puebloan ceremonial cycles, intercultural relations are dramatized in ritual dances that mimic the customs, dress, and music of other cultural groups, now in defiance or victory, now

2.2. (opposite) Comanchito de los Tewas (Albuquerque). Male San Juan Pueblo Comanche dancers use typical Plains costumes. Female dancers use more traditional Tewa dress.

2.3. (above) Comanchito de Talpa (Ranchos de Taos). Hispano Comanche dancers also use typical Plains costumes, featuring arrangements of turkey and chicken feathers.

in emulation, now in satire. These so-called "enemy dances" are performed along with "animal dances" most frequently during winter, the dormant season for agricultural activities and rituals.[3] Summer Buffalo and Comanche dances may be seen in some pueblos, but the agricultural dances predominate as crops grow. Whereas summer "Corn dances" are considered sacred, the animal and enemy dances are more social in character, although they may have sacred aspects.

Pueblo (Tewa) anthropologists such as Edward Dozier and Alfonso Ortiz were careful to point out that Pueblo "Comanche" dances are not "Plains" dances at all, but an integrated aspect of Pueblo ceremonial culture, perhaps another cultural compartment in which otherness is enacted and incorporated (A. Ortiz 1972, Dozier 1983). Dance with the enemy mimics, honors, and satirizes the enemy and s/he is no longer the same antagonist.

With local and regional variations, Comanche dances are performed at all eastern and western pueblos. In some they occur on a regular basis while in others, such as Isleta, they take place only once in a great while, due to lingering bitter memories (Cummings 1998). The descriptions here are based on observations of Comanche dances in the Tewa Pueblos of Tesuque, San Ildefonso, Santa Clara, and San Juan, as well as on literature concerning the same locations (Kurath and García 1970; Sweet 1983, 1985, 1999). The dances are also known by the Numunuh term *kwítara* in San Juan and other pueblos, while in neighboring Santa Clara they are also called *franci,* because of the influence of "fancy dancing," a Powwow tradition (Singer 2001).[4]

As in other Tewa dances, two long parallel lines of dancers move back and forth across the plaza. Women dress conservatively and alike in typical Tewa costumes, black manta dresses with shawls and sashes, carrying ears of corn or sprigs of evergreens or arrows. The men, on the other hand, are individually dressed in stunning and colorful Plains-style costumes, complete with breastplates, roaches, eagle-feather warbonnets, and several colors of face paint. As Sweet (1985:39) notes, "The difference in costume is echoed in the execution of the dance steps; the men exaggerate Tewa movements and frequently let out loud yelps while the women remain demure and perform their movements as they would for any other Tewa dance." Participants speak of their enthusiasm for the dance and refer to past relations of both enmity and amity with the Comanches (A. García 1999, Vigil 1991). The theme of past warfare is also reflected in the participation of veterans in the dance. There are reports that soldiers send back banners to place at shrines for this dance (Kurath and García 1970:233).

* Additional notes on musical transcriptions may be found in Appendix III.

Kwítara (Tewa Comanche) Song

Sung by Andy García and Vinton Lonnie of San Juan Pueblo

drum roll 1. We ya je ya je yo ja we na, we ya je ya je yo ja we na
intro 2. Santa Fe ya je yo ja we na, Ameri- cana ya je yo ja we na

1. we ya je ya je yo ja we na, we ya je ya je yo ja we na
2. Santa Fe ya je yo ja we na, Ameri- cana ya je yo ja we na

we ya je ja we yo o je o je e ne o je e ne e ya

2.4. Comanches de San Juan (San Juan Pueblo, ca. 1895–1900). Tewa Kwítara or "Comanches" appear both in the winter "enemy" dance cycle and at the San Juan Pueblo feast on June 24. Typical Plains-style regalia is seen on the plaza, including the characteristic single-row feather headdress. Photo by Christian G. Kaadt. Courtesy Museum of New Mexico. Neg. no. 42424.

Usually performed at a saint's day feast, the dance serves as a rite of thanksgiving, a celebration of life, a supplication for community health and prosperity. Kurath and García continue and offer a conclusion:

> The Tewa say specifically that they emulate the ferocity of the Comanche, and they sometimes insert Comanche words into the songs. They have not integrated the dance into their ceremonialism and their style as completely as the Buffalo dances. *Kwítara* would appear a more recent import, without ecological meaning. (284–85)

Kurath and García (1970) give no possible translation of any "Comanche" words heard, including *kwítara* or other words like *wiketaya* which are included in the lyrics. Sung in unison by a men's chorus to the rhythm of one or two drums, Pueblo Comanche songs have much more in common with other Pueblo songs, such as the Buffalo dance songs, than they do with the musical traditions of the Numunuh.

aLLí viendn Los comancHes

19

2.5. Triunfo de la Santa Cruz (Chimayó). The Holy Cross is a symbol of Christian pride and militancy. It is captured by the Moors for ransom in the play. The Christians take it in battle instead.

Numunuh-Sac and Fox ethnomusicologist Ed Wapp (1998) has observed that the Pueblos are often unaware of the exact meanings of the Numunuh words in their songs. He identifies one with the following refrain: *Nʉmʉnʉ kima, Nʉmʉnʉ kima* (the Comanches are coming). Tewa singers expressed surprise when he shared his translation with them. At a 1998 symposium on Indo-Hispano culture on a panel of Numunuh, Pueblo, and Hispano-Comanche participants, all expressed surprise and laughter when they learned the translation of the word *kwítara,* which is used without explanations in the anthropological literature and without the general knowledge of Tewa speakers.[5] *Kwítara* in Numunuh is diplomatically translated as "that musky, excremental smell of women and men when they are sexually aroused." In this case of cross-cultural mimesis, the satirical elements can work both ways, just like sex! (Wapp 1998 and Bigby 1998).

If the Pueblo paradigm of confronting cultural alterity is "dancing with the enemy," the Iberian counterpart is "sparring with the enemy" in ritualized mock combat (Gutiérrez 1993). For the Spaniard, the archetypal antagonist and cultural Other is the Moor. In the centuries-long Reconquest of Spain, mock battles between *Moros* and *Cristianos* (Moors and Christians) are documented as far back as 1150. By 1600, the noble elites had tired of royal spectacles and courtly tournaments, and they were adopted into popular celebrations (M. Harris 2000:61).

In the conquest of Mexico and the Americas, the mock battles served a military and ideological purpose. *Moros y cristianos* was regularly staged as an *auto de entrada,* or triumphal entry play, both for celebrations and for instilling in the Indians a proper fear of warhorses and firearms. The natives were further "edified" by the touching spectacles of defeat, forgiveness, and religious conversion of the Moors to Christianity at the end of the play. The play was used so frequently that the Indians developed their own "hidden transcripts," or subversive readings of the it (M. Harris 1993, 2000:27).

After the colonizing expedition of Don Juan de Oñate crossed the Río Grande into New Mexico in April of 1598, a formal act of possession was celebrated, including an equestrian display with the *Moros y cristianos* theme (Villagrá 1992:131). In the Tewa Pueblo of *Oke Owingee,* which the Spanish-Mexicans named San Juan de los Caballeros and made their first settlement, a full production with a specially composed text by soldier-dramatist Farfán de los Godos was performed (Villagrá 1992:150, Kanellos 1984). The colonial text did not survive, but the tradition did, in the neighboring village of Alcalde, until the 1920s (Austin 1928), and into present times in the village of Chimayó, just across the Española Valley from San Juan Pueblo. There *Moros y cristianos* is still occasionally celebrated on the feast days of Santiago (July 25), patron saint of Spain and the Reconquest, and during the feast of Santa Cruz (May 3), the Holy Cross (Luján 1992).

The plot structure of the modern text is simple and understandable even without a knowledge of Spanish. Most *Moros y cristianos* plays in both Spain and Spanish America are unscripted or rely on ad-lib dialogue, but the New Mexico version is one of a few that have retained their scripts, although it is impossible to determine its antiquity. In the opening scene, the Moors deceive the Christians, stealing the Santa Cruz by tempting a watchman with wine. In the following dialogue from the Chimayó performance, a Christian knight laments the theft, while a sultan gloats over his prize. Although only twenty-four or so actors and horses are on the field, the texts invite the audience to imagine a cast of more than eighty thousand.[6]

Federico:

¡Alarma, noble españól!	*Sound the alarm, noble Spaniard!*
Que ya el turco	*For the Turk has already*
Se ha robado la Santa Cruz	*stolen the Holy Cross*
Y ya tiene el castillo amurallado	*And has the castle walled in*
Con ochenta mil soldados	*With eighty thousand soldiers*
Sin la guarnición de adentro	*Not counting the garrison inside*
Que es de quinientos paganos.	*Which is of five hundred pagans.*
Eduardo, borracho está,	*Eduardo is drunk,*
Perdido y hasta descalabrado,	*Lost and undone,*
Riesgo corre de morirse.	*And runs the risk of dying.*

Sultán:

Ya la prenda está ganada	*The prize has been taken*
Cautiva la prenda rica	*Captive the rich prize*
Que entre los cristianos	*That among the Christians*
Es la prenda de más estima.	*Is their most esteemed sign.*
Y les juro por Mahomá	*And I swear by Mohammed*
Que si de oro la Turquía	*If they brought me all the*
me traía	*gold of Turkey*
Se la llevarían sin fatiga	*They could take it without care*
Y si no en esa torre	*If not in this tower it*
permanecerá cautiva.	*remains captive.*
Retírense a descansar	*Retreat and rest*
y esa prenda	*and this prize*
Como mía a cuidar.	*I will care for as my own.*

After a furious battle between riders of both sexes (in Chimayó many of the Moros are women), the cross is recaptured. The merciful King Alfonso frees the Moorish prisoners, and the Sultan repents, begging on his knees to become a Christian. This memorable scene projects the most indulgent Christian fantasy of all, the Muslim defeated by faith and arms.

Don Alfonso:

Oh, triunfo de los cristianos.	*Oh, triumph of the Christians.*
Cautiva te veo ahora	*Captive I see you*
entre los moros	*among the Moors*

2.6. El Gran Sultán en Batalla (Chimayó). The Great Sultan is surrounded by Christian knights in furious battle. He is forgiven in the end and joins his former enemies.

Pero ya ahora te veo
entre mis manos.
Pudiera yo hoy explicar
El elevado regocijo
Que siento en mi corazón
Sólo dando a Dios las gracias.
Y así las doy humillado,
Soberano Dios eterno.

Sultán:
Cristiano, ya tu valor
Me tiene a tus pies postrado.
Te pido por vuestra Cruz
Y por tu Dios venerado
Que me des la libertad
Que estoy desengañado—
Que sólo tu Dios es grande
Y Mahomá todo engaño.

But now I see you
in my hands.
If today I could only explain
The highest joy
That I feel in my heart
Just giving thanks to God.
And thus I humbly give it,
Sovereign eternal God.

Christian, your valor
Has me prostrate at your feet.
I beg you by your Cross
And by your venerated God
That you give me liberty
Because I see the light—
Only your God is great
And Mohammed is all lies.

aLLí vienen Los comanches

23

Don Alfonso:

No me la dieron mis brazos
Sino la gran providencia de Dios
Y así por El, por este Leño Sacro
Te concedo libertad
A ti y a todos tus vasallos.

My arms did not give it to me
Rather God's great providence
And so through Him and this Holy Tree
I grant you liberty
To you and all your vassals.

Sultán:

Agradezco tus finezas, Alfonso,
Que en sumo grado Dios te premie
Y que sigas su ley como
fiel vasallo.

I am grateful for your mercy, Alfonso,
May God reward you handsomely
And may you follow his law as
a faithful vassal.

(Lucero-White Lea 1953:107–12; my translation)

The melodramatic acts of contrition and compassion did not go unnoticed by the Pueblo Indians, who by 1598 had already learned the gestures of cross veneration from previous explorers. The lesson was clear: all those who do not submit to the True Cross could expect the flash and fury of cannon and horses.

2.7. "Sólo tu Dios es Grande y Mahomá todo Engaño" (Chimayó). At the moment of his repentance and conversion, the Great Sultan shouts, "Only your God is great and Mohammed all deceit."

Unlike Native groups in Mexico who embraced the drama and incorporated it into their own rituals, the Puebloans of New Mexico chose to remain spectators. Although Aurelio Espinosa reports some Indian participants at the turn of the twentieth century (A. Espinosa 1976:23), the Pueblos were never particularly interested in adopting *Moros y cristianos,* allowing the play to retain its intensely Spanish character. The drama of conquest that was adopted by the Pueblos was the Matachines dance, which was subsequently laden with hidden transcripts and embroidered with symbols of cultural survival and resistance (M. Harris 2000:237–50).

The dramatic paradigm of the *auto de entrada,* or equestrian victory play, remained unchanged and was familiar to all viewers. The hostile cultural Other is confronted and defeated through militant, military response. Then, instead of annihilation, the antagonist is integrated and assimilated. The progression of dramatic and symbolic elements of the paradigm include:

- The capture of a Christian symbol. In a moment of weakness, the Santa Cruz is captured and held for ransom.
- Military confrontation. The armies of Christianity and Islam face each other on the field of battle.
- Victory over the enemy. As preordained, the Christian forces prevail over a formidable foe, in spectacular skirmishes.
- Recuperation of the symbol. The Santa Cruz is not just recaptured, it is surrendered personally by the Sultán.
- Repentance of the vanquished enemy. The Sultán prostrates himself in humiliation before the Santa Cruz and King Alfonso, begging for clemency.
- Christian forgiveness of the antagonist. King Alfonso graciously pardons the Moros and forgives them.
- Conversion to Christianity. A mass conversion of the Moros is a grand and moving spectacle.
- Atonement. Through military and spiritual struggle, everyone is delivered.
- Religious and cultural assimilation. Convinced of the error of their ways, the Moros become Cristianos.
- Identification with the former antagonist. The Cristianos accept the Moros as brethren under the sign of the Santa Cruz.

In keeping with Spain's imperial strategies of conquest and assimilation, the cultural Other in the end resigns his otherness and becomes a subject of Crown and Cross. In this tradition as practiced in New Mexico, the element of cross-cultural mimesis is limited to dressing and acting like the cultural Other, bravely resisting, and then becoming the cultural self again. In its contemporary performance tradition, *Moros y cristianos* is a vehicle for Hispano cultural pride and historical memory in a hostile Anglo-American cultural environment (M. Harris 2000:166). Over four centuries, the discourse of colonial power becomes a discourse of resistance.

In most surviving performances of *Moros y cristianos* in Latin America, the finality of Spanish triumph is extenuated by hidden transcripts and alternative indigenous readings that subvert and mitigate the victory. When modern Nuevo Mexicanos enact the *autos de entrada*, are they merely exulting in the Spanish triumphs of the past, or are they celebrating their own cultural survival? Concerned with the decline of the *Moros y cristianos* tradition in New Mexico, Harris (2000:166) speculates on the range of meanings the play generates:

> If it becomes the site for more pointed resistance to the dominant Anglo culture, it may well flourish. If it does not, it too may slowly disappear. In this respect, the history of the *moros y cristianos* in New Mexico is instructive, for the tradition has thrived in so many different geographical and chronological contexts because of two factors: its flexibility of historical referent and its capacity to mask hidden transcripts. Flexibility extended its life in Hispanic New Mexico. The lack of a hidden transcript may bring about its demise.

When cultural critics observe New Mexican actors in folk plays and pageants dressed in the garb of Spanish crusaders or conquistadors, the worst is assumed—that the actors are somehow performing a fantasy heritage that exalts ruling elites at the expense of the rest of society.[7] I would argue that the mimetic emulation of imperial Spanishness by working-class Nuevo Mexicanos is much more than elitist hispanophilia. A hidden transcript of cultural survival and resistance invested in text and enactment creates "conquistadors" who are as ambivalent as they are complex.

Looking back to sixteenth-century New Mexico, the epic struggle of Islam and Christianity was less remote and much fresher in the imagination of the Spanish-Mexican settlers. To revel whole-heartedly in the glories of the past helped in facing up to the grim threats of the present. It was on the basic plot structure and dramatic paradigm of *Moros y cristianos* that a new victory play would be built in the eighteenth century, *Los comanches*. Unlike its literary cousin, it would never be used for threatening, edifying, or converting cultural Others. Its primary purpose was the enactment of the hopes and fears of the one of the most critical periods of New Mexico history, the Comanche wars of the late eighteenth century.

After the conflicts were resolved, the play reconfigured itself through performance to confront the cultural challenges of relations with Anglo-Americans. The new political equations of the American era would also involve cross-cultural mimesis, emulation, and even appropriation and commodification after the remainder of the Spanish Empire was inherited by the United States, in 1899.

Since *Los comanches* is based on actual historical events, it is time to consider the chronology of the Comanche encounter with the Pueblos and Spanish-Mexican colonists of the Río Grande Valley, as it is inscribed in documents, and as it is remembered and recounted by the people themselves.

3

The Numunuh in New Mexico

COMANCHE STORIES AND TALES

El Comanche y la Comancha	The Comanche man and wife
Se salieron a pasear,	Went out for a walk,
El Comanche lleva el arco	The Comanche carries his bow
Y la Comancha el chimal.	And his wife carries his shield.

—*Versos Comanches/Comanche Verses (A. Espinosa 1907:20)*

To understand Indo-Hispano cultural hybridity and the ritual performances in which it is enacted, the narrative stage can now be fully set with documents, legends, and oral histories to provide the resonance and ambivalence they produce in the community.

Embedded in this cumulative narrative are key moments that help define historical contexts and consequences. There have been many decisive and precarious narrative moments in the history of New Mexico, when the future as we know and experience it today was truly in the balance. Compassion, cruelty, chance, and ambition have all played a part. Would Don Juan de Oñate have allowed Acoma Pueblo to be destroyed in 1599 if the young Juan de Zaldívar, who died on the mesa, had not been his nephew? In the final siege of Santa Fe during the Pueblo Revolt of 1680, what possessed Pueblo and Apache warriors to show mercy to the surviving colonists, letting them escape to the south, when they could easily have annihilated them? During the Mexican-American War of 1846, why did General Manuel Armijo order his militia to disband, when they had such a fighting chance of overwhelming the exhausted and half-starved American Army during the invasion?

In the eighteenth century, the relations of the Comanches with the Spanish-Mexican and Puebloan peoples of New Mexico were just as decisive. The Comanches held the future of the province in their hands. The economic and political hegemony they established on the southern Plains was without parallel. They were convinced that the Numunuh, the People, were the most numerous and powerful humans on the face of the earth as they knew it (Noyes 1993:215). Acquisition and mastery of horses, which they termed "god-dogs," transformed their society from abject poverty to great wealth (Boulris 1983). Better armed than the presidial soldiers, the militia, and the Pueblo auxiliaries, it was within their power to have driven everyone from their homes and destroyed the province completely, had they so desired. Two centuries later, Hispano and Pueblo New Mexicans still remember the name of Cuerno Verde, his reign of terror, and his braggadocio. At Jemez Pueblo, he is recalled with sinister humor. Cuerno Verde boasted that New Mexico belonged to him, that he could destroy it if he pleased, but he needed to keep some Mexicans to tend his horses and some Pueblo Indians to water and grind his corn (Sando 1998).[1]

No one knows what possessed the Numunuh to spare Taos Pueblo in the spring of 1760, when they completely destroyed the Villalpando hacienda near Ranchos de Taos, the most heavily fortified citadel in New Mexico after the Palace of the Governors in Santa Fe. Their army of three thousand warriors could easily have routed everyone from the Taos Valley. And what if Cuerno Verde, in the summer of 1779, had not believed himself to be invincible and had exercised more caution in leading his forty best warriors in a headlong attack against Governor De Anza's army of more than six hundred?

To appreciate "Los comanches" requires knowledge of a backdrop of nearly three centuries of events and narratives about those events. Stories based on documents, on revisioning of those documents, and stories from living Pueblo, Hispano, and Numunuh sources must be heard. Accounts exaggerated by human suffering and by obsessive narrative practices that privilege violence and warfare need to be put into perspective. Notions of honor in general, defending honor, and honoring need to be defined.

An entire cadre of historians have admired and emphasized the military prowess of the Numunuh, contributing to the stereotype of the invincible and noble savages, the "Lords of the Plains," which is precisely their status in the Hispano popular imagination. Comanches are not usually given much credit for their enterprising spirit as masterful traders and networkers. On the darker side, the pervasive legend of the Comanches as thieves, kidnappers, and murderers is stubborn and persistent, with few attempts to understand different cultural concepts of property, family, honor, and ritual vengeance.

Curiously, in their analysis of honor, social historians have largely excluded analogous Native value systems. Honor is defined as a particularly Mediterranean code of values and behavior that distances indigenous peoples, who were perceived by the Spanish as lacking the capacity for honorable action (Gutiérrez 1991:176–240). In engaging each other in daily struggle, the mutual understanding of Native and Spanish men resonated across cultural difference in the very nature of their most desperate actions. James F. Brooks (2002:9) notes "[A] particular resonance between

Map labels: Vale de Sn Antonio. · Alcaldia de · taos. · Castillo · el hondo · Piedra del Carnero · R° de Luzero · RIO DEL NORTE · taos · R° de D. Fernando de las Trampas · R° de el ojo Caliente · Poblaciones arruinadas por Los enemigos Cumanches · la Meza · Pecuris · el Cobre · Alcaldia de · Embudo · la Villa de San- · trampas · Abiquiu · Joaya · Rio arriba · ta Cruz de · chimayo · quemada · Cuchilla · S. Juan · Cupdigo · Valkcillo · Chama · Sta Cruz de la Cañada · Cundiyo · Dolbadena · St. Clara · Mesilla · la Cañada. · Sn Ildefonso · LOS BACAS · Pujuaqui · Nambe · tesuque · Caja del Rio · l S. Cruz · Sta Fee Capitl y Presidio · Alamo · Alcaldia de la Villa de Santa Fee · Pecos · Sn Marcos · Galisteo

3.1.   Bernardo Miera y Pacheco Map of New Mexico, 1779 (detail). In the most violent years of the Comanche wars, many New Mexican settlements lay in ruins. The legend of the map includes an account of the 1760 Villalpando massacre and laments the poor defenses of New Mexico. Courtesy of University of New Mexico Press.

THE NUMUNUH IN NEW MEXICO

indigenous and European notions of honor and shame, of male violence and exchange imperatives in the region . . ."

The reputation and social standing of men was based on their capacity to sustain, protect, and control the well-being of their families and communities. In conflict, this common ground became a cruel no-man's-land. Brooks continues (2002:40):

> Struggling to preserve and protect the integrity of their power within families and communities, men from both sides . . . negotiated interdependency and maintained honor by acknowledging the exchangeability of their women and children. Disguising necessity in sacred artifice, they produced a mutually recognizable world of violence and retribution, of loss and redemption that drew the protagonists together while forcing them apart.

The single most illustrative eighteenth-century document on the desperate state of affairs in New Mexico is the beautifully drawn Miera y Pacheco map of 1779. Nestled in the mountains and valleys of the upper Río Grande, and indicated with carefully drawn boxes, are the principle buildings of all the settlements of the province. Nearly half had lines crossed through them, indicating that they were in ruins. Vast settlement areas, such as the entire Chama River Valley had been abandoned.

☙ *Documentos de la Guerra:* Comanche Wars and History 1706–1875

According to Eurocentric narrative practices, the history of the Numunuh begins in 1706, with their first appearance in colonial documents. Their fame as warriors preceded them. Although Spanish-Mexican settlers and their Pueblo neighbors in the Taos Valley had not yet encountered them face to face, they already knew they were cousins of the Utes and were already bracing themselves for a hostile encounter (Noyes 1993:xix). The chronicle of the next hundred eighty years is distilled in the following summary (based on John 1975, Kavanagh 1996, Kenner 1966, Noyes 1993, and Thomas 1932).[2]

The "Comanches" as they were christened, entered the stage as accomplished horsemen, indicating that they had already conducted their own "encounter" with European cultural resources by equipping themselves with horses (Richardson 1933:19).

Historians speculate that maneuvers of European colonies far to the east and north had displaced them southward (John 1975). The shifting alliances of royal succession and war, a world away in Europe, were creating political pressures that could be felt on the Plains of North America. Native sources counter that they were deeply attached to their horses, wanted to acquire more, and fell in love with the Río Grande Valley in the meantime (Bigbee 1998). They were arguably the best and most agile horsemen in the North America, according to the accounts of amazed observers (Ewers 1955:9, Noyes 1993:xxv–xxviii).

Prior to European contact, the Numunuh were a scattered Shoshonean society wandering the Great Basin, composed of small nomadic family units that dug roots, gathered berries, and hunted small game. On a seasonal basis, they gathered for larger group activities, which provided the opportunity for socializing and fostered a linguistic common ground. When they entered or were forced onto the Plains, their cultural resources were resilient enough to make the best of changing resources and new possibilities.

On their journey southward, they encountered their linguistic cousins, the Utes, who introduced them to the beautiful rolling country of the upper Arkansas and Platte Rivers. This was also a Jicarilla and Paloma Apache homeland, with agriculture and villages. The opportunities for taking horses and captives proved irresistible, as was the curiosity to see where the horses came from.

The Comanches first rode into the Taos Valley with the Utes, attracted by the commerce that was to fascinate them for the rest of the century. The Spanish-Mexicans speculated that they came form the legendary land of Teguayo, which lay west of the legendary land of Quivira, on the Great Plains (G. Anderson 1999:204). From first contact, they were impressed with Comanche customs, individualist demeanor, and warrior culture (Noyes 1993:26–32).

Leaving the Utes to their territories to the west, the Comanches moved into the valleys of Colorado's Front Range and ever southward, toward first the upper and then the lower Río Grande, displacing Apaches and other native populations on the way. The Nuevo Mexicanos were as afraid of them as they were fascinated by them, and were grateful to have a buffer zone of discontented Apaches in between (Noyes 1993:30). Comanche attacks came to the Taos Valley in 1716 and 1719, and the first large-scale military campaign was mounted against them. Governor Valverde assembled a force of more than six hundred *presidiales,* the leather-jacketed soldiers of the Santa Fe Presidio, auxiliaries of the Pueblo militias, and Apache volunteers, in an unsuccessful effort even to locate the Comanches, let alone engage them (Noyes 1993:11–14).

As geopolitics began worrying the colonial government, there was concern that the French might be arming and influencing the Comanches. The Spanish Crown wished to keep the dangerous lands of the Comanchería securely between themselves and the French. A military expedition led by Pedro de Villasur in 1720 went to the upper Platte to find evidence of French penetration and was dealt a disastrous defeat by Pawnees and Otos (Noyes 1993:17–18).

In the aftermath, the government decided against building a presidio at Cuartelejo, on the Arkansas River, and withdrew. The Apaches of Cuartelejo were obliged to abandon the Plains forever and took refuge in the mountains of New Mexico, where they remain to this day. To further aid the Apaches, the government allowed them to take refuge in improvised settlements near Pecos and

Galisteo. Jicarillas settled at Trampas de Taos by 1733, a town later to be called Ranchos de Taos (WPA 1989:287).

In the meantime, the Comanches built the most dynamic economy that the southern Plains had ever seen. Based on horse raising, buffalo hunting, the preservation of meat, and hide tanning, it was labor-intensive and involved an ever-growing workforce. Trading contacts and ties in New Mexico were pursued aggressively. In the trade fairs that the Spanish government established for them as early as 1723 in Taos, the Comanches discovered a booming demand for slaves, both for domestic service and for the rich silver mines of Chihuahua, Parral, Zacatecas, and beyond. Since there was a ready supply of Apache captives at hand, the Comanches were content to supply them to enterprising Nuevo Mexicanos, who had already come to the cynical realization that the richest commodities to be had in New Mexico were not mineral but human (G. Anderson 1999:206).

The trade fairs at Taos Pueblo and later at Pecos Pueblo became annual events protected by a truce, or *Paz de Dios* (God's peace), and the government intervened to try to regulate prices and keep the peace. A key feature of the fairs was the slave markets, or *rescates,* a euphemism referring to the slave price as a "ransom" or "rescue." Several laws were put into effect to smooth the roughest edges of the slave trade, but the economic advantages it provided were too alluring. One law excluded Pueblo Indians from participating and benefiting by the trade, and their relations with the Comanches were damaged by it (G. Anderson 1999:206).

By mid-century, a class of captives, slaves, and culturally displaced people emerged that by 1776 comprised a third of the population. These Hispanicized Indians were called *genízaros,* an Old World name for the janissaries (literally "new troops") of the Ottoman Empire, who were young Christian captives (F. A. Chávez 1979, Gutiérrez 1991:149–56). They occupied the lowest social rung of colonial society, becoming herders, servants, and concubines. Better opportunities came as New Mexico's own "new troops" served as scouts and soldiers. Military service to the Crown was rewarded, and the first Genízaro towns established in 1740 at Valencia and Cerro de Tomé and in 1749 at Abiquiú.

During this entire period, relations were tense and often broke down into hostilities. Since slaving was accomplished by raids, there was much discontent and bloodshed in the land. The next large military campaign to punish the Comanches was mounted in 1751, by Governor Vélez Cachupín. He had learned the value of negotiation and the cultural practice of gift exchanges, but relied on military action after Pecos Pueblo was overrun in November. He caught up with the offenders at a frozen lake in the Arkansas Valley, killed one hundred, and later freed forty survivors with presents of tobacco. The next year, the Comanches agreed to leave the Apache settlements near Pecos and Galisteo alone, in return for having better access to the Taos rescates. The truce lasted nearly a decade, and the governor personally attended the Taos fairs to smoke with Comanche leaders and prevent unfair trading practices (Noyes 1993:53).

The next disaster happened in Taos, precisely because a group of Comanches had been fired upon and cheated by settlers and Pueblo people at the rescate. Adding insult to injury, a Taos scalp dance was held in their presence, with identifiable Comanche scalps. When three thousand angry warriors appeared in late summer for revenge, they vented it on one hundred sixty settlers, who had taken refuge in the fortified Villalpando hacienda, near Ranchos de Taos, which had four *torreones,* or defensive towers. All the men and several women were killed, and fifty-six captives were carried off. Several months later, interim Governor Manuel del Portillo y Urrisola demanded their return, got eleven back, and captured ten Comanche leaders in the negotiations (G. Anderson 1999:209). At one point the Comanches signaled their desire to negotiate further by erecting a burning cross, but the army mounted a surprise attack that killed three hundred Comanches and took four hundred captives (Noyes 1993:55).

On the international front, with the 1762–63 Treaty of Paris and the end of the Seven Years' War (known in America as the French and Indian War), France ceded Louisiana to Spain. But the larger political scene was eclipsed by the local violence.

In the next decade, things went from bad to worse, with the installation in 1767 of Pedro Fermín de Mendinueta, who instituted a policy of all-out war. Since Comanches had no central command, but rather were organized in autonomous groups, not all would be hostile at the same time. Instead of continuing to use diplomacy with cooperative bands, war was waged against all, with disastrous results.

In 1768, the colorful and irascible chief Cuerno Verde appeared in a failed attack on Ojo Caliente and was killed. His son and namesake picked up his curious green-horned battle helmet and swore vengeance on New Mexico, a promise that he kept over the next eleven years. Perhaps in imitation of the Spanish elites, he reportedly behaved with regal demeanor and was escorted by retainers and bodyguards, who held up a canopy of buffalo skins to give him shade as he rested (Noyes 1993:62).

The bloodshed continued and reached its peak from 1770 to 1779. Roving bands of four to five hundred warriors struck both in the north and in the south without warning. Hundreds of casualties resulted, with additional hundreds of captives taken. In 1774, a number of engagements culminated in a large punitive expedition led by Don Carlos Fernández, a retired captain called up by Governor Mendinueta. His army marched east and north of Santa Fe and surprised a large camp of Comanche families, who may or may not have been involved in previous predations.[3] No trouble was taken to find out, because the governor was not interested in diplomacy. Trapped and protected only by a small wood and a deep pond, the Comanches were caught in a murderous cross fire. More than four hundred were killed, wounded, or captured, and Fernández's force only lost one Pueblo auxiliary, with twenty-eight wounded. This massacre is important, because it is alluded to in the victory play to come, "Los comanches" (Noyes 1993:64–65).

By the next year, 1775, Comanche retaliatory attacks were occurring on the very outskirts of Santa Fe. It was clear that the policy of extermination would never succeed. In spite of all the official victories, New Mexico was in ruins, the militia was exhausted, and arms and horses were in short supply. A new herd of fifteen hundred horses was desperately requested in 1775, but it did not arrive until 1778. The future of the province as a productive place to live and raise a family was seriously in doubt.

Into this atmosphere of desperation and distrust came the illustrious young governor, Don Juan Bautista de Anza, and an elite corps of troops from the presidios of Sonora. A native of Sonora, he was fresh from expeditions to California, which included the founding of the city of San Francisco. His first big initiative as governor was to mount a huge military campaign in his first year, much to the dismay of the local militia. Fortunately for New Mexico, his diplomatic skills would prove to be more important than his military prowess. But first, some scores had to be settled with Cuerno Verde and the Yamparicas. After the death of the first Cuerno Verde, his son had been conducting a reign of terror. His raids were so frequent and so devastating that some scholars suspect there may have been a third Cuerno Verde in operation (Kavanagh 1996:92).

In the summer of 1779, de Anza assembled 103 presidial soldiers, 225 militia, and 259 Pueblo auxiliaries, equipping them as best as he could. Instead of heading up the main road north to Taos, they went west, up the Chama Valley, then north by the ruins of Ojo Caliente, where the first Cuerno Verde had been killed eleven years before. As they reached the Conejos River and the westernmost part of the San Luis Valley, over 200 angry Utes and Jicarillas joined them. Traveling at night to avoid detection, they marched over Poncha Pass and skirted north, then east around El Capitán (later Pike's Peak).

To the south, along the Río del Sacramento (later Fountain Creek), they captured the main winter camp of Cuerno Verde's band. Enough tipis and provisions were there to support an estimated 1250 people for the winter. Many of the warriors were out raiding with Cuerno Verde in the Taos area. De Anza captured 64 women and children, and the other men fled south to summon their chief. A pack train of more than a hundred mules carried away the mountains of booty, and a captured herd of five hundred horses followed close behind. The army crossed the Arkansas and waited near Green Horn Mountain for Cuerno Verde. The invincible chief, his shaman, oldest son, four captains, ten elders, and forty warriors were lured by a clever series of running tactics and feigned retreats right into a trap. With no possibility of escape, they charged a well-placed army of eight hundred. Their horses foundered in a swamp, and they fought fiercely to a man, until the end (Noyes 1993:74–79). De Anza sent his trophy, the famous green horn helmet, to Spain, and it reputedly rests today in some forgotten corner of the Vatican Museum.

Were it not for the tireless diplomatic campaign that followed, this victory would have been as hollow as those that preceded it. Despite the rich spoils of war taken home to New Mexico, what use were stolen goods in the face of the retaliation that was sure to follow? These cynical views surface as satire in the last scene of "Los comanches," still performed to this day.

CHAPTER THREE

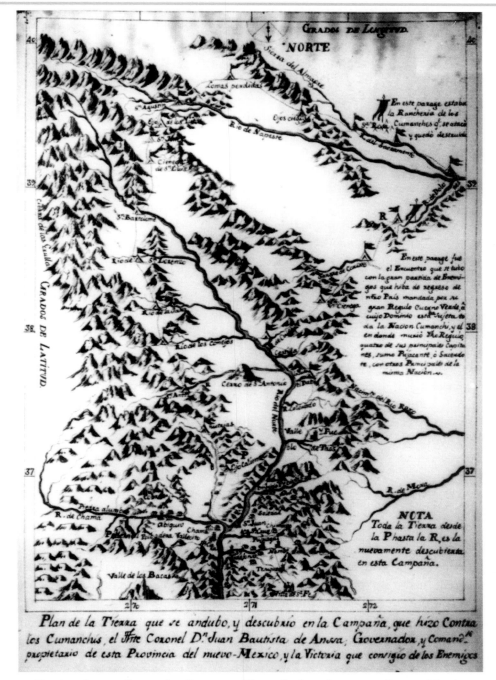

3.2. De Anza's 1779 Comanche Campaign. To outflank and surprise Cuerno Verde, De Anza traveled west and north to the San Luis Valley and over Poncha Pass, turning south at El Capitán (Pike's Peak). Each campsite of his army is marked with a flag. Courtesy Spanish Colonial Research Center, National Park Service.

Back at the Palace of the Governors in Santa Fe, in clouds of tobacco smoke, De Anza generously entertained delegation after delegation of visiting Comanches, showering them with gifts of trade goods and tobacco, for which thousands of pesos a year were invested (Kavanagh 1996:181–92). The Numunuh, in their wisdom, saw the benefit of continuing the arrangement with the Spanish government. Dozens of autonomous bands recognized the leadership and authority of chief Ecueracapa, named for his leather cape, who negotiated the treaty of 1786 with De Anza. The treaty was celebrated in Pecos Pueblo with a trade fair (Noyes 1993:80–81). Despite the example of Cuerno Verde's defeat, the Numunuh negotiated from a position of strength, not weakness. Their descendants today claim that their ancestors were never defeated by the Spanish, but decided on a "mutual protection" pact, with guarantees of annual gifts and continuing access to the trade fairs and rescates (Bigbee 1998). They would also be hired on as mercenaries in the continuing campaigns against the Apaches, especially the tribes of the south.

With minor adjustments, the "Pax Comanche" held into modern times in New Mexico (Noyes 1993:309, 339). When the Comanches warred with the Pawnee in 1790, Santa Fe sent military assistance to help out. There were misunderstandings regarding the Apache settlement policies the government was also negotiating, and there was discontent in the 1820s, when shrinking budgets stemmed the flow of gifts, but the alliance held. Historians see the treaty of 1786 as the high point of Comanche-Spanish relations. What is not generally recognized is that this date also marks the high point in the development of the widespread trading network of the Numunuh (G. Anderson 1999:205).

The American government tested the strength of the alliance by also trying to buy the confidence of the Comanches with gifts, insisting that there would be more on the way from the United States than from Mexico. This cynical move did not impress the Comanches, who had good reason to distrust Americans. By 1829, pitched battles had been fought with American armies along the Santa Fe Trail (Noyes 1993:138). And in 1830, the U.S. Congress passed the Indian Removal Bill, which would remove thousands of Cherokees, Creeks, Choctaws, Chickasaw, and Seminoles to "Indian Territory," in the heart of the Numunuh homeland (Noyes 1993:236–37). The appearance of the duplicitous Anglo Texans inspired more rancor when, in the infamous Council House fight of 1840, an entire delegation of southern Comanche leaders came to a peace conference to exchange captives in San Antonio and was summarily ambushed and executed (Noyes 1993:280–84).

When the Texas Republic drew its map, the western border was set at the Río Grande, without consulting with the New Mexicans. The entire eastern half of New Mexico was designated as "Santa Fe County." In 1841, an army with the innocuous name of Texas-Santa Fe Expedition was sent from Austin to occupy Santa Fe, establish trade, and begin collecting revenue.

Along the entire journey, Spanish-speaking Indians who they could not identify continually harassed them. It was the Numunuh, defending New Mexico. They reported the approach and positions of the splintered groups of Texans to

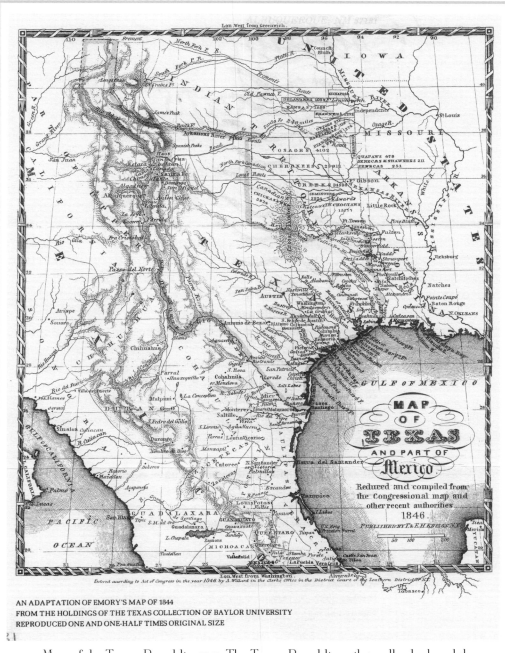

AN ADAPTATION OF EMORY'S MAP OF 1844
FROM THE HOLDINGS OF THE TEXAS COLLECTION OF BAYLOR UNIVERSITY
REPRODUCED ONE AND ONE-HALF TIMES ORIGINAL SIZE

3.3. Map of the Texas Republic, 1841. The Texas Republic unilaterally declared the Río Grande as its western boundary. Comanches warned the New Mexican authorities of the approach of the Texas Army. Courtesy UNM Map and Geographic Information Center.

Santa Fe authorities, who prepared a trap (T. Chávez 1978:135). The Texans were so exhausted upon arriving in New Mexico that they were captured with no resistance and sent to Mexico City in chains. The victory was celebrated in the nineteenth-century folk play *Los Tejanos,* in which an Indian character plays a key role in a plot to capture the Texans without a fight (A. M. Espinosa and J. M. Espinosa 1944:219–24). Later on in the century, after the implacable raids on the American and German settlers of west Texas (Kenner 1966:212), the Comanches would go west to the Río Grande to attend the feast day hospitality of their friends and allies, the Pueblos and Spanish-Mexicans.

After the Civil War, the first reservation was formed, with Fort Sill constructed to oversee it. The last Numunuh resistance was crushed at Palo Duro Canyon, south of Amarillo, in 1874. The capture and slaughter of ten thousand horses by the U.S. Cavalry there effectively ended the hostilities of the Red River War (Noyes 1993:309). When Quanah Parker surrendered at Fort Sill, in 1875, Comanche freedom on the southern Plains ended. They were confined to reservations and would not resume their much-anticipated yearly visits to New Mexico until decades later.

In the twentieth century, the isolation of the reservations was alleviated through an increased participation in the life of the nation by means of military service and relocation programs. With the convenience of roads and highways and the vehicles to travel them, the Numunuh resumed on a small scale their annual pilgrimages to New Mexico, which had been reduced to the cherished memories of a few elders. Now, at the harvest feast of San Gerónimo at Taos Pueblo, the venue for the trade fairs of previous centuries, rows of pick-ups with Oklahoma plates can be seen. After decades of absence from New Mexico, the Numunuh express their amazement at the range of celebrations in their honor, a topic that will be revisited in the conclusion.

⟲ New Perspectives: Ethnogenesis and Transculturation

After reviewing the documented war narratives of the Spanish-Mexicans and the Numunuh, it is time to consider the largely undocumented cultural consequences and manifestations of generations of struggle.

One of the greatest legacies of the conflict was the pragmatic and historic alliance of the Spanish-Mexicans and the Pueblos. The bitter differences of the past concerning religion and forced tribute were set aside in the face of a new struggle. After the 1693 Spanish Reconquest and all during the next century, the necessities of survival created a new cultural dynamic. The consequence of military alliance was cultural accommodation and mutual respect. The Pueblo cultural and religious strategy of "compartmentalization" was one of the results. Now tolerated by pragmatic Spanish-Mexican authorities, Pueblo beliefs and practices were insulated and separated from European ways (Dozier 1954, 1957). The depth of this friendship was articulated in folkways and in official discourse as well. The political, social, and economic rapprochement was such that by 1812, the wealthy rancher Pedro Baptista Pino could write, in his report to the Cortes de Cádiz, that the Pueblos "casi no se distinguen de nosotros [are hardly distinguishable from us]," unusual words for a conservative monarchist (Pino 1995[1812]:2).

The cultural landscape of New Mexico was further enriched by the growing class of Genízaros, the captives, slaves, and orphans detribalized and assimilated as they were taken from the enemy. As *criados,* or persons literally raised in the intimacy of Spanish households, they became more thoroughly Hispanicized than the Pueblos. As they moved into their own communities, they evolved their own cultural style made a major contribution to the culture and folk Catholicism of the region. The Hispano-Comanche cultural celebrations featured in subsequent chapters are part of the Genízaro legacy.

The dark side of the story is the abuse and degradation suffered by members of an underclass. There are numerous examples of the most practical solution to this dilemma—flight. Genízaros unhappy with their fate exercised the option of returning to their cultures of origin. Gary Anderson (1999:249, 224) notes that:

> [F]light became the simplest way to protest treatment, and genízaros frequently fled to the plains to rejoin their original Comanche captors. Pedro de la Cruz, for example, fled in 1746 along with four genízaro women. When apprehended, they revealed that their destination had been the 'infidel Nation of Comanches.' The records that do exist strongly imply that some Genízaros [sic] viewed life with the Comanches more favorably than with the Spanish, and this was probably true for some *vecinos* as well. . . . It is somehow lost to history that so many Spaniards and Spanish-controlled Indians wished to "become Comanche" rather than fight them.[4]

But the forced transculturation experienced by captives has partly obscured a larger process that most scholars have scarcely imagined—ethnogenesis. Historians finally noticed that the tremendous growth of Comanche culture was due to more than the increase of biological reproduction and adoption of captives. It has become clear that Numunuh was as much a cultural revolution as it was a culture. In the space of a few generations, the Numunuh had culturally reinvented themselves several times over. They embraced the strategy of ethnogenesis as a part of their survival.

Cultural revolutions have an economic base. The Comanche economy, based on horses and the produce of hunting and raiding, was the most fruitful the southern Plains had ever seen, and was the envy of many. As a result, the Numunuh absorbed many of the ethnic groups that surrounded them. Spanish, French, and later American travelers noticed that several languages were spoken in Comanche encampments, including Wichita, Caddo, and Pawnee, as well as Spanish. The linguistic diversity of Numunuh society is much more than what an

3.4. "His-oo-san-ches" (Jesús Sánchez). "The Little Spaniard." Field sketch by George Catlin. Reproduced from George Catlin, 1844, Letters and Notes on the Manners, Customs, and Condition of the North American Indians. New York, 2:68–69. Like many Spanish-Mexican captives, Jesús Sánchez completely integrated into Comanche culture and used his Spanish language skills to the advantage of his adopted people.

isolated captive might add to the mix (G. Anderson 1999:216–20). Anderson's conclusion (1999:225) is that a process of ethnogenesis was at work:

> While the language and cultural practices of Comanche bands were already formed when they reached the plains, by the early nineteenth century these bands constituted people from many different ethnic and linguistic backgrounds. A growing number of genízaros, mission apostates, Spanish "deserters," captives, and various others joined a core of what once had been Shoshone mountain people to form a more vibrant and sophisticated society. The seasoning process that each captive faced, imbued in them a strong sense of Comanche identity.

Many cultural practices associated with hunting, warfare, horsemanship, and ritual all added up to a strong sense of belonging. The "defections" and "adoptions" that took place must be understood as part of a process of transculturation, whether voluntary or as part of the incorporation of captives or the socialization of captive as well as natural children. The family of Numunuh was hybrid and diverse, and in the nineteenth century even Anglo-Americans were thrown into the mix. The list of famous Numunuh statesmen includes many half-breeds and ethnics. Jesús Sánchez, the "Little Spaniard," whom the artist George Catlin immortalized in his painting of the same name, helped negotiate a treaty with the United States because of the Spanish he remembered from his boyhood in New Mexico (Kavanagh 1996:237). Quanah Parker, the last chief to surrender, was the son of Cynthia Ann Parker, an adopted and well-integrated captive (Kavanagh 1996:50).

✑ Historias de la Gente:
People Speak, Write, and Remember the Comanches

As will be seen in chapter 4, the theme of captivity is so prevalent in Indo-Hispano culture that it develops its own poetics. To conclude this story-telling session on the Comanches, it is time to consider three stories from two different eras. The first is inscribed in the report of Pedro Baptista Pino, New Mexico's delegate to the *Cortes de Cádiz* in 1812, which articulates very clearly the Comanche stereotype in the Spanish imagination. The other two are Comanche stories from the oral tradition—one from San Juan Pueblo and the other from Tomé, which articulate the fascination and ambivalence felt by the Spanish-Mexicans and their Pueblo neighbors for the Numunuh others.

Don Pedro Baptista Pino had harsher words for the Comanches than for the Pueblos, for his home community of Galisteo, southeast of Santa Fe and southwest of Pecos, was a favorite target for the depredations and retaliations of the previous century. As a young man, he personally participated in a number of the campaigns of the 1770s and frequently defended his family and flocks from attack. Two Pino women were taken captive and several relatives were killed in the 1777 attacks still remembered in oral history (A. Espinosa 1907:11). Don Pedro had a hard-earned respect for the Comanche and paints a positive picture of them for the king. Of course, by 1812, the Pax Comanche was in full effect, to the benefit of all New Mexicans. There could be no more convenient scapegoat or justification for the barbarism of New Mexico than the Comanches, but Pino resists assigning blame.

Although he describes in detail the natural and cultural landscapes of New Mexico in his report to the king, Pino considerably underplays the prevalence and importance of the slave trade. His descriptions of the Comanches and their culture neither idealize nor denigrate them. He is familiar with the details and symbolism of their dress, for practical reasons. A principal battlefield tactic was to distinguish and target chiefs as quickly as possible, to demoralize the younger warriors. The Comanche "[I]s known throughout the area for his robust and gallant presence, his frank martial air, his honest dress. . . . On their heads they wear plumage, and the color and height of the feathers distinguish their rank . . ." (Pino 1995[1812]:45).

Pino's assessment of Comanche social and political structure shows evidence of the adaptations the Numunuh had made to subordinate the autonomy of separate bands to the general good and negotiate treaties with the Spanish government as a group.

> Their government is democratic, united more by necessity than through law because if they were not united they would be attacked by those surrounding nations with whom they have never sought peace nor alliance. Their authority is divided among subordinate captains, one of whom is named general-in-chief on the basis of his talent and bravery. He governs them militarily. (Pino 1995[1812]:46)

Pino's account of the military tactics of the Comanches is tinged with awe and respect. He had met them many times in battle.

> None of the other nations attempt to match their forces with those of the Comanche. Even when [the other nations are] allied, they have been vanquished repeatedly. . . . They prefer death to that of subjecting themselves to the slightest humiliation. In their acts of war they never attack by taking advantage, nor by trickery, but face to face and after having signaled with their whistles. Even though their principal weapon is the arrow [pacta] they also use lances and firearms like our soldiers, and vary their tactics in all their maneuvers.
>
> The wars that they have had with us have always been tenacious and bloody. They kept the province in a state of watchfulness until 1783 [read 1779], when Governor don Juan Bautista de Anza resolved to confront them . . .
>
> Since that date they have maintained peace and harmony with us, endeavoring to observe what is contained in our treaty. For our part we also strive to observe it in order not to offend their pride. (Pino 1995[1812]:47–48)

Given the nominal concern of the Spanish Crown for the treatment of indigenous groups, Pino was also quick to emphasize the forthrightness of the Nuevo Mexicanos and their abhorrence of treachery. Their former enemy is a powerful and noble one. But nowhere is there any evidence in the report of the root source of Comanche influence, their extensive economic ties with surrounding tribes and with New Mexico. By 1812, the government had already issued licenses for groups of traders known as Comancheros to actively venture out to the plains instead of waiting for the Comanches to come in for trade fairs. Both with what he includes and what he omits, Pino articulates the major stereotype of the Comanche in the Hispanic imagination—the mystification of the military aspects of their warrior society, and their reputation as "Lords of the Plains," an image that later loomed large in the Anglo-American imagination as well. A close reading of Pino is necessary, because he is the prime candidate for authorship of the bittersweet victory play *Los comanches,* to be examined in the next chapter (A. Espinosa 1907).

One of the extraordinary features of Comanche stories has been their profound resonance in the historical memory of the people of New Mexico. More than two centuries after the dark days of warfare and more than a century after their banishment from New Mexico and confinement on reservations in Oklahoma, Comanche stories are still being told. Charles Briggs has charted the astonishing historical consciousness of the Nuevo Mexicanos, identifying several types of historical discourse as a popular part of the oral tradition (Briggs 1988:59–99). People are well versed in their own genealogies and community history, because the knowledge is still the basis of individual and social prestige.

One of the most widely acknowledged and celebrated oral historians and traditional singers of Tomé, New Mexico, was Edwin Baca Berry (1924–99). After returning from World War II, he revitalized the *Calvario,* or Calvary shrine, on the Cerro de Tomé, a hilltop sacred site that is one of the most important pilgrimage destinations in New Mexico. On many occasions both private and public, he performed his extensive repertory of religious and secular songs, either a capella or accompanying himself on the *tombé,* or Indian drum.

Edwin sang many *inditas,* a broad genre of songs thematically and musically evocative of Indo-Hispano relations. In a 1993 interview before and after singing one of his Comanche songs, he shared the following narrative (my translation). Where I have added the dates in brackets, the key date of 1777 is well remembered in Tomé, because of a notorious Comanche attack in which every resident present in the village on a fateful day in May was killed (Adams and Chávez 1956:154):

> At the time of the Indian Rebellion [1680] Tomé Domínguez de Mendoza and all of his people left fleeing from here to Chihuahua. His sons went to the mines of Santa Eulalia. It had always been dangerous here because of the Apaches and the Navajos, so for a long time after the return to New Mexico of Don Diego de Vargas and his people [1693], only wagon trains and travelers passed by the Cerro de Tomé. They say that some Genízaros made a petition for a land grant here [1739],

3.5. Edwin y su Trompeta (Tomé). A grateful Edwin Berry returned from Italy and World War II with a bride and a promise to rebuild and guard the Calvario atop Cerro de Tomé.

and they let them come, because they were very good with their arms and could defend themselves from the Indians. Soon, they built their church with big and strong walls to seek refuge from the attacks.

In those times, the Comanches came here to the valley through Abó Pass and Cañón del Comanche every year at harvest time. They were friends with the people, because they treated them very well. Another thing that united them was the hatred they had for the Apaches. The Comanches always brought horses, buffalo robes, and jerky to sell. From here they got biscuits, *pinole*, blankets, and Mexican tobacco. That's where the song "Hermanito comanchito" comes from, I was told, because they would wait for the corn to grow and for the melon fields to be full.

The full text of "Hermano comanchito" is included in the discussions of chapter 4. Despite some violent undertones, its general theme is brotherhood and kinship with Comanches, and it expresses the positive sentiments of the people as they looked forward each year to the visit of the Comanches to their valley. Next, the plot thickens, and sets the stage for the tragedy to follow:

They say that the richest man back then was Don Ignacio Baca. He made friends with one of the Comanches who always brought his family. Baca had a beautiful daughter and the Comanche had a good-looking son. They got along well, since they saw each other every year. One time the men decided that it would be right for them to marry someday and gave their word. But when she was grown, the girl, whose name was María, decided that she didn't want to go to the Plains with the young man. She cried to her mother, who told her she was not obligated to keep the promise.

When the fall of 1776 came and the Comanches were on their way, Don Ignacio found out they were bringing horses and gifts to give for the bride. When they arrived, the girl hid with some people in Valencia, and her father, with tears in his eyes, told them that she had died that summer. He showed them a fresh grave in the *camposanto* [graveyard], crying, so that the Comanches would believe. They returned to the Plains without her.

Nobody knows how, but that winter the old Comanche found out that he had been deceived. Perhaps some envious person had told him. Anyway, he was furious, and they decided to take their vengeance. Besides, that year things were very bad in all of New Mexico, because of the wars everywhere with the Comanches. They returned to Tomé in late May, when many people had gone to Isleta Pueblo and Alburquerque to visit friends for a feast day. Since they were celebrating, they had no reason to expect an attack, and their guard was down.

When the Comanches arrived at Tomé, everyone was at mass in the church. The Comanches burned the door and killed everyone inside. They killed the priest with arrows, as he stood at the altar. The only ones who were not killed were in Isleta and Alburquerque. When they returned to Tomé, everything was in ruins. Their houses were burnt, and the Comanches had taken all the animals and things they wanted.

The girl María had gone to Isleta also. In the wars that followed, they took her captive to the Plains, and it is said that she married the same Comanche boy who had loved her so much. She lived with them for many years afterward. They also say that her grandson, a Comanche named Pueró returned to Tomé during one of the campaigns with the Navajos. He died fighting in that war. (Berry 1993) [my translation][5]

Beyond the name of Don Ignacio Baca in the census and the list of the dead in church records in Albuquerque, there is no documentary substantiation of the details of this legend, nor of whether the Comanche attackers were known to or knew their victims (A. Espinosa 1907:11).

The love-story plot is telltale evidence of the motifs of the romance narrative, so popular in the nineteenth century, whose characters epitomize in allegorical fashion the historical drama that surrounds them (Dekker 1990:23). Such narratives follow two tracks—the romantic quest for a maiden and the historic quest for land and justice. Typically, the romance portrays the demise of a heroic society from the perspective of the conqueror, focusing on dramatic moments of transition between two distinct ways of life and modes of production. "The conqueror thus condescends to see the 'enemy,' that is, the precapitalist society, as 'heroic' but primitive and even as unfortunate and abused by local authorities" (Dekker 1990:15).

Perhaps the romantic sentimentalization of the horrendous events of 1777 helped survivors deal with the memories. In any case, there is a clear lament for the loss of a friendly alliance, destroyed by the larger war that beleaguered New Mexico. The ambivalence expressed in this story is typical of the Hispano fascination with Comanche culture, complicated by revulsion for the horrors of war. As will be seen in the conclusions of chapter 6, Tomé is not the only tragic episode that is framed with the romance.

The following Comanche story from the Pueblo perspective was collected in 1999 from Andy García, a prominent singer and cultural activist from San Juan Pueblo. Before singing a Kwítara, or Comanche, song, he shared the following story to offer insight into the Comanche social-dance tradition as it is practiced in the Tewa pueblos. There is also considerable ambivalence expressed, fascination mixed with great trepidation:

Way back, what they are saying, what I heard is that the Comanches were around our area, and they did do trading with them. They traded with Comanches, our people. But then, some of them also found out and realized that some of them are very sneaky, the Comanche, they were sneaky. Some of them were not as honest, I guess, put it that way. Mr. Bird from Santo Domingo would tell this story about Comanches, how they went right up here in the Pecos area, where there

3.6. Andy García, Vinton Lonnie, y sus Cantos Kwítaras. Many Kwítara, or Tewa Comanche, songs incorporate Numunuh and even Spanish words. Male Pueblo Comanche dancers use full Plains regalia.

were some Comanches. So they went over there to trade with them, and they were from Santo Domingo. But they took a tall man with them and he understood the Comanche language, and when they got over there they talked to them. They said,

"We would like to trade horses or items that we brought." Like their pottery, like their jewelry, whatever things they make they took along with them. Probably their bread and cookies and pies and things that they make.

When they were there, there was a young lady that came out from a tipi that they had set up where they had camped, and when she came out she started singing a really beautiful song. And the Santo Domingo people said that, that song was so beautiful, and they said,

"I wish we knew what the words meant, what she was saying." And all this time, this tall man that they took with them was hearing the song as to what she was saying. After their trading and all they said,

"Well, we can go ahead and leave and going on the way we'll camp somewhere after we do our business here with these people, the Comanche."

So when they left, the tall man stayed around, hearing what they were saying. So in the meantime, they said,

"Bring the finest horses that we have."

"But those are our finest horses."

"Yeah, we know that, but we're going to get them back. We'll take it away from them again."

See, this is what was going on, but this tall man was hearing all these things, what was happening. So,

"—Bring them and we'll trade but we'll bring them back, we'll get them back again."

So wherever they're going to camp. So after they got to that camp, the tall man came and was explaining to them what they were saying. So he made the Santo Domingo people really aware of what could take place. In the meantime, one of them asked,

"Well, what was that lady [saying], the one that came out singing the beautiful song." The tall man said,

"What she was singing in the song was that it was the Pueblo people who killed her husband. What she was singing in the words, what she was telling her Comanche brothers there to kill the Pueblos who were there. That's what she was singing."

This tall man went and made them ready. So the Santo Domingo people said,

"Well, what are we going to do? There's just a few of us, but there's a lot of those Comanches." The tall man said,

"Well I know that there are some Comanches not too far from here that are camped, that are staying around here, and they're the good Comanches. We can ask them and see if they can help us to fight off these other ones, if they come to attack us."

So that's what they did, they moved, they started going. So they came to this camp where the good Comanches were, and they told them exactly what was going to happen, and this good Comanche said,

"If they come, well, we'll be ready for them. If this is what they're going to do, we'll be ready for them. If this is what they're going to do, we're going to help you. Because you are good people. Because we have been trading with you for a long time."

So that's how they got the help. So when the other Comanches came, that's when the attack took place, and these Comanches went after them. Those other ones they stopped, and they told them,

"You leave these people alone, because these people, we've been trading with them, they've been good to us, and just because you came here not too long ago, and this is what you're trying to do? We have good relations with these Pueblo people, so you leave them alone."

And that's how they left them and they went on. And this story goes on, this man, Mr. Bird, that's how he talked. He's gone now, but this is what he was talking about.

CHAPTER THREE

The first part of this story is set not in San Juan, but farther south, between the Keresan pueblo of Santo Domingo, also located on the Río Grande, and Pecos Pueblo, which was located on the principal route from the Plains to the central Río Grande Valley. The characters in the story are also from Santo Domingo, as is the teller, to whom Mr. García attributes the story. The historical record is clear that Pecos suffered more attacks than any other pueblo, one of the factors in its eventual abandonment. The Pueblo perspective of ambivalence and fascination is clearly expressed. The Numunuh were a people composed of many different bands, and each had distinct relations with their neighbors. Some could be trusted and some cannot. The story continues to involve San Juan Pueblo directly:

> So the Comanches around the area, like in San Juan, they would come. They would be on horses, and they would be coming in for trouble. And as far as I heard, their Comanche chief was knocked down by the Pueblos. And when he fell, all the braves that he had, they started crying for their Comanche chief after he was knocked down by the Pueblos. That's why there's no grass around the San Juan baseball diamond. In that area there is no grass growing because all the tears of the braves started to come and it started to be like a stream. It came through there and nothing used to grow there. It killed everything. Nothing, not even a weed would come up in that area. And now it's a ballpark and that area is still there.

This story is not fixed chronologically, but from the tenor of the relations described, may be placed in the 1770s, if not before. The historical record indicates that 1774 was a very bad year for raids. In June, San Juan was attacked and fiercely defended. Several Comanche high-ranking warriors were killed, and many younger ones were driven into the river. However, on this particular occasion they got what they came for—five hundred horses, San Juan's entire herd (Noyes 1993:63). What is fascinating in the story are the references to local topography. Everyone knows where the baseball field is in San Juan, given the popularity of softball. This very familiarity, of course, lends credence to the story. With the Pecos and San Juan incidents as preface, Mr. García then explains the Pueblo fascination with the Comanches and their mimetic tradition of including them in their cycle of ceremonial dances:

> And this is the reason why, because our people had seen the Comanches with their beautiful outfits that they were wearing like the headdress, the paint that they had on them, the buckskin, the feathers, how they had them. So that fascinated our people, the way that they were dressed, so they decided to do a Comanche dance. When the Comanches paint themselves from the foot to the head, that means that if the put red, all this paint on, that means war. And they look so good, the way they paint themselves, the colorful costumes that they wear. That's how the Comanche dance came.

So they said, "Well we can do a Comanche dance." And so the Comanche dance has been going on now for we don't know how long. (A. García 1999)

Listening "between the lines," the key concepts are fascination, respect, emulation, and relief that one of the most uncertain eras in New Mexico history had been positively resolved. Formal history and Pueblo oral accounts agree on their assessment of the past: the two most important events in the history of New Mexico are the 1680 Pueblo Revolt, which secured the survival of Pueblo culture, and the end of Comanche hostilities, formalized in the Treaty of 1786 and signed in Pecos Pueblo by Don Juan Bautista de Anza and Ecueracapa. After the traditional greeting of rubbing their faces together and smoking tobacco, the Comanches ceremoniously dug a hole in the ground and "buried" their enmity with the Spanish-Mexicans. De Anza gave Ecueracapa a saber and a banner. More gifts were exchanged, and a trade fair was celebrated to honor the peace that lasted into modern times (Noyes 1993:80–81). The celebration of this Pax Comanche has continued into the present, not as a phantom remembrance of the past, but as an intercultural force that still shapes identity and ethnic relations in New Mexico.

4

Cuerno Verde y Sus Hijos

text and performance in an eighteenth-century folk drama

Yo soy aquel capitán,	I am that selfsame great captain,
no capitán, poco he dicho,	No, sire, few words I've devised
y solo por Gran Señor	Of all tribes I am the leader
de todos soy conocido.	And by all am recognized.

—Cuerno Verde, *Los comanches*[1]

W hen recollection becomes collective and simultaneous, the plaza/stage is set for the action that the spectacle of folk drama and ritual performance unfolds. Cast in the mold of the auto de entrada, the equestrian victory play in the genre of *Moros y cristianos,* the folk drama of *Los comanches* has evolved over a two-century performance tradition to generate socially specific meanings for the communities that perform and promote it. At the time of its inscription in the late 1770s, it was celebrated as an ambivalent victory play in a ferocious war that had not yet reached its resolution. An important battle had been won, and a fearsome war chief had been annihilated, but peace would still be a long time coming and was by no means guaranteed. The Numunuh were the most formidable foe faced by anyone in New Mexico.

Nineteenth-century performances were less troubling. In his memoirs, Rafael Chacón recalls seeing the play before the Civil War, when it was a celebration of victory and peace as well as a demonstration of the indomitable character of the Nuevo Mexicanos, who by then were living under American occupation:

At other functions *Los Comanches* were held, a composition of New Mexican origin, in order to commemorate the conquest of the Comanche nation by the New Mexican Spaniards. One part represented the Comanches under their captain, Cuerno-Verde (Green Horn), and the Spanish were represented under a chief, Don

Carlos, who was the one who guided them. This comedy was shown in an open field with all the pomp, style, raiment, and arms of those times. (R. Chacón 1986:76)

After a hiatus in the last decades of the century (A. Espinosa 1907:19), another chapter in the performance tradition of *Los comanches* was stimulated by Anglo interest in colonial Spanish culture after the 1898 victory over Spain. With the spoils of the remainder of the Spanish Empire,

> [T]he new hegemony was institutionalized in public architecture, monuments, and civil ceremonies that incorporated fantasies of the Spanish Empire. War-time Hispanophobia quickly shaded into Hispanophilia, for about the same time that Anglo Americans were at war with Spain, they were also beginning to celebrate highly idealized elements of Spanish culture, including food, music, and so-called colonial architecture. (Márez 2002:8)

This mimetic impulse is what became the Santa Fe style (Wilson 1997), or the New Mexico version of the same "fantasy heritage" that on the West Coast became the California Mission style (McWilliams 1990). Sensing the prestige value of imperial nostalgia, Nuevo Mexicano elites not only embraced the cultural Hispanophilia of the times, but also competed with Anglo elites for the legitimacy and authenticity of the perceived Spanish colonial heritage (Márez 2002:10). The rediscovery of *Los comanches,* thanks to the critical edition of Aurelio M. Espinosa (1907), provided a bona fide episode for the many civic pageants and festivals that were being invented to celebrate the cultures of New Mexico. But this mediated revival of the play only lasted through the 1930s.

Meanwhile, in the villages of northern New Mexico, an autochthonous revival of *Los comanches* was underway, in which Nuevo Mexicanos articulated their own response to the cultural climate and political challenges of the twentieth century. In the hands of the people and through the process of oral transmission, the text of the eighteenth-century play evolved to project a different set of aspirations and intentions. At this point it began attracting the attention of a new generation of revisionist scholars interested in recovering the U.S. Hispanic literary heritage.

In a seminal essay in the first volume of Recovery essays, Genaro Padilla thoughtfully questions the forays of Chicano criticism into the colonial period in search of roots, wondering, "Is this a move to invent continuity between colonial Hispanic and Chicano literary discourse—the first a hegemonic discourse of possession and domination, the second a counterhegemonic discourse generated by dispossession and subordination?" (G. Padilla 1993:32). In the case of *Los comanches,* there is no need for invention or critical artifice, because the record of its evolution becomes complete, if an ethnographic gaze is cast beyond the play as published text to the play as cultural enactment and socially symbolic performance. From this perspective, the metamorphosis from a discourse of power to a discourse of resistance is complete.

This transformation of the play's range of meaning offers a fascinating glimpse into the dynamic process of cultural mestizaje, what postcolonial theory terms "a rethinking of the forms and forces of 'identification' as they operate at the edge of cultural authority" (Bhabha 1986:149). As seen in the other types of mimetic and intercultural Comanche celebrations in the subsequent chapters, a wide range of subjectification is present, from the military confrontation of the Comanche as cultural Other to the identification of Comanche as part of cultural self. In the context of the upper Río Grande, this complex is popularly known in all of its facets as *Los comanches.* To distinguish the victory play from other "Comanches" celebrations, the people sometimes call it *Los comanches de castillo,* in reference to the "castle," or base area, the Spanish-Mexican soldiers used in the play (F. Gonzales 1992).

In an equestrian display only equaled by the New Mexican *Moros y cristianos,* the play is an ambivalent celebration of the defeat of the great chief Tabivo Naritgante ("brave and handsome") in the final campaign of the Comanche wars of the late eighteenth century. Famous for his distinctive battle headdress with a single green-and-gold buffalo horn, Cuerno Verde is the name the Spanish Mexicans gave both him and his father, whose death he avenged in a series of raids until his own defeat, in early August of 1779. He and most of his Spanish-Mexican dramatic and historical antagonists can be found on the pages of chronicles and letters from the period (John 1975, Thomas 1932:62, 99, 309). Carlos Fernández led a 1774 campaign for Governor Mendinueta (Thomas 1932:62); José de la Peña was one of the founders of Peña Blanca, south of Santa Fe (Thomas: 99); Salvador Ribera was a first ensign in the De Anza campaigns (Thomas 1932:319); and Toribio Ortiz was a relative of De Anza (Thomas 1932:309).[2]

❧ Synopsis, Scenes, and Texts

The most complete script of the play (dated 1864), and the only one with staging directions, was published by Arthur Campa in 1942.[3] As Márez (2002:15) notes, this script casts a more Spanish frame around the play, beginning in the Spanish war camp and ending with the death of Cuerno Verde. The script that Espinosa published in 1907, and which dates to the 1840s and 1850s, begins with the entrance of Cuerno Verde and ends with a demented soliloquy of Barriga Duce, the battlefield clown and robber of the dead. Although the majority of the texts are identical, the frame itself suggests a substantially different meaning for the play, especially since there is no Cuerno Verde death scene in it. Before engaging in any additional speculation, the production must be visualized.

The set is an open field with a Spanish fort, or *castillo,* on one side and the Comanche camp on the other. Two *Pecas,* or captive girls from Pecos Pueblo, cower in the shadows of the fort. The cast of mounted braves and soldiers meet in their respective camps, then on the field of battle, to exchange fierce arengas, or military harangues, in a dazzling verbal display. They recount their deeds, declare their loyalty and desire for vengeance, then confront each other to exchange taunts and prepare for battle.

A messenger from another group of Comanches who are negotiating a peace treaty with the government arrives at the last minute but is unable to intervene in the inevitable conflict at hand. In the final scene, the battle rages, ending in a rout of the Comanches. In the confusion of the skirmish, the Pecas are rescued. In some versions, Cuerno Verde dies, and in others he remains. A disturbingly enigmatic and burlesque character named Barriga Duce watches the captives, robs the dead on the battlefield, and ridicules the entire spectacle. Although not noted specifically in the text, the action may be divided into seven fast-paced scenes:

1. Danger Approaches.

The Spanish camp is warned of approaching warriors by Barriga Duce (Sweet Belly), a clownlike camp follower, who throws balls of dough to get their attention. The initial gag is that he has threatened the Comanches with his *maza* (battle-axe) and then threw dough, or *masa,* at the Spanish (both are pronounced the same way in New World Spanish). The *capitán* sounds the alarm, the bugle is heard, and Don Carlos emerges with a battle flag for the *sargento* to carry. He announces it is time for an attack, since the Spanish have Faith on their side.

4.1. Arengas de Cuerno Verde (Alcalde). On the field of combat the arenga, or battlefield harangue, proves that fighting words and threatening gestures are just as important as weapons.

2. Enter Cuerno Verde and Don Carlos Fernández

Cuerno Verde makes a dramatic appearance at full gallop and delivers his famous arenga, with its invocation to the four directions. He exults in brash boasts and bristling threats to inspire his warriors and intimidate his enemies:

Desde el oriente al poniente,	*From the east to west horizons,*
Desde el sur al norte frío	*From the south to northern cold*
Suena el brillante clarín	*Rings the blast of that bright trumpet*
Y reina el acero mío.	*Where doth reign my steel so bold.*
Campeo osado, atrevido,	*I do battle daring, last,*
Y es tanta la valentía	*And such is the valor reigning*
Que reina en el pecho mío . . .	*Here within my breast held fast . . .*

He and the other Comanches constantly compare their valor to that of the animals of the mountains and plains.

Refreno al más atrevido,	55	*The most daring I restrain,*
Devoro al más arrojado;		*The most dauntless I devour;*
Pues con mi bravura admiro		*And in my bravura admired*
Al oso más arrogante,		*The most arrogant bear and*
Al fiero tigre rindo . . .		*Fiercest mountain lion do I conquer.*

Cuerno Verde then evokes the reason for his vengeance—the vision of a flowery field. Some critics read this as a threat of the damage he will wreak, but I am convinced he is making a historical reference. The red blossoms are the spilled blood of Comanche men, women, and children, a reference to Carlos Fernández's September 1774 campaign fifty leagues north and east of Santa Fe, characterized by historians as a merciless slaughter (Noyes 1993:65). The unburied bones of more than four hundred victims could be seen at a place called Orejas del Conejo (Rabbit Ears). The surviving captives were taken as slaves to Cuba and never heard from again (Chaves 1906:9).[4]

Y sólo los españoles	100	*And only the Spanish refrain*
Refrenan el valor mío,		*My valor which doth shine.*
Pero hoy ha de correr		*But today blood shall flow*
Sangre del corazón vengativo.		*From this vengeful heart of mine.*
Me recuerda la memoria		*It recalls to mind and memory*
De un español atrevido	105	*A daring Spanish soldier*
Que ufano y con valentía		*Who, full-proud and filled with valor*
Y con tanto osado brío		*And with unsurpassing furor*
El campo vistió de flores		*Dressed the battlefield with flowers*
En sangre de colorido.		*Crimson and with scarlet red,*
De los muertos la distancia		*Of the men, women and children*

Hombres, mujeres y niños	111	Killed at distance, fully-dead.
No pudiendo numerarse		We could not begin to number
Ni contarse los cautivos . . .		Nor to count the captives claimed.

In the exhortation of his warriors, Cuerno Verde makes a revealing reference to the brave Genízaros that are fighting in his service. Could they be captives, or are they apostates or simply refugees that have decided to cast their lot with the Numunuh, as so many other neighboring groups had done on the Plains? Cuerno Verde continues the list of allies: Kiowas, Arapahos, Quechas, Kansas, Jumanos, and Yamparicas. The last is the name of his own band of Numunuh.

Ea, nobles capitanes,	114	Your attention, noble captains,
Genízaros valerosos,		Valorous janissaries,
Que se pregone mi edicto,		Let my edict be proclaimed,
Que yo como general		That I, as your general speaking
He de estar aprevenido . . .		Must be well-prepared and seize . . .
Que suene el tambor y pito.	126	Beat the drum and play the fife!
¡Al baile, y punto de guerra!		Start the dance and launch the battle!

The poet may be putting words into Cuerno Verde's mouth, but if he is a veteran of these battles, as historians think, he undoubtedly heard the screaming harangues of the battlefield. The dauntless bravura of the character in the play

4.2. (opposite) Furia de Don Carlos Fernández (Alcalde). Called up from retirement to meet the Comanche threat in 1774, Capitán Fernández attacked the first group of Comanches he found. His wife was from Alcalde.

4.3. (above) Cuerno Verde y Don Carlos Fernández I (Alcalde). In Los Comanches, Capitán Fernández is credited with the defeat and death of the Numunuh war chief, although Governor Juan Bautista de Anza conducted the final campaign.

matches the historical descriptions of the chief himself and the fearless tactics of Comanche warfare.

In this key scene, a venerable and dignified Don Carlos Fernández responds to Cuerno Verde's challenge face to face, touting the imperial power of Spain, before whom all nations tremble. His curious mention of the "four poles" of Spanish power is a counter to Cuerno Verde's invocation of the "four directions."

¿Qué no sabes que en la España	190	Don't you know, in Spain by law,
El señor soberano		The most Sovereign Lord of Heaven
De los cielos y la tierra		And of all the earth right here
Y todos los cuatro polos		By the four poles thus enclosed
Que este gran círculo encierra?		Within this unending sphere
Brilla su soberanía,		Shines in majesty and splendor?

CUERNO VERDE Y SUS HIJOS

Y al oír su nombre tiemblan	*And when His name's heard withall,*
Alemanes, portugueses,	*Tremble Portuguese and Germans,*
Turquía y la Inglaterra,	*Turkey, as does England all,*
Porque en diciendo españoles	*At the mention of us Spaniards,*
Todas las naciones tiemblan... 200	*Every single nation quakes...*

Don Carlos scoffs at Cuerno Verde, saying that he has already heard of him. Later in the speech, he recognizes him and realizes they have met on the field of battle before. Although there is no documentary proof, this has led some historians to believe that Fernández and Cuerno Verde had fought in 1774. So many raids were attributed to Tabivo Naritgante that some historians believe that there may have been more than one (Kavanagh 1996:92).

Si quieres saber quién soy, 205	*If you'd know my appellation,*
Te lo diré porque sepas	*I'll reveal it to you such.*
Que no es la primer batalla	*This is not the first engagement*
Esta que tú me demuestras.	*On the battlefield for us.*
Las que he hecho son infinitas,	*The campaigns I've fought are many,*
Siempre he pisado tus tierras	*I've always trodden your lands*
Aunque ya avanzado en años, 210	*Although now advanced in years,*
Y me veas de esta manera	*You still see me in the ready*
Siempre soy Carlos Fernández	*Carlos Fernández am I always.*
Por el mar y por la tierra,	*O'er the land and o'er the sea*
Y para probar tu brío	*I'll challenge your pride and mettle*
Voy a hacer junta de guerra.	*And now prepare to give you battle.*

3. Councils of War

As both mounted figures part, both go to hold their respective councils of war with their men, who swear obedience, brag about their deeds of valor, and show impatience for the upcoming battle. Since battle tactics are so difficult to portray dramatically, plenty of forceful words would have to do.

Don José de la Peña boasts that not even a hundred opponents will faze him, and that he will fight to the end rather than fall into their hands as a captive. He has no doubt heard of the cruel punishments that the Numunuh were capable of inflicting on their prisoners of war. It was well known that Cuerno Verde himself presided over the tortures. De la Peña will never surrender or submit, knowing this.

En un número crecido 279	*Though the number be dire high*
Siendo cien hombres de guerra	*Be they a hundred men in battle*
No me daré por vencido	*There, unvanquished shall be I*
Pues tengo bien conocido	*I have always known this truly*
Y me late el corazón	*And my heart beats very fast*

4.4. Cuerno Verde y Don Carlos Fernández II (Alcalde). In the merciless Comanche wars of the 1770s, Cuerno Verde and Don Carlos Fernández met more than once in battle. In the eighteenth century, he would have been wearing leather armor.

Que jamás seré cautivo	Knowing I shall not be captured
De esta bárbara nación	By this savage nation cast.
A ganarles el terreno	To retake the ground is best now;
Es lo mejor que se puede	It's what we can do; 'tis fate
Para salvar nuestro reino	To safeguard our kingdom here
Que nuestra patria venera	Since our homeland venerates
Aquel príncipe Miguel	Blessed Michael of nine choirs;
De las nueve jerarquías	The hierarchies he allays
Será nuestro gran sostén . . .	He will be our intercessor . . .

(line 290 is marked beside "Aquel príncipe Miguel / Blessed Michael of nine choirs;")

By invoking the warrior Archangel San Miguel, he invokes not only the power of his sword, but also in the same allusion demonizes the enemy, associating him with the serpent of Evil that Saint Michael and the nine hierarchies vanquish.

4. Boasts and Threats
In the next scene, the war councils end and soldiers and warriors begin taunting each other directly, trying to incite their rage and provoke them into battle. Cabeza Negra (Black Hair) brags about his bravery in taking captives and his compassion

4.5. Consejo de Guerra (Alcalde). Both the Comanches and Spanish-Mexicans call war councils during the play, to decide their course of action, invigorate morale, and prepare for imminent battle.

at taking good care of them, a story that is sure to infuriate his interlocutor, Don Salvador Ribera.

Yo saqué de los Cristianos	350	It was I who from the Christians
Dos niños que cautivé,		Took two children that caught,
Y con mis fuerzas mostré		And with all my might I showed thee
El valor a tus paisanos.		And thy countrymen quite fair
Sin hacerles ningún daño		That I did not ever harm them
Los mantuve con mis bienes.		But sustained them with my wares.

The braggadocio quickly turns into threats. Oso Pardo (Gray or Brown Bear) says he will no longer delay. Like his namesake, he is a wild beast and will cut the heads off the arrogant Christians.

No hay que detenerse un punto,	368	There's no need to sue for favor
Que como bárbara fiera		Since, like a barbarous beast
Con esta lanza animosa		With my great, bloodthirsty lance
Le he de cortar la cabeza		I would lop the head at least
A aquel cristiano arrogante.		Of that Christian who's so haughty.

As the threats escalate and Zapato Cuenta (Beaded Shoe) asks who in the world will answer to his rage, Don José de la Peña answers forth, mocking the Comanche practice of gorging after battles. The reference to buffalo lard may be an insult, because Comanches were disgusted by the idea of eating lard and used it mostly for other purposes (Noyes 1993:30). Around them the final battle rages.

Zapato Cuenta:		*Beaded Shoe:*
El oso más arrogante	430	Even the most arrogant bear
Se encoge de mi fiereza		Shrinks from my vengeful rampage
El tíguere en las montañas		Even the lion of the mountains
Huye en la oculta sierra.		Can be made to hide and flee.
¿Quién se opone a mi valor?		Who opposes my own valor?
¿Quién cautiva mi soberbia?		Who'll entrap my pride that be?
Don José de la Peña:		*Don José de la Peña:*
Yo quebrantaré la furia,	440	I shall shatter all his fury,
Que soy la más alta peña.		As my last name indicates.
Soy peñasco en valentía,		I am rock in might and valor,
En bríos y en fortaleza.		Which my strength ne'er moderates.
Esas locas valentías		Your exalted gallantries are
Son criadas de la soberbia.		Born and bred of foolish pride.
Que tanto infunde el valor		Spurred and infused is your valor
En vosotros la manteca		From that lard you have inside

Que coméis con tanta gula	*Gleaned from buffalo and eaten*
Y con ella criáis la fuerza	*With such healthy appetite*
De vuestras disposiciones . . .	*To engender strength within you . . .*

Don José in the next verse makes an interesting reference to the battle tactics of the Numunuh, who preferred to minimize their losses by avoiding direct engagements, unless they were of sufficient numbers or battlefield advantage to prevail. This regard for the lives of warriors is distinct from the willingness of European soldiers to engage each other directly, whatever the cost (Noyes 1993:223).

Nace el sol y luego muere,	453	*The sun rises and it sets then,*
Porque nunca cuerpo a cuerpo		*And you've never, hand to hand,*
Habéis hecho resistencia.		*Fought with any force behind you.*
En un choque que tuvimos		*In a skirmish on this land,*
Siendo cien hombres de guerra		*Although we were but a hundred*
Siendo el número crecido		*And many more warriors had ye,*
De tu bárbara nación		*With all your barbarous nation,*
La victoria no fué vuestra.		*You could not win victory.*

Don José is probably referring to the same September 20, 1774, massacre at Orejas de Conejo that Cuerno Verde had referred to. Comanches did outnumber the Spanish-Mexicans, but that was because so many families were in the encampment.

5. A Call to Arms

The provocations have reached their culmination, and Don Carlos screams out the call to arms in one of his classic arengas. He exhorts his troops with their totem animal, the Spanish imperial lion, with the battle-cry invocation of Santiago, the patron saint of Spain and the Reconquest, who had the reputation of appearing on the battlefield to aid beleaguered Spanish troops on to victory.

Y así esforzados leones	502	*And so my indomitable lions,*
Todos al arma, guerreros.		*To the fight my noble warriors.*
Suénese tambor y guerra		*Sound the drums of war*
En el nombre de Santiago		*In the name of Saint James*
Y de la Virgen María.		*And of the Virgin Mary.*
Márchense pronto al campo . . .		*March forthwith to battle . . .*
¡Santiago y cierre España!		*Saint James, and close in Spain!*

Soldiers a begin to skirmish with the warriors and then retreat to the castle momentarily. Behind their backs, the Comanches take two captives being held in the castillo. Strangely enough, on the sidelines there is a trading session going on between Barriga Duce and some of the Comanches.

6. A Last Chance for Peace

At the last moment, Tabaco Chupa Janchi (Tobacco-Smoking Janchi) arrives at full gallop with news from the Napestle country, the Arkansas valley stronghold of the Numunuh to the north. He alludes to his role in negotiating peace treaties in Taos and tells Cuerno Verde and his warriors of his bravery in proposing peace with the Spaniards. Ritual use of tobacco is always part of the negotiation process, hence his name. He sees that the possibility for peace is nil in this confrontation and wishes them well. As ambassador, Tabaco then advises Don Carlos and his soldiers that Cuerno Verde, Oso Pardo, and Cabeza Negra were determined to fight, a fact that had not escaped them. As Tabaco leaves at full gallop, a pitched battle begins.

7. Spoils of War—Death of Cuerno Verde

To provide some carnivalesque comic relief, Barriga Duce, the camp follower, begins to loot the battlefield, boasting of the booty he will take home to his wife. The meat and green chile she will cook him is also laden with erotic innuendo. In performances, he plays both fool and coward, taunting the warriors, then hiding when the battles began. After the fatal rout of 1774, contemporary reports mention the rich booty taken home by both Spanish and Pueblo Indian combatants (Noyes 1993:76). The capture of Cuerno Verde's winter camp in August 1779 was another notable bonanza of booty.

4.6.   Tabaco, el Indio Embajador (Alcalde). Prior to the battle scene, an emissary arrives in haste from Taos, in a last try for peace. Treaty negotiations were customarily marked by smoking tobacco.

CUERNO VERDE Y SUS HIJOS

63

4.7. (above) La Batalla Final (Alcalde). Threats and intimidation eventually escalate to full-scale mounted combat. In the Alcalde production, nobody dies. All the combatants leave the battlefield together.

4.8. (opposite, top) Cautiverio de la Peca (Alcalde). The presence of pecas, or female captives (from Pecos Pueblo), is an indication of what was at stake for combatants—their own children.

4.9. (opposite, bottom) "Soy de Todos Conocido" (Alcalde). "I am well-known to all." Cuerno Verde was anxious to avenge the death of his father in 1768. Note the yearly changes of actors and costumes.

Que mueran, que para mí	620	*Let them all die, for to me then*
Todos los despojos quedan.		*All the spoils will then stay!*
Tiendas, antas y conchelles		*Tents, skins, and bedrolls also*
Para que mis hijos duerman.		*For my kids to sleep away.*
Y la carne, a mi mujer		*And the meat, my wife, I'd ask her*
He de hacer que me la cuesa		*To prepare it nice for me,*
Y me la guise con chile		*And to season it with chile*
Que es una comida buena.		*As a dish most heavenly.*
¡Apriéntenles compañeros!		*Push on forward, dear companions,*
Que de eso mi alma se alegra.		*For it warms my heart and soul!*

As he eats and loads up his plunder, he sees that in spite of all the boasts of Spanish arms, the liberated Peca children who had been in the hands of the Spanish are now with their captors again. In the confusion of the battle scene, he frees them once more. In his hands they are just more booty.

In the climax of this final scene, Cuerno Verde is vanquished, bringing the last great campaign against the Numunuh to its conclusion.

Capitán:		*Captain:*
Ya mi vista no te pierde,	691	*You cannot hide from my vision,*
Indio traidor, inhumano.		*Traitorous Indian inhumane.*
Serás muerto por mis manos:		*By my own hand you shall perish:*
¡Muera, muera Cuerno Verde!		*Death to Green Horn and his name!*

Gone are the touching scenes of repentance, forgiveness, and conversion that characterize *Moros y cristianos.* Gone also is the moral allegory and the classical allusions that embellish the siege of Acoma in Villagrá's 1610 epic *Historia de la Nueva México.* Here the defiant Comanches are soundly defeated, and the play is a victory celebration. Neither demon nor prince, Cuerno Verde appears as the haughty and formidable enemy that he was. What is gravely missing is his redemption.

∾ In Search of Juan Bautista De Anza and Pedro Baptista Pino

Although five generations of scholars acknowledge that *Los comanches* is a folk play, and several of them actually witnessed it, there are no contemporary performance studies to date. The most complete contextual study was recently drawn by Curtis Márez (2001), who examines the politics of cultural representation in New Mexico in the wake of the Spanish-American War of 1898. The majority of the scholarship concerns itself with the play's origins and the plethora of tantalizing historical references (Austin 1927, 1933; Brown 1939; Campa 1942, 1979; Englekirk 1940, 1957; A. Espinosa 1907, 1976; Kavanagh n.d.). Four more recent scholars have examined the literary structure of the play (R. Anderson 1989, Dahlberg 1996, Lamadrid 1993, Roeder 1976).

The consensus among them concerning the historical record is that the play combines or conflates two distinct campaigns against the Comanches, both outlined in the previous chapter. In September 1774, following a violent summer of raiding and successful retaliation, Governor Mendinueta implemented his zero-tolerance policy of extermination above diplomacy and dispatched Don Carlos Fernández with a rag-tag force of six hundred poorly equipped presidial soldiers, militia, and Pueblo auxiliaries. A large encampment composed of Comanche families was surprised well north and east of Santa Fe, and over four hundred were captured or slaughtered. For the next five years, the Comanches exacted their vengeance on Nuevo Mexicano settlers, who paid a terrible price for this and other controversial victories in a badly miscalculated policy (Noyes 1993:62–65). In August of 1779, newly appointed Governor De Anza was faced with bringing closure to the genocidal policies of his predecessor before initiating his own ultimately successful efforts at diplomacy. He captured an even larger camp of Cuerno Verde's people on the *Río del Sacramento* (Fountain Creek, south of present-day Colorado Springs) after most of them fled and left behind all their winter supplies. The warriors were off raiding in northern New Mexico. Returning from the raid, forty Comanches desperately charged the Spanish-Mexican army of eight hundred, and Cuerno Verde, his son, and all his chiefs were annihilated (Noyes 1993:74–79).

The absence of the victorious De Anza as a character in the play is a conundrum that has puzzled scholars. Early scholarship attributed the presumed inaccuracy to a folk aesthetic more interested in dramatic spectacle than in historic fact (A. Espinosa 1907, Campa 1942). Those more concerned with dating the play have speculated that it may have been written between 1774 and 1779, adding Cuerno Verde's death as a codicil (Englekirk 1957). Recent scholarship has noted that the exclusion of the newcomer De Anza actually adds to the drama of the play, since Cuerno Verde was familiar with the veteran Carlos Fernández and yearned for the opportunity to avenge himself personally for the Orejas del Conejo atrocities of 1774 (R. Anderson 1989:116). The Comanche losses there cried out for vengeance, especially since it is doubtful that the victims were responsible for the raids they had been accused of. Governor Mendinueta wanted blood, and Carlos Fernández delivered him a bloodbath. With the Cuerno Verde campaign at hand, the militia and auxiliaries in 1779 assumed that De Anza wanted more of the same.

The poet feels great ambivalence toward the brash new governor. Would the victorious campaign against Cuerno Verde just be another disastrous episode in an escalating cycle of violence? Was he impatient or skeptical with the emerging diplomatic campaign? Was he yearning for new victories and the possibility for more personal vengeance and more booty? It is difficult to say. Soldiers had access to wealth in the form of all the animals, goods, and captives they took in warfare. If the poet was indeed the diplomat Pedro Baptista Pino, was he a party to the conspiracies to discredit De Anza and deprive him of his well-earned fame? After De Anza took office, he caused some popular discontent when he ordered a reduction of missions and a concentration of outlying settlements into defensible plazas (Noyes 1993:155). Encouraged by the discontent, Felipe de Neve, the interim comandante general from 1782 to 1784 actively tried to discredit De Anza during the most critical period of the negotiations for peace, moving them from Santa Fe to Béxar for a time (Noyes 1993:155).

In any case, the name that resounds to this day in the popular memory is that of Don Carlos Fernández, while the name of De Anza lives on only in books. If the play's intent was to erase him from the popular consciousness, it succeeded. "Native son" sentiment is always a factor in northern New Mexico, especially in

Alcalde, where the only surviving performance of *Los comanches* is staged. Critics have overlooked what community historians have noted all along—the marriage of Don Carlos Fernández to one of the daughters of Sebastián Martín, the original settler of Alcalde, whose descendants are still present in the area (Chaves 1906, Brown 1939).

Sandra Dahlberg, the newest critic to join the debate, uses careful textual scrutiny to posit De Anza's exclusion from the play as a clever and calculated protest of government Indian policy and a personal objection to the flamboyant style of the young outsider:

> Fernández is not only personifying the Anza administration's lack of regard for the Comanche people and the Spanish intent to conquer the Indians . . . he is also reflecting authorial disapproval of Anza's personal involvement in the war with Cuerno Verde's Comanches. The use of the personal pronoun rather than relying on the established empirical power, exposes Anza's self-pride, his need to flaunt his power, a tendency supported by Anza's own notes on the engagement. (Dahlberg 1996:140)

The hilarious but disturbing speeches of the comic character Barriga Duce take on new significance in this critical light. He is much more than a stock *gracioso* providing humorous relief from the heroic action. He is clearly the dramatic vehicle that at once veils and reveals the author's cynical view of the futility of the Comanche campaigns and the complicity of the Nuevo Mexicano settlers as they greedily divide up the spoils of war, rich as it was in the Cuerno Verde campaign. Honor and the quest for peace were the justifications, but "a simple tally of the booty colonists seized in their raids unmasked their true intent" (Gutiérrez 1991:152).

The other critical dilemma of *Los comanches* concerns authorship. All but one scholar (Englekirk 1957) agree that based on the wealth of cultural and historical detail in the text, the author of *Los comanches* in all probability was a participant observer of the Comanche campaigns of the 1770s. Critical speculations as well as oral historical sources indicate that the author may have been none other than Don Pedro Baptista Pino of Galisteo, the New Mexico representative to the Cortes de Cádiz of 1810. Amado Chaves, the donor of the first manuscript to be published, reported to Aurelio Espinosa that descendants of Pino by family tradition claim him as the author (Chaves 1906:9). Pino was a participant in the campaigns, and Comanches attacked his ranch several times. Two family members were taken captive and others perished in the Tomé massacre of 1777.[5] Despite these personal tragedies, he writes favorably, even admirably about Comanche culture in his 1812 *Exposición sucinta y sencilla de la provincia del Nuevo México*, the document that he personally delivered to the Cortes. The most convincing case for Pino's authorship is provided by Dahlberg's (1996:133–47) close reading of the opinions expressed in the *Exposición* and the opinions implicit in *Los comanches*.

In terms of literary origins, there is unanimous critical agreement concerning the dramatic inheritance of *Los comanches* from its parent, *Moros y cristianos.* The analogous dramatic action and staging is evident to anyone who has seen both plays in New Mexico. Opposing mounted armies face each other across the battlefield, then enter into combat to rescue the Santa Cruz in one case and the Peca captives in the other. However, the ideological differences stand in sharp contrast. In *Moros y cristianos,* the symbolic action progresses from challenge, to conflict, to defeat, and then culminates with forgiveness, conversion, and assimilation. The irony of *Los comanches* is that it truncates the dramatic paradigm of heroic folk theater. The play ends abruptly with utter defeat and no mention or possibility of redemptive closure, the moral sanction for *guerra justa,* or the "justified violence" of war. This lack of symbolic resolution supports Dahlberg's (1996) analysis of the play as a political protest cloaked in the familiar and popular guise of the auto de entrada.

‿ *Los Comanches de Castillo:* Text and Performance

What is evident in performance is that the ancient paradigm of heroic drama is fulfilled beyond the text and ambivalent climax of *Los Comanches de castillo.* Resolution and closure are expressed in the other manifestations of Comanches and Matachines celebrations in the larger regional context, where the values of forgiveness, redemption, and inclusion are not only realized, but also surpassed, in a process of transculturation that proceeds through emulation to identification.

Like other literary phenomena of frontier and borderlands areas, *Los comanches* occupies a space defined by inscription but contiguous with oral tradition. Testimonial accounts from both the nineteenth and twentieth centuries suggest that the drama has led a dual existence, one in the careful conservation, circulation, and hand copying of manuscripts, and the other in the more dynamic and subjective process of oral transmission, revivals, and actual performance.

The trail of paper has many branches, but it can be traced to two sources, both published in the *University of New Mexico Bulletin.* The photocopy given to me by my wife's tía Phil from the State Records and Archives Center was from handwritten copy one J. J. Vigil made *"Verbatim et Literatim"* sometime between 1840 and 1850, given by Amado Chaves of Santa Fe to Aurelio Macedonio Espinosa (1907). The other source was the more complete 1864 copy made by one Miguel Sandoval, given by Rafael Lucero of El Pino to Arturo Campa (1942). This second manuscript adds opening speeches by Barriga Duce and Cuerno Verde's death scene at the end. Unpublished manuscripts gathered by Mary Austin (n.d.), Frank M. Bond (1972), Lorin Brown (1937, 1939), Lester Raines (1936), José Alvarado Roybal (n.d.), and John D. Robb (1980) are close relatives of these two.[6]

The popularity of the play undoubtedly enhanced its oral transmission. In his memoirs, Rafael Chacón recalls spirited performances prior to the U.S. military conquest of 1846 (Chacón 76). Aurelio Espinosa (1907:19) also testifies to its popularity and then its decline by the turn of the century. In 1907 he declared that, "Up to some twenty years ago, it was produced in many parts of New Mexico, during the Christmas holidays or other important feast days. The popularity of the play during the last century is confirmed by the fact that very few New Mexicans over fifty years of age are not able to recite portions of Los Comanches from memory" (19). I discovered this to be just as true seventy years later. Additional substantiation of the play's dual literary and oral existence is suggested by the skepticism of John Englekirk (1957:238n7) as to the antiquity of the play. He noticed that Espinosa's and Campa's manuscripts show little textual evidence of having been in the oral tradition at all.

After the global trauma of World War I and the cultural shock of the returning troops, the decline noticed by Aurelio Espinosa in the performance tradition became a lapse, corroborated by oral-historical accounts (Vialpando 1992). In subsequent years, two kinds of revivals of *Los comanches* would surface: promotional and autochthonous.

After the Spanish-American War and by the 1920s, the emerging Anglo art colonies in Taos and Santa Fe had noticed the "primitivist" vitality of Nuevo Mexicano folk art and folklore. An undated manuscript of *Los comanches* appeared in Mary Austin's collection of folk plays about the same time that she and the Spanish Colonial Art Society began encouraging the work of traditional santeros. She and her friends, such as Ruth Laughlin Barker, Blanche Grant, Alice Corbin Henderson, and Frank Applegate, waxed poetic about "Spanish colonial" plays. All of them find the Comanches dramatic tradition praiseworthy, but discreetly, none assume direct credit for actually promoting it.

Then in the summer of 1929, Taos history attorney and history buff Francis T. Cheetham, with the support of the Taos Lion's Club and local boosters (Roeder 1976:218), enthusiastically promoted a performance spectacular enough to attract the attentions of tourists and folklorist Arthur Campa (1979:232):

> *Los Comanches* . . . was staged in the open spaces, where a battle on horseback could be enacted, and the plains of Galisteo and the high mesas around Taos were favorite sites where both audiences and participants could enjoy the drama. Real Indians often took the parts of the Comanche braves, and as the battle that is the climax of the play opened, both sides became caught up in the action. When the summer tourists visiting Taos in 1929 witnessed the drama on the mesa between Taos village and Ranchos de Taos to the south, hundreds of warriors and soldiers took part on both sides. They presented such a realistic scene, to the accompaniment of rifle shots and arrows, that the visitors took cover, thinking that real warfare had broken out.

The role of Cheetham and the businessmen of Taos in encouraging the 1929 Taos performance, or Cheetham again in the initial 1935 Galisteo staging, is curiously unacknowledged by Campa or by WPA fieldworker and writer Cleofas Martínez Jaramillo (1980[1941]:46), who wrote on the same productions as if they were totally spontaneous community events.

CHAPTER FOUR

The local Taos newspapers, however, contain the full credit line for the pageant productions. Under the masthead "Boosting for Taos and Vicinity," the September 26, 1929, *Taos Valley News* report of the event ends with this suggestion (*Taos Valley News* 1929a): "Another time this is given, it would be best to put on the play while the visitors are here, as most of the outsiders had gone home by noon, and their presence would give fine advertisement.")

The paper was clearly interested in the touristic, and therefore economic value of *Los comanches*. Since the art colony and members of the Spanish Colonial Arts Society were less directly obsessed with profit, they enthusiastically and dutifully documented the cultural aspects of the same productions (R. Barker 1931:237).

One of the high points of this era was an Albuquerque production of *Los comanches* that was incorporated into a civic pageant entitled *The First American*, in 1930. In his report of this urban spectacle, Campa (1942:18–19) seems more aware of the promotional hype and responds with sarcasm:

> Pageants of this sort so arouse the feelings of the actors that when Indians are used, as they are used in *Los Comanches*, they are advised to observe certain limitations. An audience witnessing a pageant of *The First American* in Albuquerque in 1930 got its money's worth when the Indians shot their arrows into the Spanish army and unhorsed a number of actors, who had to be given medical treatment immediately. In the remaining performances, the arrows were bound with tape and the Indians urged to shoot up in the air, in order to prevent further mishaps

Interestingly, Campa does not indicate whether the Indians involved were actors impersonating, or Natives participating in the play. The players are all unidentified. The reference to multiple productions is an indication that the producers wanted a return on their investment.

With the editorial help of researchers at the University of New Mexico and the support of the Coronado Cuarto Centennial Commission, the sizable archive of WPA field reports was distilled into a State Tourist Guide, complete with information on local history, place names, and festival calendars. Perhaps due to the lack of tourist infrastructure in villages such as El Rancho, travelers were routed to "Tour 3" and Ranchos de Taos, with the recommendation to see the "annual play, *Los comanches*." "[I]n co-operation with the adjoining village of Llano Quemado. This play in Spanish, enacted on horseback, has as its plot the rescue of two children captured by Comanches. The play ends with a grand entrance into the church" (WPA 1989:287). By the time the New Mexico guide was published, in 1940, the Cuarto Centennial was over, and the promotional performances of *Los comanches* were already a thing of the past.

After the initial Anglo promotion and the validation of the plays by Anglo and Hispano cultural elites, subsequent performances of *Los comanches* in rural communities took on a life of their own, as evidenced by their reincorporation into the traditional Christmas performance slot of regional Comanches celebrations.

John D. Robb (1980:602) described an impressive December 1955 performance in Taos, an indication that summer tourism was no longer a factor. Whatever the popular interest generated by these promotional revivals, none seems to have survived the Great Depression and World War II, which were followed by the relinquishment of traditional culture and folkways in the postwar boom. With a yearly cycle of Indian dances and the new fad of skiing, the tourist industry had no more interest in quaint eighteenth-century spanish folk plays.

ᑎᕉ *Los Comanches* de Alcalde

The revival of *Los comanches* that has survived into the present is an autochthonous one from Alcalde, New Mexico. Another local performance tradition of the play, in Los Ranchos (Roybal n.d.), twenty miles to the south, lasted into the 1950s and is well known through Loren Brown's lively description of a 1938 performance in his WPA writings (1939; Brown, Briggs, and Weigle 1978:40–41).[7] As in all the northern New Mexico villages, the World Wars and the intervening economic turmoil forced many families to leave the community to seek work in migrant labor and distant mines, interrupting performance traditions. A vital link in the transmission of the play was formed by a few performances staged immediately following World War II. Returning Nuevo Mexicano veterans had suffered the harsh conditions of the Pacific Theater and horrific episodes such as the Bataan Death March. Many made personal *promesas,* or solemn vows, to rededicate themselves to their religion and the traditions of their community. However, the pressures of the 1950s created another yet another lapse in the observance of cultural traditions, one that lasted into the 1960s.

In response to the requests of a curious new 1960s generation of Chicano cultural activists, a teacher named Roberto Vialpando Lara, his associate Adelaido Chacón, and friends and neighbors answered the call. They were instrumental in reviving the two Indo-Hispano folk celebrations previously observed in tandem in Alcalde: *Los matachines,* an Indo-Hispano ritual dance drama, and *Los comanches* (Montoya 1993, Sánchez 1992, Vialpando Lara 1992).[8]

Relying on childhood recollections and the memories of aging musicians and actors, the texts, choreography, and music were reconstructed to reintroduce these traditions into a community eager to reestablish its cultural roots. Since performances of *Los matachines* could still be observed in neighboring pueblos and *placitas,* and since the Alcalde melodies were still in living memory, the revival mostly involved the training of new dancers and musicians. The restaging of *Los comanches* was more of a challenge, because the community's script had been lost. Despite the availability of the two published texts of *Los comanches* (A. Espinosa 1907, Rael 1942), a painstaking effort was made to recover the authoritative Alcalde version from memory and oral tradition.

Vialpando and his cousin Feliberto López conducted extended interviews at Medina's Cantina and at private homes with Elfido Gonzales, Eduardo Edmons, and others who had acted in turn-of-the-century productions directed by Macedonio Chávez and his associate Noé Martínez. Adelaido Chacón's childhood memories of the play were clear enough to reconstruct the stage directions. Everyone remembered how carefully the horses were trained and rehearsed. Vialpando recalls a particular sorrel horse, an *alazán tostado* of his uncle's, who would gracefully kneel before the image of San Antonio to pay reverence before the play began.

An almost primal sense of authenticity has been reclaimed for the Alcalde production, given its proximity to San Juan Pueblo and San Gabriel, the very first settlement of Spanish-Mexicans in the land. Vialpando was always told that the very first Comanches and Matachines celebrations came from Abiquiú, the Genízaro town just up the Chama River Valley from Alcalde. From there he traces their dispersal to Ojo Caliente, Alcalde, Ojo Sarco, Chamisal, Las Vegas, Belén, and Socorro. One of the current performers is from Canjilón, where performances were staged when he was a child (Montoya 1993).[9]

Vialpando Lara attributes his knowledge of these traditions to Bozor Lara, an ancestor of his grandmother's. A key person in his paternal lineage was his grandfather Mónico Vialpando, a captive raised by Indians. Mónico's father, Juan Antonio Vialpando, was himself a Navajo raised by the Spanish-Mexicans. Since so many children were lost to raids, the colonial authorities gave the settlers permission to capture and raise Indian children as their own.

Vialpando Lara believes that the Comanches are celebrated because they were "fiercer than the Navajo," and their 1779 defeat was earlier and more definitive. The final victory over the Navajos did not come until 1865, well into the American period. He claims that each community performed its own distinct versions of *Los comanches.*

Matachines and Comanches celebrations were performed together in Alcalde because the costumes and mystery of the Matachines served to attract the attention of the Indians, while the purpose of the Comanches was to "pacify" the Indians. In Alcalde, *Los comanches* is staged immediately following the Matachines dance, which is organized yearly by *mayordomo* sponsors as a part of the *Función,* or patronal feast day, which in Alcalde is December 27 (Sánchez 1991).[10] Participants in Matachines are motivated by strong personal faith, the hope for blessings, and devotional promesas. Actors in *Los comanches* are motivated by a deep sense of cultural pride and dedication to community, whose original spirit is expressed in the play. All are young and middle-aged Nuevo Mexicano men involved in everything from ranching to work at the National Laboratory in Los Alamos. All are accomplished *jinetes,* or horsemen, who take great pride in their skills and their animals.[11]

Performances are staged for the *vísperas* (vespers) celebrations in the early evening of the December 26 at the old plaza and San Antonio chapel, then twice on the December 27—after morning mass in front of the new church and again in the afternoon, either at the house of the mayordomos, the old plaza, or in front of the Casanova, a community dance hall. Although the traditional feast day of San Antonio de Padua is June 13, a priest moved the fiesta decades ago. On July 26, 2000, in a special observance, the entire fiesta of Matachines and Comanches was celebrated for Santa Ana, the other patron saint of Alcalde, in the millennium jubilee year.

Every other year, on the morning of December 27, San Antonio is taken in procession to a vantage point where he too can watch the festivities. The spirit of the Alcalde Matachines is devotional, yet festive. The twelve masked spirit captains dance in graceful rows and crosses, all to the accompaniment of violin and guitar music. The Monarca directs the dance drama and the interactions of the other characters, which include the spirit guide Malinche, dressed as a little bride, and the Torito, with horns and cowhide, both played by children. On the periphery, the masked Abuelo monsters tease the crowd and fight and subdue the Torito, which they kill with a rifle and castrate, at the end of the dance. The Matachines is a conquest drama that in its most universal interpretation represents the encounter and conciliation of European and indigenous spirituality. Like the Comanches celebrations, it is a regional Indo-Hispano celebration with a range of meanings from sacred to burlesque, depending on the particular performance contexts of Hispano placitas and Indian pueblos (Rodríguez 1996, Romero 1991).

4.10.   Abuelo, Malinche, y Matachines (Alcalde). In triumph, the grandfather monster leads Malinche through rows of kneeling spirit captains.

Many of the actors of *Los comanches de castillo* are also Matachines dancers and occasionally participate in both.

After the Matachines finish and retire, the musicians and Abuelos remain on the scene to provide the music and crowd control for *Los comanches.* Still clowning with the crowd, the Abuelos, with their short *chicote* whips, help clear the crowd from the performance space to be used by the horses and riders. The musicians are called on later in the play, after the Comanche war council, when Cuerno Verde calls out for music. As the action begins, they play a short prelude to focus the attention of the crowd.[12] The Indio Embajador, here with the Christian name of Juan Antonio Romero, comes racing in at a full gallop, shouting that an armed confrontation between Comanches and Españoles is at hand.

The costumes of the players are as imaginative and colorful as they are stereotypical. The Comanches dress in a varied assortment of jeans, breechcloths, and bright ribbon shirts, with vests and saddle blankets sporting "Indian" designs. Cuerno Verde often has stark black-and-white face paint, while the others wear smudges of *almagre,* or traditional red mineral paint. Headdresses include simulated warbonnets, a recreation of the famous green-horn helmet of the protagonist, Cuerno Verde, and an occasional (technically illegal) eagle feather, gifted from Indian friends. The Spanish soldiers wear costumes, metal armor, and plumed helmets, all borrowed from the Española Oñate fiesta. The Hapsburg-style armor lends an anachronistic touch, since soldiers and militia of the eighteenth century used armor sewn from layers of rawhide and leather. But the Coronado-style helmets so emblematic of the Spanish imperial past are worn with pride and lend authenticity to the production, even though they come from a previous century.

Close examination of the earliest video recording made in Alcalde in 1978 and several made in the 1990s reveals performances that stay well within the parameters of the Vialpando Lara text of 1963. There are several moments that lend themselves to improvisations, but all the major arengas are delivered in similar style. Through the years, roles are circulated and new actors join the group, although several, such as Alfredo Montoya, Galento Martínez, and Tomás Sánchez and his late brothers Juan and Leo have been performing for more than two decades and have played all the parts. There seems to be no directorship role, but the more experienced actors do take the lead.

The oral recovery of the Alcalde text reveals a fascinating process of reduction, realignment, and modification that permits the play to reflect the social desires of its performance community. The script is reduced to 273 octosyllabic verses, as compared to 347 in the El Rancho production (Roybal n.d.) versus the two published versions with 515 in A Espinosa (1907) and 714 in Campa (1942). In the original historical battles, the Spanish significantly outnumber Comanches. In the Espinosa cast they are evenly matched, at six to six, and in Campa's there are seven Spaniards to five Comanches. As might be expected in the streamlined Alcalde production, the list shrinks from fifteen to ten characters, but the reduction is not proportional. In Alcalde, with six to four, the Indians become the majority. Alcalde eliminates four Españoles: Don Salvador Ribera, the Capitán, the Sargento, and most importantly, Barriga Duce.

The disappearance of the battlefield buffoon in Alcalde is notable. His Rabelaisian excess and repugnant antics cast a disparaging, even cynical light on the gallantry of the events and the notion of Spanish military honor. Although he follows the Spanish camps, neither his name nor his behavior conforms to Spanish standards. With time, Barriga Duce's original subversive critique is blunted and finally eclipsed by the slapstick comic function of the character. In any case, his absence insures that heroism as redefined for the Alcalde audience retains a central role unchallenged.

In his analysis of the 1938 El Rancho performance of *Los comanches,* Márez (2002:16) interprets the clowning of Barriga Duce as a satire of the Hispanophilia of the pageants of the Anglo and Hispano elites:

> Barriga Duce parodies the hegemonic performances of "Spanishness" that emerged in the wake of the Spanish-American War. . . . And while he makes brave speeches threatening the Comanches, when faced with battle Duce flees in comic terror. Indeed, audiences reportedly took great pleasure in this portion of the play, laughing uproariously as Duce in effect made a fool of the Spanish Empire. By laughing at Spanish clowns, audiences indicated their critical distance from ruling-class uses of the colonial past to legitimate domination in the present.

In Alcalde, the presence of the matachines Abuelo clowns at the edges of the performance may have subsumed the role of Barriga Duce. Their challenge to hierarchy and hegemony serve both ritual performances in the Alcalde fiesta.

Another notable revision in the Alcalde text is the virtual disappearance of the rhetoric of empire and its twin ideological pillars of dynasty and religion. The abundant allusions to imperial dominion and invocations of divine right and miraculous intervention all but vanish. The only direct mention of the king is ironically on the lips of Cuerno Verde:

Está el Rey en su lugar	45	*The king is in his place*
Como todo el Cristianismo. [sic]		*As is all of Christendom.*[13]

Only one of the Españoles, Toribio Ortiz, mentions the regent in passing, taking pride in his own financial independence:

El Rey le sirvo a mi costo,	176	*I serve the king at my cost,*
Con un esmero especial.		*With special pride and attention.*

In the original versions, the Españoles swore allegiance to the Crown with almost every other breath. In Alcalde, only Toribio Ortiz invokes Christian divinity:

Santiago, La concepción de María,	200	*Santiago, Conception of Mary*
Sean mi norte y guía.		*Be my north star and guide.*

It might be argued that this attrition is merely a factor of the economy of orality (Ong 1982). What is more probable is the shift in what Benedict Anderson calls the "imagined community" (1983[1991]:20—35). As the Spanish Empire crumbles, the discourse of imperial power is abandoned. A regional Nuevo Mexicano identity formation emerges in its place, consonant with the shifting political landscapes of nineteenth- and twentieth-century New Mexico.

Perhaps the most celebrated feature of *Los comanches* beyond the prodigious equestrian display are the stirring arengas, in which the opponents match their rhetoric and wits. What Espinosa noticed at the beginning of the twentieth century was still true at the end. The elders in northern New Mexico (my own family included) can still quote Cuerno Verde's stirring invocation, which is also a prayer to the four directions.

Given the lofty diction in the Comanche speeches in all the published and manuscript versions of the play, it is curious that one Alcalde character would slip into stereotypical or pseudo-pidginized "Indian Spanish." The Indio Embajador, or lowly messenger of the first scene, speaks in burlesque "dialect":

Dende tan lejo yo vene	1	*From so far I comin'*
Oh tata Gobernado!		*Oh pappy Govnor!*
Vengo a traete esta noticia		*I come to bring you this news*
Que alla en mi pelbo [sic] paso.		*That happun in my twon.*

All the other Comanche speeches use the same diction, imagery, and elocutionary figures as their Spanish opponents. All the warriors liken their ferocity to the wild animals of the sierra and link their strength and fury to the forces of nature.

Likewise, all observe the honorable decorum of the battlefield. Only chief Cabeza Negra (Oso Pardo in Campa 1942 and A. Espinosa 1907) briefly transgresses the protocols of heroic discourse, when he threatens to cut of the head of his opponent. Even though warriors and soldiers contest each other on stage, they do so with the same voice. Is the author's aim to ennoble himself by elevating the discourse of his enemy? Michel de Certeau (1986:78) reminds us that "The written discourse which cites the speech of the other is not, cannot be, the discourse of the other." If dialogue is the communication of difference, then monologue is the contemplation of identity.

One of the moments of highest drama in *Los comanches* is the confrontation of the two principal antagonists, contrasting the brash challenge of Cuerno Verde with the seasoned response of Don Carlos Fernández. In Campa's manuscript, Cuerno Verde delivers 108 verses and Don Carlos 76. In Alcalde, the exchange is composed of 45 and 38 verses, respectively. What is most extraordinary about Don Carlos's Alcalde response is that it is a total appropriation and adaptation of the second half of Cuerno Verde's speech in the longer manuscript. Don Carlos calls out to his troops with the very words of Cuerno Verde on his lips:

Ea, nobles capitanes!	76	*Hear, noble captains!*
Que se pregone este grito!		*May this edict be proclaimed!*
Que yo como General		*That I as general*
He de estar aprevenido:		*Will truly be ready:*

There is no disjunction in the discourse or in the action. The only break is in the distinction between cultural self and cultural Other. Cuerno Verde does not die in the skirmishes of Alcalde. In the display of valor and resistance, a new cultural sign is forged for the battles of the twentieth century. The old differences and oppositions dissolve into a new synthesis in the edifying spectacle. At the play's conclusion, Comanches and Españoles ride off together.

Cultural othering is part of the ideology and psychology of warfare. But the conflicts of the eighteenth century created sociological consequences that blurred the category of otherness. By the census of 1776, fully one-third of the Spanish-Mexican, non-Pueblo population of New Mexico were Genízaros and

4.11. Herencia de Españoles y Comanches (Alcalde). The Indo-Hispano legacy is defined by pride and perseverance. Historical memory is deep and abiding in New Mexico.

their descendants—war orphans and victims of the colonial slave trade, raised by and serving their Spanish-Mexican families (Gutiérrez 1991:171). Although the majority of the Genízaro population of New Mexico came from Navajo, Apache, and Ute stock, the 5 percent of Numunuh origin are symbolically significant beyond their numbers. With the extended Pax Comanche that began in 1786, the notion of the Numunuh as antagonists and cultural Others becomes ambiguous and obscured. An implicit recognition emerges that they are also a part of the extended cultural family as "Comanches," a cross-cultural category that recalls and invokes them even as it includes their Hispanicized mestizo and maroon descendants.

Santo Niño y Sus Cautivos

THE POETICS OF CAPTIVITY AND REDEMPTION

A mí no me lleva el río	The river won't take me
por muy crecido que vaya,	no matter how high its flood,
y yo sí me llevo al Niño	I'll take the Child away
con una buena bailada.	with a good dance . . .
Al Santo Niño de Atocha	To the Holy Child of Atocha
le encargamos por favor,	we entrust you please,
cuide de sus comanchitos	care for your little Comanches
que no olvide cuántos son.	never forget how many there are.

—*"Los comanchitos," Bernalillo (Lamadrid and Loeffler 1994:191).*

The tragic wars of the eighteenth century scattered everyone's children of all groups in New Mexico—Spanish-Mexicans, Pueblos, Athabascans, and Comanches. When society is traumatized, symbols of spiritual reintegration are necessary to pick up the pieces and resume the life of the group. El Santo Niño de Atocha, the mestizo Son of Guadalupe, will never forget how many "Comanchitos" there really are, how many lives and families have been broken, nor will He abandon them, regardless of the degree of their innate or acquired Spanishness or Indianness. As James Brooks (2002:26) has noted, the sufferers of personal tragedy and loss in times of war find refuge and meaning in the sacred:

> The exchange of culture-group members fostered accommodation, eroded linguistic and cultural boundaries, and concomitantly placed stress on the production and preservation of in-group identity. So painful were these pressures that they found expression in terms of the sacred, where beauty and danger, death and healing, tragedy and romance reflected in the spiritual realm the violence of everyday life.

The desire to capture and "adopt" the Santo Niño and never let him go is only understandable in this frame. There are many lives to repair, and the future of New Mexico is in the balance. These are the themes of the religious Comanche celebrations, especially those clustered around Christmas and the birth of the Santo Niño. To understand just how they bring atonement and closure to the conflict with the cultural Other, the symbolic progress that has led to this point must be recapitulated.

The grim realities of warfare with no quarter are a shock to the spirit and the imagination. The military victory dramatized in *Los comanches de castillo* was found in the previous chapter to be entirely bereft of religious themes. Since the goal of warfare in the 1770s was the annihilation, rather than the conversion, of the enemy, victory was heroic but hollow. The only Christian symbols or allusions are in the form of battle cries and supplications for victory: "*Santiago y la Virgen María sean mi norte y mi guía* (May St. James and the Virgin Mary be my north star and my guide)." Cuerno Verde, the antagonist, does the same, invoking the power of the four directions, the sun, and the wild animals of the land. Although victory against him is achieved, it is an unsettling victory, ending in death and pillage.

The audience of the autos de entrada is accustomed to and expects the edifying scenes of conversion and forgiveness that lead the dramatic paradigm to its culmination and closure. What goes wanting in *Los comanches de castillo* is fulfilled in the other regional Comanches celebrations, most of which are laden with strong religious themes. The Alcalde performance tradition takes a first step toward resolution by the elimination of the death of Cuerno Verde from the play.[1]

Before charting the geographical and calendric distribution of Comanches celebrations, the question must be revisited of why the Comanches were singled out, when there were several other hostile tribes in the region to contend with. If there was enmity at one time or another with Apaches, Utes, Navajos, and even Pawnees, why did none of those cultures become so entirely synonymous with invincibility, unredeemed wildness, or barbarity? In response to the question, Arthur Campa (1942:15) writes: "Despite the fact that these Indians were the scourge of the *Mexicanos,* they were so impressive and daring that tradition accorded them an unique place seldom given to enemies," although their prowess as traders also helped to make them so memorable. In contemporary interviews, several Pueblo and Nuevo Mexicano observers have noted that the Comanches "were the most fierce" (Vialpando 1992), "the most flamboyant and fascinating" (A. García 1999), or "the most formidable and admirable" (A. Ortiz 1991).

But perhaps it is the inclusive nature of Numunuh culture itself that inspires others to invest the cultural category of "Comanche" with such a range of meanings.[2] Through their own ethnogenesis, the Numunuh assimilated other ethnic and linguistic groups to their language, lifestyle and economy. "Comanche" culture becomes iconic, a repository for the ascribed power of wildness, whose source is outside the walls of towns and cities and emanates from the land itself. The Numunuh perception of this attribution is generous and proud: "We accepted marginal and downtrodden groups and let them identify with us. It was all right with us" (Bigbee 1998).

The other native cultures alluded to in the region's celebrations of cross-cultural mimesis are Navajos, Apaches, and Chichimecas. The Navajo dance, as performed in the Tewa pueblos, is a full burlesque of stereotypical Navajo dress, mannerisms, and even drunkenness (Sweet 1978, Kurath and García 1970:283). Other mimetic traditions are more dignified and emulative. From northern Chihuahua to central Mexico, there are ritual dances termed "Apache" by their participants, but with little cultural or historic connection to the Ndeh (tribal Apache) survivors of the genocidal campaigns conducted against them by Spain, Mexico, and the United States (Redfield 1930:120).

Genocidal warfare was more successful against the various cultural groups in northern Mexico generically called Chichimecas, from a Nahuatl term meaning "barbarian." Numerous communities from Tortugas, New Mexico, south to the states of Aguascalientes and San Luis Potosí, Mexico, feature "Chichimeca" celebrations, whose choreography and costumes are similar to those of the Matachines of Tortugas (New Mexico), El Paso (Texas), and the lower Río Grande Valley (Cantú

5.1. Devoción de los Apaches (Juárez, Mexico). Some dance troupes identify with Chichimeca and Apache warrior tribes of the past, demonstrating with their devotional dance that all indigenous people love Guadalupe.

CHAPTER five

82

5.2. Matachines Chichimecas (Tortugas). The regalia of the southern matachines and Chichimeca dancers include gourd rattles, bow-and-arrow clackers, reed aprons, and Plains-style warbonnets.

1995, Sklar 2001). In La Mesilla (Aguascalientes), the annual feast of San José (March 19) features a "Danza de los Indios," which participants refer to as a Chichimeca celebration. Curiously, the dance leader who directs the choreography as well as the mock battle with Spanish soldiers is called "El Comanche" (Medrano de Luna 1999). The dance captains of the Matlachines (compare spelling to *Matachines*) dances of San Luis Potosí are also called "Comanches," probably the southernmost use of the term in ritual dance.

The Chichimecas dancers of Tortugas Pueblo make no allusions to Comanches by name, although it could be argued that a reference point is present in costume, because of the many Plains-style warbonnets they use.[3] Before settling Tortugas in the 1850s, the Tigua, Piro, and Manso peoples lived in the El Paso and Ysleta del Sur area, to the south. In the eighteenth and nineteenth centuries, they frequently engaged in armed conflict with both Comanches and Apaches (Kohlberg 1973:29, Gerald 1974:40). The farthest historical penetration of the Numunuh into Mexico was Monclova (Coahuila) in the southeast, Zacatecas in the south, and Durango in the southwest. The reputation and fame of the Numunuh obviously penetrated much farther south than their raids or trading expeditions did. In the oral histories of the region, the Mexicans still remember the Numunuh as "indios de trenza," or braided Indians, since they could easily be distinguished from other groups by their distinctive hair style (Punzo 2002).

✑ Geography and Hagiography of Indo-Hispano Celebrations

In the northlands, *Comanches* is by far the most common reference point or icon for the "wild or savage cultural Other," and is celebrated by both Pueblo and Nuevo Mexicano communities. As already pointed out, all Pueblo groups have Comanche celebrations, especially the eastern Pueblos, and the Tanoan more than the Keresan, mostly due to geographical proximity (Sweet 1985:86–87).

The topic of Pueblo and Nuevo Mexicano Comanche dances will be revisited in the next chapter. Here the focus will be on the more overtly spiritual Comanches Nativity celebrations observed in Indo-Hispano communities all across central New Mexico, including Bernalillo; Cochití/Peña Blanca;[4] the Albuquerque-area communities of Los Ranchos, Los Griegos, Atrisco, and Arenales; Tomé and Estancia; and western New Mexico, including Seboyeta, Grants, San Rafael, Atarque, and San Mateo. Two northern communities observe their "Genízaro," or general "hispanicized Indian" roots with ritual celebrations, including Abiquiú, where the "Genízaro" rubric includes a variety of tribes that lived there, and Ranchos de Taos, where the Genízaro heritage is specifically associated with Comanches. The Nativity Comanche play was celebrated in Ranchos de Taos many years ago (B. Chavez 1988), but its text has not been recovered.

As the map is surveyed, so must the calendar be, because the selection of Indo-Hispano feast days has specific significance to the themes of transculturation. In all the Indo-Hispano fiestas of the upper Río Grande, children play prominent roles in the rituals that reenact the mixed cultural origins of their communities. The maternal saint that protects and nurtures these children is María herself, as Guadalupe, her own indigenous aspect, an Indian woman who is spiritual mother and patroness to all peoples of the New World. The devotion to Guadalupe began among the Mexican creole elite in the struggle for independence, and they took her image into the thick of battle (Lafaye 1976). Soon she moved in from the cultural fringes of syncretism to her place at the altar, the enduring and essential emblem of indigenous and mestizo identity and the emergence of Indo-Hispano culture. In Mexico and New Mexico, she is omnipresent, presiding in some degree over all religious feast days and cultural celebrations (Sklar 2001).

Much has been said of the complexion of Guadalupe. Less obvious is the Aztec sash tied around her belly, the sign of her pregnancy and portent of her Son to come. It goes without saying that His heritage is mestizo, for he comes for all the people. In her mission to the Américas, Guadalupe represents and sanctifies both cultural and racial hybridity. The other aspect of María most prominent in the prayers, hymns, and devotional art of New Mexico is Dolores, Our Lady of Sorrows, the consoling Mother to a frontier people well versed in suffering. Most

CHAPTER five

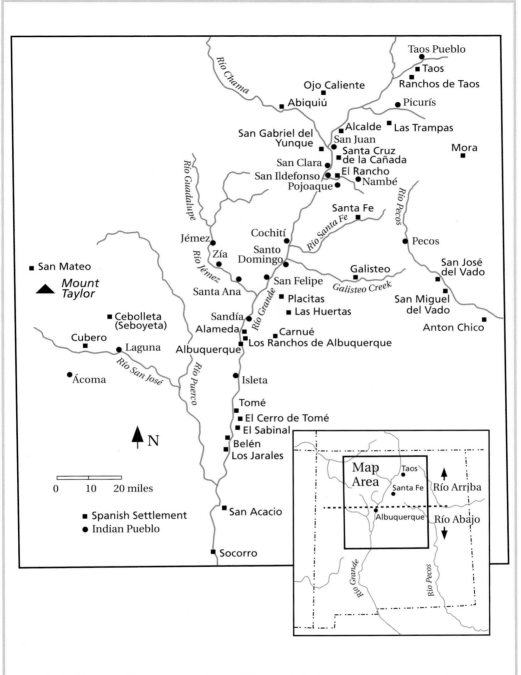

5.3. Indo-Hispano Communities of New Mexico. Indo-Hispano expressive culture is most pronounced in communities located near pueblos and in the dangerous outlying frontier areas of the seventeenth and eighteenth centuries. Map by the University of New Mexico Press.

5.4. General Chichimeca Azteca y la Virgen (Tortugas). To the Aztecs, the word
"chichimeca" was a generalized term synonymous with "barbarian," but Guadalupe
unites all indigenous peoples of greater Mexico.

prominent in the yearly cycle of feasts is Guadalupe's day on December 12,
although the entire Marian calendar is celebrated at the parish level.

The mestizo Son and Holy Child of indigenous Guadalupe is the Santo Niño de
Atocha, whose devotion began and is still based in the Mexican state of Zacatecas,
the historical point of departure for the colonization of New Mexico. The child
Jesus appears as a five- or six-year-old, dressed in the garb of the medieval pilgrim,
with hat, staff, and the cockleshell emblem of Santiago, patron saint of Spain and
fierce warrior of the Reconquest. According to legend, in the Old World this Child
regularly slipped by Moorish and Turkish guards to offer bread from his basket and
water from his gourd to Christian captives. In the New World, he became the
devoted patron and best hope for the deliverance of Indian captives. In New
Mexico, the Santo Niño receives devoted pilgrims at two destinations—the famous
Santuario de Chimayó as well as at Zuni, where a pueblo family with a very old
image of the Child opens their home for visitors from all the western region of the
state. Santo Niño's compassion also extends to the Natives who revere and associate Him with the Hero Twins, Sons of the Sun, whose Nativity is also celebrated
on the Winter Solstice (Gutiérrez 1991:162). One of the Comanche verses from San
Mateo contains a tantalizing reference to this duality.

5.5. Santos y Niños (Chimayó). In identification with the Santo Niño de Atocha, there is a popular custom in Mexico of dressing young children in the garb of the Holy Child, in hopes of receiving his blessings.

De las estrellas del cielo	*Of the stars of the sky*
tengo separado dos,	*I have two set apart,*
una para el Santo Niño y	*one for the Holy Child and*
otra para el Niño Dios.	*another for the Child God.*

(D. Salazar n.d., San Mateo, N.Mex.)

El Santo Niño's dual feast is not only Christmas, but New Year's as well, in the form of the child Manuel, the incarnation of all the ancient prophecies, who is especially honored by the Hispano-Comanches of Ranchos de Taos.

The Epiphany, on January 6, is traditionally the occasion for the recognition of secular and colonial power and transfer of authority. With its theme of the Three Kings from the ends of the earth, it is the occasion for the ritual exchange of gifts, which missionaries used to their advantage in subverting native systems of reciprocal exchange (Gutiérrez 1993:76, 84). In the pueblos, Comanche and animal dances are celebrated, and in Hispano communities, Comanches and Matachines dances take place. When the "Comanches" show up to pay homage to the Santo Niño on Epiphany Eve, instead of the Three Kings, the meaning of the feast shifts accordingly. In their indita songs, the "Comanches" explain how the Three Kings themselves guided them to Bethlehem. It goes without saying that the "Comanches" got there first.

Several other saints figure prominently in the Indo-Hispano pantheon. Credited as being the first Christian convert, the example of San José was so central to the missionary efforts to Christianize indigenous peoples that he was declared the first patron saint of the Americas. In Mexico the popular devotion to San José is much more significant than it ever was in Spain. In New Mexico, he takes his place beside the Virgin on the altar of every church in the region (Chorpenning 1992). In the Christian calendar, San José is assigned the key date of March 19, near the spring equinox. But since it falls during Lent, not many festivals are dedicated to him.

Of all of the disciples, Santo Tomás the Apostle was the one who most severely tested his faith by doubting Jesus. He traveled the farthest by taking the gospel to India and ministering across cultural differences as vast as those between Spanish missionaries and their Native charges in New Mexico (Córdova 1973). The winter feast at Abiquiú is dedicated to Tomás.

Another apostle saint historically celebrated in Indo-Hispano communities is San Pablo, not in his role as church father, but for the January 25 feast that celebrates his conversion in an explosion of light on the road to Tarsus, from the intransigent and skeptical Saul to Paul, the true believer. The *custodio,* or Franciscan administrative region, that included New Mexico was named El Custodio de la Conversión de San Pablo in 1621, a measure of the importance of this feast and the missionary quest for the conversion of all the "gentile savages" (Kessell 1987:103).[5]

The other saint prominent in Indo-Hispano dance traditions is the young seventeenth-century Italian Jesuit San Luis Gonzaga, who is the patron of devotional (and social) dance. How his devotion began in New Mexico is a mystery, but his June 21 feast is observed in central and western New Mexico with the singing

La Jeyana

(FRAGMENT OF INDITA DE SAN LUIS GONZAGA)

Sung by Rosanna Otero of San Acacio

A na je ya na a na je ya na

A na je ya na yo je ya na yo je ya na yo

1. A na je ya na je ya na a na je ya na je yo,
2. Di-cen que las go-lon-dri-nas de un vo-lido pa-san el mar.

1. A na je ya na je ya na, a na je ya na je yo.
2. Di-cen que las go-lon-dri-nas de un vo-lido pa-san el mar.

of indita hymns and chanted vocable choruses, with devotional dancing quite reminiscent of Puebloan traditions (Lamadrid 2002:175–82).[6]

ᥩᥩ Conversion and Transculturation

Conversion in the example of San Pablo or more forcefully portrayed in the dramatic paradigm of *Moros y Cristianos* may be seen as a spiritual analogue of transculturation. In becoming a cristiano and embracing the Santa Cruz, the Moor closes the gap between self and cultural Other, as does the Christian in forgiving him. In *Los comanches de castillo,* there is no Santa Cruz or any other Christian symbol, beyond the fierce war cry invocations of Santiago. What justifies the battles of *Los comanches* are the two captive Pecas, or young women from Pecos Pueblo, the Towa pueblo attacked more times by Comanches than any other. Traditionally played by children of either sex, although passive and mute, they recall and signify the primordial experience of forced transculturation. Captivity is the greatest trauma, the most rigorous test of faith and character, and it is at the symbolic focus of all the Indo-Hispano celebrations.

As the spiritual themes of the Comanches Nativity plays of San Mateo, Seboyeta, and Los Griegos begin to close the final gap between cultural self and other in Indo-Hispano culture, the importance of the *Santo Niño* as Ideal Captive child becomes clear. The Comanches fall in love with Child and Mother as they offer their music and dance at the altar, and plot to kidnap him and raise him as Comanche. But instead of assimilating to the culture of his abductors, he captures their affections and they follow Him. The Comanches Guadalupanos of Los Ranchos de Albuquerque also offer the tribute of song and dance to the Indian Mother and the Indian Child, approaching her through their surrogate, Juan Diego, the Aztec man who first recognized her. In Bernalillo, all the lost children come home as *comanchitos,* little Indians, who follow the rounds of Las Posadas processions to dance at the main altar on Christmas Eve.

Although most of the Indo-Hispano communities surveyed emblematically

El Nanillé

Sung by Floyd Trujillo of Abiquiú

link the theme of captivity with Comanches, others (such as Tortugas, San Marcial, Placitas, and Abiquiú) further universalize the motif, perhaps because they were geographically vulnerable to warfare with other groups as well, namely Apaches, Navajos, and Utes. As already noted, in their devotions for Guadalupe, the dancers of Tortugas allude to Comanches through costume only. In the holiday *velorios,* or prayer vigils, celebrated in the southern village of San Marcial for Christmas, Epiphany, and the feast of Santa Rosalía, *padrinos,* or godparents, would stand over the Santo Niño all night long, to guard against anyone who would take Him captive, Indians or not (DeFlice 1999).

The festival narratives collected by the WPA Writers' Project in Placitas, New Mexico, also contain numerous references to Christmas vigils full of intrigue and drama (Rebolledo and Márquez 2000:214–15).

> On each side of the altar stood an ever watchful guard, a man and a woman. They were the padrinos and they must watch the Infant. . . . After the young people had prayed in twos at the altar, the children followed, likewise in pairs. Thus the remainder of the night wore on. At about the hour of midnight the padrinos feigned drowsiness. The worshippers appeared to nod their heads in sleep. The padrinos

5.6.   Una Indita del Nanillé (Abiquiú). An eagle feather in each outstretched hand. Nanillé dancers soar into freedom, honoring the captive children of the past in a community full of captivity stories.

made efforts to keep awake and guard the Infant. But at last sleep overpowered them, and the Child was left unprotected. It was then that one secretly chosen by the padrinos stole furtively into the room and tiptoed noiselessly to the altar and snatched the padrinos' charge and as quietly crept from the room with it. The seconds passed and within the room all was as silent as death. Then in due time a noisy roar from a gun aroused the slumbering ones. They looked at the altar to behold the vacant spot where the crib had been. With the padrinos in the lead they dashed from the room to find the house from which the gun had been fired. There they would find the Infant. The padrinos made a good pretense at aiding in the frantic search but to no avail. But at length the Infant was found in the house of the one who carried him away. Shouts of gladness rang out on the night air. Now the padrinos must redeem the Child. The unlawful possessor must name the price. No set ransom was insisted upon in this game, though usually the one who stole the Infant asked for a dollar, a baile to be given for him at the date he named, or for a rosario to be said on a certain date for a departed relative. When the ransom had been promised by the padrinos, the Infant was given into their hands, and they led the procession back to the house from which it was stolen and restored it to the altar.

The plot is structurally identical to the Comanches Nativity plays, but without specific reference to Comanches, only to the constant threat of abduction and captivity.

In the Genízaro village of Abiquiú, home to converts from more than half a dozen tribes, the rituals of captivity are also universalized. For the feast of Santo Tomás on the old plaza there, all eyes are on the cautivos, the captive children who dance in front of the church to the drums and ancient chant of the Nanillé.[7]

Outstretched arms and hands clutching eagle feathers lift them above their captivity and into the hearts of their parents, both lost and found. Radiant of hope and resiliency, children have the power to transcend the conflict and cultural struggles of past and present.

⤜ Lullabies and Laments

As might be expected, the cultural memory and trauma of captivity inevitably make their way into popular lullabies. Like other indita melodies, they are so musically hybrid that they are not easily described within the parameters of Western music. As for content, Indo-Hispano children are frightened by their parents' suggestions (or veiled threats), that they will be given away or sold to the Indians (or inversely to the Hispanos) if they don't behave. Carolyn Shaw, a coyota who grew up on a ranch on the Llano Estacado near Santa Rosa, collected this lullaby from her aunt, Leota Frizzell (Lamadrid and Loeffler 1994).

Arrullo Comanche
El cumanche y la cumancha

Comanche Lullaby
The Comanche and his wife

se fueron pa' Santa Fe,	*went to Santa Fe,*
se fueron pa' Santa Fe,	*went to Santa Fe,*
a vender al cumanchito	*to sell the little Comanche*
por azúcar y café,	*for sugar and coffee,*
por azúcar y café.	*for sugar and coffee.*

The fascinating scene of the Comanches selling their children for fancy imported goods from the tropics seems almost comic at first.[8] But then the anxiety sinks in. Are they really the parents of the children, or could they be the guardians of captive children? Would they really be so cruel and selfish? (Would my parents do the same?) And so on. The questions multiply in the mind of the child falling asleep in the

Arrullo Comanche

Sung by Leota Frizzell of Santa Rosa

El co- man- che y la co- man- cha, el co-
man- che y la co- man- cha se fue- ron pa'
San- ta Fe, se fue- ron pa' San- ta Fe, a ven-
der al co- man- chi- to, a ven- der al co- man-
chi- to, por a- zú car y ca- fé,
por a- zú car y ca- fé.

La Venada y el Venado

Sung by Floyd Trujillo of Abiquiú

E a e a e a e a   e a e a   e a e a   oh.   La ve-

na-   da y el   ve-   na-   do   se fue-   ron   pa' San-   ta

Fe,   a   ven-   der   a sus   hi-   ji-   tos   por   a-

zú-   car   y   ca-   fé.

security of his parents' arms. Historical memory is ambivalent and deep. By the 1770s, warfare and slave trading were not the only causes of bondage. Debt peonage had begun to emerge, and the droughts between 1778 and 1780 caused many people to sell their children into domestic service, a desperate and unfortunate practice that aroused the sympathy of Governor De Anza (Gutiérrez 1993:323). In Abiquiú, deer replace Comanches in the same lullaby. The Comanche lullaby that Edwin Berry used to sing in Tomé (Lamadrid archive) strikes a more optimistic note:

Arrullo Comanche	***Comanche Lullaby***
Hermanito comanchito,	*Little Comanche brother,*
te venimos a avisar,	*we have come to tell you,*
que esta noche allá en Peralta	*that tonight in Peralta*
también vamos a bailar.	*we will also dance.*

    Ay oh ay ey ay oh ay ey, ay oh ay ey ay oh ay ey

Hermanito comanchito,	*Little Comanche brother,*
si es que te quieres casar,	*if you really want to marry,*
cásate con la más bella	*marry the most beautiful girl*
y no le vayas a pegar.	*and don't dare beat her.*

    Ay oh ay ey ay oh ay ey, ay oh ay ey ay oh ay ey

Hermanito comanchito,	*Little Comanche brother,*
hoy tenemos que sembrar,	*today we must plant,*
las milpas y melonares	*the corn and melon fields*
si quieres cosechar.	*if you want to harvest them.*
Ay oh ay ey ay oh ay ey, ay oh ay ey ay oh ay ey	
Hermanito comanchito	*Little Comanche brother,*
ven para decirte adiós,	*come and say good-bye,*
hasta el año venidero	*until next year*
si estamos vivos los dos.	*if we both are still alive.*
Ay oh ay ey ay oh ay ey, ay oh ay ey ay oh ay ey	

In this playful song, there is an invitation to dance with the Hispanos, an admonition to a wild brother to avoid domestic violence, an invitation to settle down and plant crops, and a slightly ironic farewell until next year's visit, if both survive another year in what could be dangerous times. The lullaby expresses brotherhood and filial affection, along with several ambivalent assumptions—that Comanches may be violent and have no desire to commit to agricultural labor, the very same doubts about them shared by generations of Pueblos and Hispanos alike.

Hermanito Comanchito

Sung by Edwin Berry of Tomé

Her- ma- ni- to co-man- chi- to te ve- ni- mos

a a- vi- sar, que es- ta no- che en Pe- ral- ta

tam- bién va- mos a bai- lar, Ay oh, ay ey, ay

oh, ay ey. Ay oh, ay ey, ay oh ay ye.

santo niño y sus cautivos

Nevertheless, the annual visits for trading and commerce were universally anticipated with pleasure, which is also the sentiment felt by the child falling into unconsciousness, despite the yips and whoops that the singer interjects into the vocable (syllable-sung) chorus.

Despite the centrality of children, adult captives were not forgotten. More completely socialized than children at the time of capture, they were more culturally resistant, and their ordeals more daunting. Women were taken more often than men were. If Comanche captors had any particular vengeance to exact or score to settle, they could be cruel and ruthless; but captives were valuable property and were cared for and integrated as much as possible, often to the point of adoption (Noyes 1993:87–98). New captives were subjected to a kind of "seasoning" process, reported by a Ute man in 1768, who followed the war party that captured his wife and son. He observed them in a captivity dance, where captives were forced to dance in a circle. "The captives, including the two unfortunate Utes, were 'forced by the Xomanches' to dance, repeating in a droning fashion a phrase that meant literally 'they were captives'" (G. Anderson 1999:222).

An American named Burnet observed a similar ritual in 1818, a half-century later. Comanche men and women assailed the captives "with clubs, and thongs, and knives, and javelins, and firebrands" as they danced. "The repetition of the chant helped to indoctrinate the new people and show them that they would not be killed. It also brought them to accept their new position" (G. Anderson 1999:222) In commemoration of the trials of adult captivity, in Abiquiú as well as Ranchos de Taos, adults are taken captive in pantomime, forced to dance, then ransomed by their friends and relations. Nobody is forgotten.

The travails of captivity and the lament of captives may be heard in New Mexico's indita ballads, so named by the people because the majority of them have to do with relations between hispanos and indios as diverse as warfare and love (Romero 2002:62–80). Some of the earliest and latest inditas are called *cautivas,* because they sing of the travails of captivity faced by women on the frontier. From the 1720s to the Treaty of 1786, large numbers of captives were taken, up to as much as 15 percent of the population, as estimated by historians (Márez 2001:274–75).

"La cautiva Marcelina" is an indita sung by a character of the same name in the Comanches Nativity play in western New Mexico, as recalled by Pauline Chávez Bent, who played the role and sang the indita as a young girl (Chávez Bent 2000). In the communities of the eastern Plains, the song is part of the general repertory of narrative ballads. With time, Marcelina's surname dropped away and rendered her a kind of forlorn everywoman, whose fate it was to witness the murder of her family and wander the Plains with her captors, with nothing to eat but mare's meat. Horseflesh was a common enough repast for the Numunuh, but one that the Hispano would prefer to avoid, except in the direst of circumstances. Many inditas are sung entirely in the first person, but in this one the cautiva is too

5.7. Cantos del Cerro (Tomé). A call to worship at central New Mexico's holiest sacred site. Edwin Berry knew hundreds of religious and secular songs, which he sang to the accompaniment of his tombé.

5.8. La Rueda: Danza de los Cautivos (Ranchos de Taos). As the ring dance begins, captives are taken and held tightly in a ring of dancers who honor and bless them, incorporating them into the group. Families later pay their ransom.

distraught to narrate her story. Only her cries of anguish are heard. With building tension, the narrator enumerates the dead, anticipating with the rhyme of place names, who is next in the list. By the time the listener hears that Marcelina is at the *cerritos,* it is obvious that she has been deprived of her most precious company, her "hijitos." The devastation is soul-wrenching and complete.

La Cautiva Marcelina	**Marcelina the Captive**
La cautiva Marcelina	*Marcelina the captive*
ya se va, ya se la llevan,	*she is going, there they take her,*
ya se va, ya se la llevan	*she is going, there they take her,*
para esas tierras mentadas	*to those famous lands*
a comer carne de yegua,	*to eat mare's meat,*
a comer carne de yegua.	*to eat mare's meat.*
refrán:	*chorus:*
—Por eso ya no quiero	*—That is why I can no longer*
en el mundo más amar,	*love again in this world,*
de mi querida patria	*from my beloved homeland*
me van a retirar.	*they will take me away.*

La cautiva Marcelina	When Marcelina the captive
cuando llegó al aguapá,	arrived at the cattail marsh,
cuando llegó al aguapá,	arrived at the cattail marsh,
volteó la cara llorando,	she looked back, crying,
—Mataron a mi papá,	—They killed my papa,
mataron a mi papá.	they killed my papa.
refrán	chorus
La cautiva Marcelina	When Marcelina the captive
cuando ya llegó a los llanos,	arrived at the plains,
cuando ya llegó a los llanos	arrived at the plains,
volteó la cara llorando,	she looked back crying,
—Mataron a mis hermanos	—They killed my brothers and sisters
mataron a mis hermanos.	they killed my brothers and sisters.
refrán	chorus
La cautiva Marcelina	When Marcelina the captive
cuando llegó al ojito,	arrived at the little spring,
cuando llegó al ojito	arrived at the little spring,
volteó la cara llorando	she looked back crying,
—Mataron al Delgadito,	—They killed Delgadito (Slim),
mataron al Delgadito.	they killed Delgadito.
refrán	chorus
La cautiva Marcelina	When Marcelina the captive
cuando llegó a los cerritos,	arrived at the little hills,
cuando llegó a los cerritos	arrived at the little hills
volteó la cara llorando,	she looked back crying,
—Mataron a mis hijitos,	—They killed my little children,
mataron a mis hijitos.	they killed my little children.
—Por eso ya no quiero	—That is why I can no longer
en el mundo más amar,	love again in this world,
de mi querida patria	from my beloved homeland
me van a retirar.	they will take me away.

Known all over New Mexico, this ballad was collected as far south as Mexico City as late as 1914, in a version in which the female character is named *la infanta Margarita,* and whose refrain includes the memorable mention of mare's meat (Mendoza and Mendoza 1986:482). The use of the word *infanta,* or princess, lends a deeper antiquity to the ballad, an echo perhaps of an older Spanish *romance fronterizo,* or captivity ballad from the wars of the Reconquest.

Margarita ya se va,	Margarita is going off,
ya se va, ya se la llevan,	there she goes, they've taken her
a la sierra de los indios	to the mountains of the Indians
a comer carne de yegua . . .	to eat mare's meat . . .

SANTO NIÑO Y SUS CAUTIVOS

There is no sure indicator of the direction of diffusion, north or south, but the ballad has all the indications of being of some antiquity, since dates and place names have been forgotten. Many more recent captivity ballads still have enough points of temporal and geographical reference that they can be corroborated with known historical events documented in other sources. "La cautiva Marcelina," however, is more regional than local in focus. In most areas it is sung with the devastating pathos outlined in this performance.

La Cautiva Marcelina

Sung by Virginia Bernal of Ratón

La cau- ti- va Mar-ce- li- na, ya se va ya

se la lle- van, ya se va ya se la lle- van

pa- ra e- sas tie- rras men- ta- das a co-

mer car- ne de ye- gua, a co- mer car- ne de ye- gua,

por e- so ya no quie- ro en el mun- do más a- mar

de mi que- ri- da pa- tria

me van a re- ti- rar.

Famed Nuevo Mexicano singer Roberto Martínez learned the indita growing up in Mora, but with the playful, even mocking tone of a nursery rhyme, an understandable strategy, given the almost unbearable pathos at hand (R. Martínez 1985).[9] Since the focus of the ballad is on the individual suffering of la cautiva, there is no direct appraisal or particular condemnation of Indian cultures. Colonial records in the eighteenth century include numerous reports of captivity incidents, most of which involving women and children (Rebolledo, Gonzales-Berry, and Santillanes 1992:17–19). Official documents are sparse in details, containing barely more than names of people and places. It is easy to imagine the multitude of personal captivity narratives that must have circulated, and the attitudes that such anecdotes would express.

Some later and better-documented oral captivity narratives from nineteenth-century New Mexico suggest a marked tendency to interpret the experience of captivity from within a spiritual frame, as an individual test of faith (Lamadrid 2002:171–72). The earliest North American captivity narratives, from Puritans in New England and French Jesuits in Canada, are also spiritual. Thereafter, however, the stories of captives were consistently used as political propaganda to stir popular ire and raise money for Indian campaigns. In contrast, Hispanic New Mexican captivity narratives have consistently utilized a spiritual framework, right through the last Apache wars of the 1880s. Like "La Cautiva Marcelina," New Mexican women seem to have been able to survive their ordeals and mourn their dead with faith and forbearance, somehow avoiding the condemnation or vilification of the Indians. Now, to the ritual contexts of this music.

✎ Comanches and the Santo Niño: The Nativity Plays

With captives in tow and dressed in feathers and buckskin, the encounter of indigenous power and the newborn Child God ignites a powerful response whenever it is staged in the Christmas season (H. Chacón 1932). In communities across New Mexico, Comanche themes may be found to one degree or another in all the dramatic traditions of Christmas, even the processions of *Las Posadas* and the *pastorelas,* or shepherds' plays.

According to several accounts, in productions prior to World War II an enigmatic Comanche character sometimes appeared in *Los Pastores* productions alongside the shepherds in their journey to Bethlehem to see the Santo Niño (Van Stone 1933). In the well-known Griegos family production, El Comanche would keep silence until the last scenes, when he shouted *"¡Ave María, Pastores! ¡Ahora sí vamos a bailar y gozar!"* [Hail Mary, Shepherds! Now for pure pleasure we're going to dance!] (Van Stone 1933:20–21). Of even greater interest is the cycle of Nativity plays where Comanches are not merely adjunct characters but rather the central protagonists.

According to numerous written accounts, *Los comanches* is performed on

Christmas Eve, with a second window of opportunity on Epiphany Eve (January 5), when instead of the arrival of Three Kings to give secular recognition to the infant Jesus, a band of Comanches appears in the same significant role, but with a very different result. A site survey and search for origins and contemporary performance traditions of the Comanche Nativity play will contextualize poetry and performance for even deeper insights into the cultural processes they dramatize. Although the ritual Comanche dances at Ranchos de Taos are also offered to Manuel, the infant Jesus, the image of the Holy Child is not present. With over twenty songs and more than a dozen dances, the Taos Comanches, their music, and choreography, will be the subject of the following chapter.

All of the Comanche celebrations in the religious context are unified by the same electrifying energy felt at the moment when costumed characters enter a house, a plaza, or a place of worship. It is mundane and commonplace for a Christian, whether Indian, mestizo, or European, to pay homage to the Holy Child. But when a Comanche expresses a wish to do the same, a special power is invoked, an even more intense sanctity. This "spiritual power of the savage" as Michael Taussig (1987:220) defines it, ultimately stems from the redemption that emanates from defeat. "[W]ildness is incessantly recruited by the needs of order. . . . But the fact remains that in trying to tame wildness this way, so that it can serve order as a counter image, wildness must perforce retain its difference. If wildness *per se* is not credited with its own force, reality, and autonomy, then it cannot function as a handmaiden to order. . . ." The power of wildness lends strength and blessings to the spirit and is particularly efficacious in restoring health, a theme in all the *Comanches* celebrations. The carnivalesque spirit of the Christmas *Comanches,* set within a deeply religious context of vigils and rosaries, lends an extraordinary ambivalence and vitality to the rituals.

Arthur Campa wrote the first study of *Los comanches,* the Nativity play and dance drama, in his critical edition of the victory play in 1942. Before this treatment, the play was briefly documented in the WPA folklore surveys (Fordyce n.d.). A musical documentation and ethnographic account in the 1960s (Hurt 1966, Robb 1980:599–602) and two recently published folk memoirs of the play in the 1930s and 1940s (Peña 1994, 1997; Chávez Bent 2000) supplement my own field observations of the tradition in the 1990s.

When the question of origins comes up at the celebrations themselves or in the memoirs, the people's answer is typically that "We have always celebrated 'Los comanches,' it has always been part of family and village Christmas traditions." Both the Peña and the Chávez Bent memoirs go into great genealogical detail in tracing the family lineages of the celebration. Campa (1979) speculates that the ritual of uninvited Comanches showing up for Christmas first appeared at the turn of the twentieth century, in the north-central part of New Mexico; however, the attacks referred to in the manuscript he saw were perpetrated by Apaches, in the western part of the state.

5.9a. Los Comanches de Atarque (Atarque, 1936). The 1936 Comanches was dedicated to the Santo Niño in a petition for the health of young Emilio Ortiz (fourth from right). Pauline Chávez is the girl on the horse. Courtesy of Pauline Chávez Bent.

It was composed, as a manuscript states, "recalling the Indian chief Victorio who attacked in 1880 and Nana in '81," In the late 1920's and early 1930's it was presented in Arenales, a small settlement adjoining Albuquerque. It was also very popular in San Rafael, a small village on Highway 66 in western New Mexico.... According to informants who had the original manuscript, the events related in the play actually took place in San Rafael in the days when the Comanches were roving over the Southwest. (Campa 1979:230)

These statements conflate relations with Apaches and Navajos with the iconic category of "Comanche," as already discussed. Campa, Hurt, and Peña all speculate on the question of why the Comanche were singled out, since western New Mexico is an area where the major historical struggle involved Navajos, Apaches, the Keres pueblos of Acoma and Laguna, and Zuñi. There is no record of Comanche raids in the area; the main armed threat was from Apaches and Navajos. But it must be recalled that after the Treaty of 1786, the Numunuh did collaborate with government troops in campaigns against the Gileño Apaches, their first foray into western New Mexico. Since Comanches were enlisted as allies in the continuing struggle against the Athabascans, it is possible that local settlers saw them in a more positive light. As always, popular lyrics can be examined for corroboration, and one of the inditas from San Mateo is as suggestive as it is ambiguous (Salazar 1997, San Mateo):

5.9B. (opposite) Los Comanches de Félix Torres (Los Griegos, 1969). The 1969 Comanches was dedicated to the protection of soldiers in the Viet Nam war. After a hiatus of two decades, Mr. Torres (on the left) passed on the music to his friends. Photo by John D. Robb, courtesy of the Center for Southwest Research, UNM General Library, John D. Robb Collection, 000-497.

5.9C. (above) Los Comanches en el altar (Los Griegos, 1969). Visiting Comanche elders dance and sing for a well-guarded altar and the Santo Niño in his manger. Photo by John D. Robb, courtesy of the Center for Southwest Research, UNM General Library, John D. Robb Collection, 000-497.

Hermanitos comanchitos,	*Little Comanche brothers,*
pues a mí me habían robado,	*well they had taken me captive,*
estas manos navajoses	*these Navajo hands*
por qué venían alzados?	*why had they been raised up?*

The singer seems to appeal to the Comanches directly, complaining about the unrelenting and inexplicable raids of the Navajo. How many Comanches might have lingered in western New Mexico is unknown. Since by 1875 the Numunuh were confined to their Oklahoma reservation (Noyes 1993:181), the possibility of an earlier origin to the Comanches Nativity plays can be raised.

A side note illustrates how diverse the "Comanche" rubric can be in the popular imagination. San Rafael, the village where Campa observed the Comanches Nativity ritual, was the original site of Fort Wingate. This fort was the base of operations for the campaigns against the Navajos in the early 1860s, before it was moved to the Gallup area. In the last war of the Gileño Apaches, in 1881, a nearby ranch in Cebolletita Canyon was attacked, two men were killed, and the wife of one, Plácida Romero, was carried off with one of her children. When she escaped in Mexico and returned, in 1882, an indita ballad was composed to commemorate her captivity (Lamadrid 2002:166–74). To fulfill a vow made during her captivity, she organized yearly *comedias,* or plays, that portrayed her ordeal. Her daughters and grand-daughters played the captives, soldiers from Fort Wingate played the Apaches, and Plácida directed. Her granddaughter Rosa Trujillo recalled being in the play, praying in the vigils that preceded and followed it, and knew all of the inditas, such as "Indita de Plácida Romero" and "La cautiva Marcelina," connected to this celebration and the Comanche Nativity plays performed in the same community (R. Trujillo 1985).

In his thoughts on Christmas *Comanche* origins, community scholar Abe Peña observes that the elders of San Mateo he knew in the 1930s told him that they learned the tradition from their elders (Peña 1997). In a consultation with Franciscan scholar Fray Angélico Chávez, he confirmed his suspicion that the Comanches Nativity plays came from eighteenth-century experiences and traditions in communities such as Tomé and Atrisco, in the central valley of the Río Grande, where there was extensive Comanche contact (Peña 1994:19).

> Sometimes in their raids, they kidnapped young children and took them to serve as braves or as servants to increase their population, which was declining because of intertribal clashes.
>
> To keep alive the memory of their children kidnapped by Comanches in war paint and feathers, and taken to distant lands to the east, Hispanic villagers along the Río Grande began the custom of Los Comanches.
>
> In 1800, the custom was brought from Atrisco by the settlers to Seboyeta, the first Hispanic village west of the Río Grande. From Seboyeta it came to San Mateo in 1862, where the custom is still a part of our Christmas tradition.

As a complement to historical sources, it is important to consider the legends about Nativity Comanches to get an insight into the cultural imagination of the people who observe and treasure the ritual.

The legend that Campa (1942:12–13) collected also serves as an outline to the action of the play.

> It seems that the *Mexicanos* of some New Mexican village have made preparations for a Nativity play when the Comanches attack them unawares and take the Christ Child as a hostage. The entire community sets out after the Indians, following the Child's footprints on the snow.
>
> The Indians have finished their evening meal and amuse themselves at various indigenous sports when the *Mexicanos* surprise them. Upon being thus out-

5.10. Cautiva de los Comanches (Los Griegos). On the eve of Christmas or Epiphany, with captives in tow, Comanches offer their gift of dance to the Holy Child. Captive children are thought to have healing powers.

witted, the chief of the Comanches attempts a trade with his conquerors. He offers a blanket for the Child, but he is promptly rebuked for his insolence. When the white men tell him the story of Christ and His sovereignty over mankind, the chief not only agrees to return his hostage but offers Him blankets, bows, and arrows. With this scene the drama ends.

Wesley Hurt collected two legends about the Comanches Nativity play from the families and friends of Félix Torres and Vicente Carrillo, in Albuquerque in the 1960s. Since their family connections were from the area of San Mateo, it is not surprising to see the place of origin coincide with the home village of the celebrants (Hurt 1966:127).

One informant stated that the grandmother of her husband was gathering *piñones* (pine nuts) in the forest of Mount Taylor, and suddenly the songs and rituals of the Comanche Dance occurred to her. On her return to San Mateo she felt so inspired that she initiated the ceremony, which has been performed many times since. Another version states that a long time ago a woman from San Mateo was captured by Indians. Her husband and sister visited the captors and asked what they wanted for ransom. The Indians replied that they would free the captive if the Spanish-Americans on their return to San Mateo would sponsor a Comanche Dance.

In my own fieldwork in Bernalillo and Los Griegos, I was told yet another story about the Christmas Comanches.

One night around Christmas time, some Hispano villagers were traveling to another village to visit. In the middle of nowhere, they came upon some Comanches dancing in front of a little manger and the Holy Child, both of which they had stolen. Amazed, the villagers invited the Comanches to accompany them to town. Since then "Los Comanches" has been performed. (H. Bustamante 1988)

The motifs that emerge from all the stories are captivity and redemption. Comanches fall in love with the Santo Niño, take Him captive, and bring their own

Los Comanches de San Mateo

Sung by Las Hermanas Salazar of San Mateo

Á- bran- se e-

sas puer- tas es- ta no- che de e- ne- ro, y

de- mos pa- so de en- tra- da se- mos bue- nos ca-

ba- lle- ros, e na je yó e na je yó e

na je ay ne ay ne yo.

spiritual energy into the spiritual circle of the community. The themes unfold in the processions, the singing of inditas, the dancing, and the capture of the Holy Child. There is no script, only a sequence of events. Campa (1942:13) minimizes the importance of the lyrics, saying they are of "little consequence" and mostly unrelated to the action. I believe they merit closer attention.

Las Inditas del Santo Niño: *Texts and Performance*

Complete indita texts from San Mateo (V. Salazar 1997 and D. Salazar n.d.), Los Griegos (Hurt 1966, Robb 1980:599–602), Bernalillo (Lamadrid 1992b), Atrisco (A. García and G. García n.d.), and Cochití/Peña Blanca (Tafoya n.d.) will be compared, along with additional fragments from San Rafael (Campa 1942), Atarque (Chávez Bent 2000), and San Mateo (Peña 1994, 1997). Just as Campa observed, each text is unique to its own community, with verses composed to match the occasion and the participants; however, many of the principal verses can be found in each version. The singing is in unison, to the beat of a *tombé,* or Pueblo Indian drum. The entire group of Indian impersonators in buckskin and feathers arrive and is permitted to sing and dance. The music, in typically hybrid indita style, uses an array of diatonic, chromatic, pentatonic, and modal melodies, punctuated with shouts and syllable chanting, a Hispanic attempt to reproduce or at least emulate Indian music. The resulting synthesis is so complex that the expertise of an ethnomusicologist is needed to understand what the ear intuits.

The Epiphany Eve performances I documented in the Albuquerque area (Los Griegos and Four Hills) were presented by four sisters of the Salazar family, originally from San Mateo: Rafaelita Baca, Eufemia Trujillo, Vangie Armijo, and Ida Segura. Local references and mention of individuals in attendance abounded in the verses (Salazar 1997, San Mateo):

Aquí estamos en su altar	*Here we are at your altar*
pa' que no estén con deseos,	*so you will not be wanting,*
semos pobres comanchitos	*we are poor little Comanches*
de la plaza de San Mateo . . .	*from the village of San Mateo.*
Desde San Mateo he venido	*From San Mateo I have come*
pa' apreciar este lugar,	*to appreciate this place,*
denme razón del Niñito	*tell if you've seen the Child*
que le prometí bailar . . .	*who I promised to dance for . . .*
Oígame usted, doña Mary,	*Listen to me, lady Mary,*
no le van a perdonar,	*they will not forgive you,*
el Niño también quiere	*the Child also wants*
que usted se pare a bailar.	*for you to get up and dance.*

The exhortation to "doña Mary" is a trick, because she is the *Madrina,* or

5.11. (opposite, top) Las Madrinas del Santo Niño (Los Griegos). These godmothers form a tight defensive ring around the Holy Child, as the Comanches fall in love with him. Their plans to abduct him are revealed in their songs.

5.12. (opposite, bottom) Los Padrinos del Santo Niño (Four Hills). The Holy Child is guarded all night by his godparents, especially watchful and suspicious when the Comanches come in to dance.

5.13. (above) Entrada de los Comanches (Los Griegos). With drums in hand and singing praises, a band of Comanches is granted entrance to the Nativity scene after convincing their hosts of their good intentions.

Godmother, of the Santo Niño, sitting to one side of the altar, guarding it. If the Comanches can distract her, the Infant may be stolen more easily. In the midst of the fun, there is serious intent as well. Several verses are dedicated with great sentiment to individuals from the community who have recently passed away. They are remembered both in song and in the *sudario,* or prayer for the dead, that is recited in the rosary services that both precede and follow the dance.

The narrative elements common to all the texts examined are as follows. As in the tradition of the *canción,* or lyrical song, verses are fairly autonomous units that float in and out of performance, sometimes independently of the poetic unity of a particular song. Looking at component verses of several songs does not break their unity, but rather demonstrates the range of expression and the most common themes. An important rhetorical feature of the verses is their dialogic quality—the Comanches are almost constantly addressing their hosts and the Santo Niño directly.

During the Nativity prayer vigil and after the first rosary, there is a knock on the door. The hosts open it, surprised to see all the "Comanche" visitors who have arrived at the manger scene in "Bethlehem," symbolized by the gathering at the house of the *mayordomos* (fiesta sponsors).

1. After knocking, there is formal ceremony at the door, in which the Comanches greet the owners of the house, request permission to enter and dance, and promise to pay respect (G. García and A. García 1995, Atrisco):

En el marco de esta puerta	*In the threshold of this door*
pongo un pie, pongo los dos,	*I put one foot, I put both,*
a los dueños de esta casa	*to the owners of this house*
buenos noches les dé Dios.	*may God give you a good night.*

In San Mateo (Peña 1994, 1997), the Comanches are even more formal, carefully placing the right foot first, exactly as the Hermanos Penitentes enter a *morada* chapel. In the full San Mateo version (Salazar 1997), the Comanches are very forward and demanding, so the people inside answer them cautiously but firmly:

Ábranse esas puertas	*Open those doors*
esta noche de enero,	*on this January night,*
y con este paso de entrada	*and with this entering step*
semos buenos caballeros.	*We will be good gentlemen.*

Ena jeyó, ena jeyó, ena, je ayne, ayne yo.

Pasen, pasen, comanches,	*Come in, come in, Comanches,*
y díganme cuántos son,	*and tell me how many your are,*
pasen a bailarle al Niño	*come in to dance for the Child*
si vienen con devoción.	*if you come with devotion.*

2. The Comanches then recount the story of how they were lost, how they "saw the light" of Bethlehem, and how far they have come to find the prayer vigil for the Holy Child and his family (Tafoya n.d., Cochití/Peña Blanca):

Hermanitos cumanchitos	*Little Comanche brothers*
estos caminos no son,	*this road is not the way,*
pueda que en aquel pueblito	*perhaps in that village*
alguien nos dará razón.	*someone will guide us on.*

CHAPTER five

Tenemos que caminar
donde la luz está,
oiremos repicar
las campanas de Belén.

Venimos de monte a monte
buscando estas maravillas,
buscamos al Niño Dios,
a San José y María.

Parece vamos hallando
lo que tanto hemos buscado,
andando largos caminos
no lo habíamos encontrado.

We have to walk
toward where the light is,
we will hear the tolling
of the bells of Bethlehem.

We come from mountain to mountain
looking for these marvels,
we look for the Child God,
for Saint Joseph and Mary
    —G. García and A. García 1995, Atrisco

It looks like we are finding
what we've looked for so much,
traveling long roads
we hadn't found it.
    —Lamadrid 1992b, Bernalillo

In a verse reminiscent of the boasts of Cuerno Verde and his chiefs likening themselves to the wild beasts of the mountains, the Comanche chief of San Rafael (Campa 1942), San Mateo (Salazar 1997), Cochití/Peña Blanca (Tafoya n.d.), and other performances, compares himself to a mountain lion. He laments that no one will guide his way, but his fierce disposition is the likely cause. In the San Mateo text, Sierra Nevada becomes Sierra Plateada (Silvery Mountains).

Soy de la Sierra Plateada

Sung by Las Hermanas Salazar of San Mateo

Soy de la tie- rra pla- tea- da, soy de la tie- rra pla- tea- da, don- de está pin- ta- do el león, don- de está pin- ta- do el león.

Soy de la Sierra Nevada
donde fui pintado león,
vengo en busca del Niñito
y no hay quién me dé razón.

I'm from the Snowy Mountains
where they pictured me a lion,
I'm looking for the Child
but no one will guide my way.
     —Campa 1942:13, San Rafael

3. Then the Comanches quell the fears of their hosts and speak of the promises they have made to offer the Child the gifts they bring: their dance and their hearts.

No se asusten, caballeros,
porque venimos bailando;
es promesa que debemos
y ahora estamos pagando.

Do not be afraid, gentlemen,
because we have come dancing;
it is a promise owed
that now we are paying.
     —Hurt 1940, Los Griegos

Ya toditos te adoraron
todos te ofrecen un don,
yo soy pobre y nada tengo,
te ofrezco mi corazón.

Now all have adored you
all have given you a gift,
I am poor and have nothing,
I will offer you my heart.
     —Salazar 1997, San Mateo

4. Petitions for blessings and health from the Santo Niño are the indication that the Comanches are learning fast how the system of mutual obligations with the saints works. What they do not yet realize is the people's belief that their very wildness is a source of health as well. In many communities, the sick are brought forth to be blessed by la cautiva, the captive girl and daughter of the Comanche chief, also known as "el Capitán" (Hurt 1940:130–31):

Por los enfermos, Niñito,
te pido en primer lugar,
con tu mano poderosa
Tú los tienes que sanear.

For the sick, little Child,
I ask you above all,
with your powerful hand
You must make them well.

The Comanches realize that dance is a powerful offering, and want to learn which prayers the Niño wants in addition (Hurt 1940, Los Griegos):

Viene de aquel cerro alto
nos pusimos a pensar,
Santo Niñito de Atocha,
cómo haremos para orar?

[The light] comes from that high hill
we have realized,
Holy Child of Atocha,
how should we pray?

5. Miraculous cosmological signs or portents are reported by the Comanches, including messenger birds, rainbows, heavenly floral arches, and great niches

5.14. Bailando al Santo Niño (Los Griegos). When families from Tomé settled the villages around Mount Taylor, they took Comanches Nativity plays with them. The Comanches dance for the Holy Child, then take him captive.

made of billowing clouds that all frame the Virgin and the saints in their descent to earth (Tafoya n.d., Cochití/Peña Blanca):

Las golondrinas vinieron	*The swallows have come*
del otro lado del mar,	*from the other side of the sea,*
en el nacimiento del Niño	*at the birth of the Child*
nos vinieron a anunciar.	*they came to announce.*
Del cielo viene abajando	*From heaven comes down*
un arco lleno de flores,	*an arch full of flowers,*
en medio del arco viene	*and on the middle of the arch*
mi Señora de los Dolores.	*is my Lady of Sorrows.*
	—G. García and A. García, Atrisco

In the intercultural folk Catholicism of New Mexico, clouds have an additional iconographic dimension, since they represent *katsina,* or ancestor spirits, in Pueblo Indian theology. Painted clouds swirl around the saints, God, and the

Virgin, and the cloud terrace motif is present in the design of altars and church architecture (Gutiérrez 1991:163).

In the plays performed on Epiphany Eve, the Comanches even report having seen the Three Kings themselves, who show them the way from their *ranchito* to Bethlehem. Nomadic Indian settlements are referred to in colonial documents as *rancherías,* or temporary rural settlements (Tafoya n.d., Cochití/Peña Blanca):

Los tres reyes buscando	*The three kings searching*
eso yo también lo sé,	*and that I know as well,*
nos trujeron del ranchito	*they brought us from our "ranch"*
para el portal de Belén.	*to the portal of Bethlehem.*

6. Ingenuous declarations of new devotion and love are tenderly made for the Santo Niño, and the thinly veiled desire to take him captive is expressed, over and over again:

Qué bonita la cunita,	*How pretty the little cradle,*
qué bonito está el altar,	*how beautiful the altar,*
más bonito está el Niño	*how lovely is the Child,*
si yo lo pudiera robar.	*if I could only steal Him.*

—Peña 1997, San Mateo; G. García and A. García, Atrisco

Here the Comanches ask the godparents for permission to "borrow" the Child, so they can perform their dance for him. After they dance, frustrated by the distrust of their hosts, they even offer to baby-sit the Child and invite him to play while his parents sleep (Tafoya n.d., Cochití/Peña Blanca):

A los Padrinos del Niño	*To the Godparents of the Child*
también les quiero explicar,	*I also want to explain,*
que me empresten al Niñito	*they should lend me the Child*
que le prometí bailar.	*For I promised him I'd dance.*
—Hurt 1940, Los Griegos	

Al despedirnos les digo	*On taking our leave I tell you*
que si quieren descansar,	*that you may want to rest,*
que se acuesten un ratito	*go ahead and lie down awhile*
que el Niño quiere jugar.	*for the Child wants to play.*

El Santo Niñito de Atocha	*The Holy Child of Atocha*
tiene gusto pobrecito,	*has his desires, poor thing,*
seguro que quiera jugar	*surely he would want*
con nosotros un ratito.	*to play with us awhile.*

—Tafoya n.d., Cochití/Peña Blanca

5.15. Santo Niño Cautivo (Los Griegos). Tired by hours of praying, singing, and dancing, godparents let down their guard and a victorious Comanche captures the baby Jesus. He will sponsor the next year's Christmas party.

Rebuffed again, the ever watchful Comanches then offer their services to "guard" the Santo Niño from "foreigners" (other tribes of wild Indians), who would really want to kidnap him, instead of just "playing" or "borrowing" Him as they have offered (Tafoya n.d., Cochití/Peña Blanca):

Todos estos cumanchitos	*All these little Comanches*
los tenemos que cuidar,	*we must watch after them,*
de aquella gente extranjera	*to not let those foreigners*
que sí lo quieren robar.	*steal them as well.*

Finally, after all entreaties fail, the Comanches invite Santo Niño directly, asking Him to join them as fellow pilgrims, and even to take pity on their fears.

Santo Niñito de Atocha	*Little Child of Atocha*
semos unos peregrinos	*we are but pilgrims,*
que ¿no vas con nosotros?	*so, will you not come with us?*
Está muy largo el camino.	*The road is very long.*
	—Tafoya n.d., Cochití/Peña Blanca

Santo Niñito de Atocha,	*Holy Child of Atocha,*
no podemos retirarnos,	*we cannot retire,*
solitos tenemos miedo	*alone we are afraid*
si gustas de acompañarnos.	*would you like to accompany us.*
	—Lamadrid 1992b, Bernalillo

Dramatic elements observed in performance and reported in the literature are listed below. Some communities utilize all the options, and others modify the options for the particular occasion.

1. On the afternoon of the performance, costumed Comanches run through the village, breaking into certain houses and terrorizing or even kidnapping children there, with the permission of their parents (Mora 1991).
2. Processions of Comanches parade through the streets of the village or neighborhood, with stops at as many as seven houses before finding the house with the Santo Niño. The young cautiva, or daughter of the Comanche capitán, also visits the sick, since it is believed that she has healing powers.
3. The Comanches arrive at their destination and beg to be allowed entry into the house where the prayer vigil is taking place.
4. A Rosary is recited in the main house of the godparents, with solemn sudarios, or prayers for the dead, as well.
5. One or as many as three inditas are sung, including "Los Comanches," and "Soy de la Sierra Plateada" (Nevada), analyzed above, which narrate the actions and intentions of the dance. "La Cautiva Marcelina" is often sung by a character of the same name.

6. At the *comanches guadalupanos* service for the feast of the Virgen de Guadalupe, her indita is sung, and a solemn dance is offered at her altar.
7. The Comanches dance is held for the Santo Niño in double lines, sometimes straight and sometimes undulating "like a snake." To the rhythm of a tombé, or Indian drum, they sing Him their praises and fall in love with Him. A careful eye is kept on the Padrinos guarding the altar, to watch for any sign of fatigue or inattention.
8. When the chance presents itself, sometimes as they are taking their formal leave, the Comanches kidnap the Santo Niño. If the abduction takes place too soon in the evening, tempers flare and the offending Comanche is given a severe admonition from hosts and "Indians" alike, as happened in the 1997 Comanche Epiphany vigil at Los Griegos.
9. Negotiations are made for the return of the Santo Niño. The next year's sponsor of the Comanches Nativity play is usually chosen at this time.
10. Another solemn rosary is recited, again with sudarios for the departed.
11. The joyful atmosphere of the Guadalupe or Christmas or Epiphany feast party resumes.

5.16. Comanchas Todas—Las Hermanas Salazar (Los Griegos). When rural families moved to urban areas, many traditions were left behind. Years later, the Salazar sisters Rafaelita Baca, Eufemia Trujillo, Vangie Armijo, and Ida Segura revived Comanches traditions from the village of San Mateo.

The sudden appearance of the Salazar sisters Rafaelita, Eufemia, Vangie, and Ida with their captive children at the altar of the Santo Niño in Los Griegos in 1997 and at Four Hills in 1998 was memorable. Dressed in sumptuous Navajo velvet and silver, with black braided wigs, headbands, and peacock feathers, they epitomized the mimetic attributes of the Hispano Comanche. Their animated gestures, swirling dance, and sly smiles lent a carnivalesque quality to their disguise. But the echoes of the solemn rosary that had just concluded, along with the plaintive indita verses for the souls of the recently departed, lent a rare power to the spectacle.

Bernalillo's "Comanchitos": An Urban Comanches Revival

My attempts to find Comanche Nativity performances took several years, since they are only intermittently enacted in the village setting. Many of the villages in the Mount Taylor region were depopulated after World War II, as their inhabitants emigrated to nearby Grants or east to the Río Grande valley communities of Albuquerque, Bernalillo, and even farther east, to the Estancia valley. When people moved away, they took the Comanches tradition with them. In new areas and neighborhoods, the celebration that had been public and communal in the village setting now was relegated to a more private context at family prayer vigils. *Los comanches* was performed with public processions in the Los Griegos area of Albuquerque through the late 1960s. The complete play, with kidnapping and ransom scenes, is currently undergoing a revival, thanks to the efforts of individual families such as those of the Salazar sisters.

It soon became obvious that, since traditions evolve according to changing social and cultural contexts, the Christmas Comanches had not disappeared, as suspected, but had changed to meet new social and cultural circumstances. In the early 1990s, students alerted me to "new" traditions that had emerged to the north of Albuquerque, in Los Ranchos and Bernalillo (H. Bustamante 1988). At the Christmas Eve services at Nuestra Señora de los Dolores church in Bernalillo, a group of *comanchitos* was dancing. The story that emerged involves a confluence of interests and memories of the parishioners of Our Lady of Sorrows parish in Bernalillo. Many people from the area grew up in the villages of Mount Taylor and the Río Puerco watershed, to the west, and nearby villages such as Placitas, to the east. After several decades, people began to miss their village traditions and determined to recreate them, even if they needed modification to fit their new lives.

In 1987, Mr. Ezequiel Domínguez, a native of Guadalupe (a New Mexican village north of Cebolleta and south of Cuba), decided to revive one of the scenes of the Comanches Nativity play for the semiurban setting of Bernalillo (Aguilar 1991). The Coro de Bernalillo, or parish choir, offered to help with the *indita,* because so many of its singers had childhood memories of their own. Restituto Sandoval, from Cabezón, recalled being "stolen" by the Comanches one Christmas. Viola Jaramillo, from Placitas, remembered being la cautiva in *Los comanches* as a child. Her son Gilbert now plays accordion for the Comanches music. Andrés Mora grew up in Cuba, New Mexico, with the Comanches tradition, and now directs the

5.17. Posadas de los Comanchitos (Bernalillo). Las Posadas is the reenactment of the Holy Family's search for shelter in Bethlehem. In Bernalillo, the Comanchitos follow close behind Mary and Joseph.

choir, whose Comanches music was recorded for Smithsonian Folkways in 1992. Gregoria Domínguez, from Bernalillo, was the wife of Ezequiel Domínguez, the man from Guadalupe who revived *Los comanches* in Bernalillo. Unfortunately, Ezequiel died unexpectedly, in November of 1991, before he could be interviewed. What Mr. Domínguez accomplished was a clever linkage of *Los comanches* with the well-known "Las Posadas" (the inns) processions, in which Joseph and Mary seek shelter each night, nine nights before Christmas (Torres 1999:49–70, West 1988:159–60).[10] In "Las Posadas," one group of singers outside asks shelter for the Holy Family, while another group inside a house makes excuses why they should not come in. The threshold scene is a key dramatic element in the procession, for finally there is a family who gives shelter to Joseph and Mary, even though it is only a stable.

Perhaps Mr. Domínguez realized the difficulty of importing the entire *Los comanches* Nativity play to a community that already celebrated "Las Posadas." In any case, he recognized the structural similarity between the two and succeeded in making the graft. In performance, as soon as the Holy Family gains entry to a house, the Comanches come right behind them, asking permission to enter and dance for the Holy Child.

5.18. Los Comanchitos Bailan al Santo Niño (Bernalillo). On Christmas Eve, Comanche children dance in devotion to the Holy Child and to honor the memory of all captive children taken by and from the Indians.

The Bernalillo adaptation is that the group of Comanches is now a group of "Comanchitos," or Comanche children. The costumed group is composed of one young adult and between ten and twenty children, ranging from four to twelve years of age. On the ninth night before Christmas, or Christmas Eve, the processions converge at the church at about 9 p.m. The Posadas group, complete with Holy Family, a donkey, and various shepherds, gains entrance to the church, followed by the Comanchitos. After the mass, the choir begins to sing the indita "Los comanchitos" in praise of the Holy Child, as previously used in Mr. Domínguez's village.

To the beat of a double-headed tombé, the little dancers hop from foot to foot, as they pass up and down the central aisle in double file, pausing as they face the Holy Family, which consists of community actors and a live baby. Between the verses, the choir sings the choral refrain of "Ana, jeyana, jeyana, jeyó . . ." in the vocable, syllable singing style of Indian music (Powers 1987), although to a non-pentatonic melody. Toward the end of the twenty-verse song, the priest invites everyone who has made a *promesa,* or promise to the Holy Child, to come and dance with the Comanchitos. Several young and older adults then join the group and dance with the children.

Mr. Domínguez trimmed away the other events and characters of the Nativity play to preserve the central event: the dance offering made by the Comanches to the Holy Child. The gifts that a Christian might offer the Child are appreciated, but there is a particular power in the gift that comes from "barbarians" who finally recognize and praise the divinity of the infant Christ. The music is fanciful in its lyrical effort to cross cultural boundaries, and the lyrics are evocative of a people that implicitly recognize and honor their cultural origins:

Los Comanchitos de Bernalillo

Aquí estoy, Santo Niñito	*Here I am, little Holy Child,*
para cumplir mi promesa,	*to fulfill my promise,*
este grupo de comanchitos	*this group of little Comanches*
me vienen a acompañar.	*comes to accompany me.*

Coro/Chorus

Ana, jeyana, jeyana, jeyó,
ana, jeyana, jeyana, jeyó,
anayana yo, anayana yo,
anayana yo, anayana yo,
ana, jeyana, jeyana, jeyó,
ana, jeyana, jeyana, jeyó.

En el marco de esta puerta	*At the threshold of this door*
pongo un pie, pongo los dos,	*I put one foot, I put both,*
a toditita esta gente,	*to all those present,*
buenos noches les dé Dios.	*may God give a good night.*
Coro	*Chorus*

Esta noche es Noche Buena,
noche de mucha alegría,
para bailarle al Niñito,
a San José y María.
   Coro
Ahora sí vamos bailando
adonde esa luz se ve,
vamos a bailarle al Niño,
a María y San José.
   Coro
Parece vamos hallando
lo que tanto hemos buscado,
andando largos caminos
no lo habíamos encontrado.
   Coro
A mí no me lleva el río
por muy crecido que vaya,
y yo sí me llevo al Niño
con una buena bailada.
   Coro
Este portal en Belén
devisamos de aquel cerro,
pensamos que aquí tendrían
al Mesías verdadero.
   Coro
Niño lindo, Manuelito,
tú solito nomás sabes
el corazón de cada uno,
también sus necesidades.
   Coro
Quisiéramos que los padrinos
se durmieran un ratito
para que el Niño bailara
con todos los comanchitos.
   Coro
Somos tristes ignorantes,
nos falta la educación,
pero el Niño agradece,
siendo de fe y corazón.
   Coro
Esta noche es Noche Buena,
noche de comer buñuelos,

Tonight is Christmas Eve,
a night of much joy,
to dance to the little Child,
to Saint Joseph and Mary.
   Chorus
Now we are really dancing
to where that light is shining,
let us dance to the Child,
to Mary and Saint Joseph.
   Chorus
It looks like we are finding
what we have looked for so much,
traveling long roads
we hadn't found it.
   Chorus
The river won't take me,
no matter how high its flood,
I'll take the Child along
with a good dance.
   Chorus
This portal of Bethlehem
we see from that hill,
we think here they must have
the true Messiah.
   Chorus
Beautiful Child, little Emmanuel,
only you can know
the heart of each one,
and also its needs.
   Chorus
We wish that the godparents
would sleep for a while
so that the Child could dance
with all the little Comanches.
   Chorus
We are sad and ignorant,
lacking in education,
but the Child is thankful
being of faith and good heart.
   Chorus
Tonight is Christmas Eve,
the night to eat fried bread,

en mi casa no los haya
por falta de harina y huevo.
   Coro
Santo Niño Manuelito,
apruebe bien tus taquitos,
porque te quieren bailar
todas estas comanchitas.
   Coro
Oye, Niñito chiquito,
oye, Niñito Divino,
mientras Dios nos preste vida,
guíanos por buen camino.
   Coro
La damita que es la guía
la quiero congratular,
que cuide bien del año
y lo entriega en el altar.
   Coro
A todita esta gente
las gracias les quiero dar,
deseando que todos
gocen de una Feliz Navidad.
   Coro
Santo Niñito de Atocha,
no podemos retirarnos,
solitos tenemos miedo
si gustas de acompañarnos.
   Coro
Santo Niñito Divino,
te pido de corazón,
con tus benditas manitas
échanos tu bendición.
   Coro
El Santo Niño de Atocha,
la Virgen y San José,
nos han de prestar la vida
para el otro año volver.
   Coro
Nos despidimos de todos,
de todos en cambullón,
les desiamos felicidades
por su buena atención.

in my house we have none
because there is no flour or eggs.
   Chorus
Holy Child little Emmanuel,
try out your little shoes,
because all these little Comanche girls
want to dance for you.
   Chorus
Listen, little Child,
listen, divine Child,
as long as God gives us life,
guide us on the good road.
   Chorus
The little lady who is the guide
I would like to congratulate,
may she keep well the year
and deliver it at the altar.
   Chorus
To every one of these people
thanks I would like to give,
desiring that all
enjoy a Merry Christmas.
   Chorus
Holy Child of Atocha,
we cannot retire,
alone we are afraid
would you like to accompany us?
   Chorus
Divine Holy Child,
I ask you from my heart,
that with your blessed little hands
give us your blessing.
   Chorus
May the Holy Child of Atocha,
the Virgin and Saint Joseph,
give us life so
we can return next year.
   Chorus
We take our leave of all,
of all together,
we wish you happiness
for your fine attentions.

SANTO NIÑO Y SUS CAUTIVOS

Los Comanchitos de Bernalillo

Sung by Brenda Romero, Jesús Armando Martínez,
Cipriano Vigil, and Enrique Lamadrid

A- quíes- toy, San- to Ni- ñi- to pa- ra

cum- plir mi pro- me- sa, es- te gru- po de co-man-

chi- tos te vie- nen a a- com-pa- ñar, es- te

gru- po de co-man- chi- tos te vie- nen a a- com-pa-

1., 2.   **3.**

ñar.   En el...

A na je ya na je ya na je yo. A na je ya na je

ya na je yo. A na ya na ya na a na ya na yo.

A na ya na ya na a na ya na yo. A na je ya na je

ya na je yo. A na je ya na je ya na je yo.

CHAPTER five
126

Coro	*Chorus*
Al Santo Niño de Atocha	*To the Holy Child of Atocha,*
le encargamos por favor,	*we entrust you please,*
cuide de sus comanchitos	*take care of your little Comanches,*
que no olvide cuántos son.	*don't forget how many there are.*
Ana, jeyana, jeyana, jeyó . . . [11]	

The vocable choruses composed of nonlexical syllables, are the most prominent indigenous feature of all the New Mexican inditas, a cultural and musical reference to the cultural hybridity of the community. The melody itself is also hybrid, neither pentatonic nor melodic, but rather modal, in full evocation of an ancient and mixed heritage. In the lyrics of its indita, the Bernalillo "Comanchitos" recapitulates the entire plot of the Comanches morality play, the arrival at the house of the vigil, the formal entrance, the promises, and the abduction of the Santo Niño. Before the farewell verse, the Comanchitos ask a fully animated Holy Child to bless them with his little hands. The last verse is the most revealing of all, an entreaty to the Niño not to forget his Comanchitos, his little redeemed and unredeemed captive children, because only He knows how many they are. The tenuous boundary between cultural self and Comanche other almost disappears completely, the sub text of "cuántos son" (how many of them there are) is "cuántos *somos*" (how many of *us* there are).

Comanches Guadalupanos: *A Revival Tribute in Los Ranchos de Albuquerque*
The Indo-Hispano communities of New Mexico honor the Virgen de Guadalupe with ritual dance, namely Matachines in the north and Chichimeca-/Carrizo-style Matachines in the south. Although the main devotion of Comanche dancing is to the Santo Niño, the Virgin is also honored, sometimes on Guadalupe's feast day and sometimes as a part of the Comanches Nativity play. In the relocation of this tradition to urbanized areas, the Comanche tribute to Guadalupe was largely forgotten. The most popular and widespread observance of the feast of the Indian Virgin is the dramatization of her story, which has formed the basis of folk plays. "Las cuatro apariciones de la Virgen de Guadalupe" is one that was performed for many generations in New Mexico, since colonial times (Torres 1999:1–48). Since the story is so familiar, it is often represented with minimal narration, and sometimes no dialogue whatsoever, by children, who simply dress as the main characters and act out the main features of the story, as follows.

During his journey along the north shore of Lake Texcoco, on several occasions the Indian Juan Diego hears a heavenly voice from the heights of Tepeyac, the ruined hilltop temple of Tonantzin, the Aztec Blessed Mother. The proof of her request for a new temple brought by Juan Diego to the doubtful bishop was a bouquet of roses, symbolic of Mary, and a wondrous image on an agave-fiber cape. A little Juan Diego, with his colorful cape, and a little Virgin, dressed in blue, are present in almost every parish celebration.

In 1996, the community of Ranchos de Albuquerque wanted to bring the

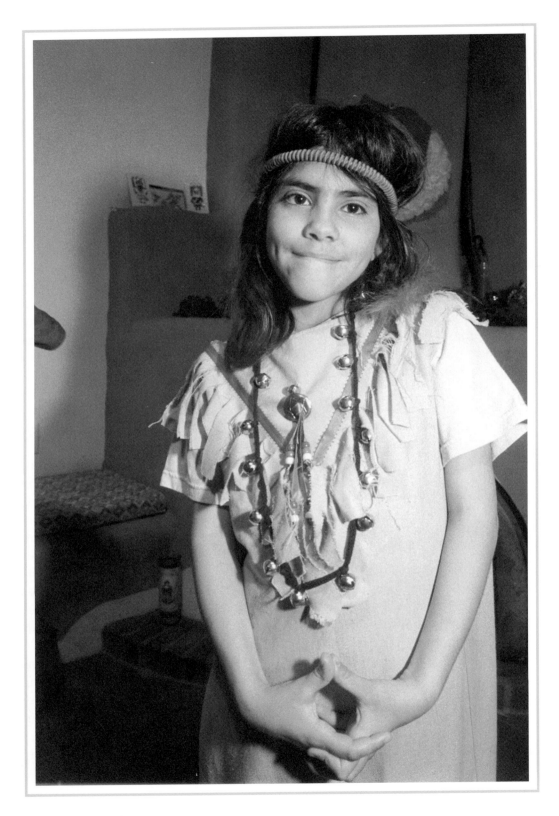

5.19.   (opposite) Una Comanchita (Bernalillo). When they moved to Bernalillo from western New Mexico, the Domínguez family introduced the music and dance of the Comanches Nativity plays to their new community.

5.20.   (above) Juan Dieguito y Guadalupita en el Altar (Los Ranchos de Albuquerque). In his heart of hearts, every boy is Juan Diego, the young Aztec Indian, and every girl is the Virgin of Guadalupe, who called to him from the heights of Tepeyac.

power of the Comanche dance back to the feast of Guadalupe. The revival came in the form of a tribute to a recently deceased neighbor, Mr. Félix Torres. Originally from Seboyeta, he directed the Comanches Nativity plays for many years in Los Griegos, because the Monte Carmel church near his home in Los Ranchos de Albuquerque lay in ruins until its reconstruction in 1973. Monte Carmel is a mission of the nearby Nativity of the Virgin Mary parish in Alameda. By the late 1960s, the Torres and Moya family performances had attracted the documentary attention of the musicologist John D. Robb and the folklorist Wesley Hurt. During the Vietnam War, the performances abruptly stopped, and three decades passed before Félix Torres realized that he needed to pass on the tradition. With the support of the Moya family, who danced with him in the 1960s, Torres taught his neighbors the late Priscilla and Eduardo Chávez and their friends the dance for Guadalupe, shortly before his death. A talented singer,

santo niño y sus cautivos

129

5.21a. (opposite) & **5.21b.** (above) Comanches Guadalupanos, Eduardo and Priscilla Chávez. Before his passing, in 1997, Félix Torres taught friends and neighbors the music of the Comanches Nativity plays that he and his family had performed years before.

Mrs. Chávez composed another indita for her, which was first sung at the Monte Carmel mission church on the night of December 11, 1996. The text is typical of many Guadalupano hymns, except for the vocable chorus, which lends a special indigenous flavor to the ritual.

Comanches Guadalupanos
En el marco de esta puerta
pongo un pie, pongo los dos,
a la gente de esta iglesia
buenas noches les dé Dios.

Si nos reciben con gusto,
si nos reciben con gusto,
hemos venido a bailar,
hemos venido a rezar.

Comanches for Guadalupe
On the threshold of this door
I put one foot then the other,
to the people of this church
may God give a good night.

If you receive us gladly,
if you receive us gladly,
we have come to dance,
we have come to pray.

Coro/Chorus
Ana jeyana jeyana jeyó,
ana jeyana jeyana jeyó,

ane ane ane, ane aneyó,
ane ane ane, ane aneyó,
ana jeyana jeyana jeyó,
ana jeyana jeyana jeyó.

En el cerro de Tepeyac,
en la ciudad mexicana,
saludó a Juan Diego
la Virgen Guadalupana,
la Virgen Guadalupana.

On the hill of Tepeyac,
in the Mexican city,
She called to Juan Diego,
the Virgin of Guadalupe,
the Virgin of Guadalupe.

Coro/Chorus

Oh, Virgen de Guadalupe,
morenita como la aurora,
eres la virtud del mundo,

Oh, Virgin of Guadalupe,
dark featured as the dawn,
you are the virtue of the world

Comanches Guadalupanos

Sung by Priscilla & Eduardo Chávez of Los Ranchos de Alburquerque

En el mar-co de es-ta puerta, en el mar-co de es-ta puerta pongo un pie pongo los dos, pongo un pie, pongo los dos, a la gente de esta iglesia a la gente de esta iglesia buenas noches les dé Dios, buenas noches les dé Dios. Ana je yana je yana je yó, ana je yana je yana je yó, ane, ane, ane, ane, ane yó, ane, ane, ane, ene, ane yó, ana je yana je yana je yó, ana je yana je yana je yo.

en la tierra y en la gloria,	*on earth and in heaven,*
en la tierra y en la gloria.	*On earth and in heaven.*

Coro/Chorus

Oh, Virgen de Guadalupe,	*Oh, Virgin of Guadalupe,*
te venimos a rezar,	*we come to pray,*
pintar con tus colores,	*to paint with your colors,*
para tu Hijo bailar,	*and to dance for your Son,*
y para tu hijo bailar.	*and to dance for your Son.*

Coro/Chorus

Oh, Virgen de Guadalupe,	*Oh, Virgin of Guadalupe,*
me despido yo de ti,	*I take my leave of you,*
estos versos te compuse,	*I composed you these verses*
pa' que te acuerdes de mí,	*so you will remember me,*
pa' que te acuerdes de mí.	*So you will remember me.*

—P. Chávez 1996

As the children Juan Diego and Guadalupe stood in front of the altar, the elderly and venerable Comanches entered with their drummer and danced lightly to the altar to pay their respects. In hybrid dress with Navajo velvet and silver, Tewa

5.22. Una Comancha y el Santo Niño (Los Ranchos de Albuquerque). At Guadalupe's altar, a Comancha holds a Holy Child with Indian features, dressed in buckskin, and tightly bound in his Apache cradleboard.

5.23. Danza de la Virgen (Los Ranchos de Albuquerque). In a short-lived revival, parishioners of Monte Carmelo Church dance for Guadalupe, to honor their Indo-Hispano traditions.

moccasins, dyed chicken feathers, and tinsel headbands, they swayed from side to side with a power and grace that captivated all.

Due to changing pastoral priorities in the Nativity of the Virgin Mary parish in Alameda, masses and feast-day services in the Monte Carmel mission have been sharply curtailed since 1996. The convocation of the Comanche devotions to Guadalupe was a unique and ephemeral event, a memorial to the passing of a Comanche elder. As in Bernalillo, Comanche music and dance was grafted onto a more contemporary ceremony. In Bernalillo, a new annual tradition was born, while in Ranchos de Albuquerque, the revival was cut short by a clergy apparently unaware of deep-rooted community traditions. In all of the case studies examined, the peace of 1786 is still alive in the hearts of the people. But in the postmodern setting of the city, the public spaces of plaza and church are no longer as accommodating to the cultural memory of the people, since they fall under the direct control of bureaucratic institutions.

Now to a discussion of a unique tradition of Hispano-Comanche dance and music that has flourished in Ranchos de Taos, despite an even greater obstacle, its association with the most assimilated, mestizo, and marginalized sector of indigenous cultures in New Mexican society, the Genízaros.

CHAPTER five

6

Los Comanches de la Serna

MUSIC, DANCE, AND HISPANO-COMANCHE IDENTITY

As long as anyone can remember, there have been Comanches celebrations in Ranchos de Taos and the neighboring villages scattered along the Río Chiquito and the Río Grande del Rancho, the southernmost valley of the Taos basin. The earliest photos of Hispano Comanches in the Taos Historic Museums Archive date to the 1920s. Earlier photographic surveys of indigenous folkways passed through Taos Valley, including that of Edward S. Curtis, but were evidently not interested in mestizo groups.

Of all the Comanche groups in this study, in Taos the process of subjectification is fully realized, and the identification between self and cultural Other is complete. Hispano-Comanche identity in Taos is enacted in ritual dance that includes dramatizations of the root experience of transculturation and captivity. As mentioned in the preface, the celebrants of this tradition refer to themselves as "nosotros los comanches" (we the Comanches). They are careful to disassociate themselves with the term *comanchero,* which refers to the traders who dealt (often illegally) with the Numunuh, and which is occasionally used to discredit them (F. Gonzales 1992).

The Comanches of Taos Valley have never claimed that they are Numunuh, nor do they claim any legal status as Indians. As far as the U.S. Census is concerned, they are Hispanic and have no tribal affiliation or rights. As will be seen, cultural workers and activists with passing knowledge of the ethnic complexities of New Mexico have been overly hasty to question their legitimacy and dismiss their very existence.[1] Cultural representation of such hybrid groups in research and in museums can be a risky business. But Genízaro groups since colonial times have been marginal and "disreputable," until, of course, they prove themselves in battle in defense of the state (Gutiérrez 1991:305–6).

According to oral tradition as well as archaeological remains, the valley of

Ranchos de Taos was originally settled by seasonal farmers from Taos Pueblo. When the Spanish-Mexicans settled in the area, it was named Las Trampas de Taos and later Ranchos de Taos. In the seventeenth century, the permanent settlements were located at Taos Pueblo, on the Río Pueblo, where natives and colonists gathered for survival and mutual defense. As population and tensions grew, the Hispano colonists founded Fernando de Taos, a few miles south along the Río Fernando (WPA 1989:287).

We know that the first appearance of the Numunuh in the historical documents of New Mexico was in 1706, when the people of the Taos Valley were ordered to prepare their defenses in anticipation of a hostile visit from these Comanches, in the company of their cousins, the Utes. In the following decades, Plains Apache groups sought refuge in the mountains of New Mexico. The government decision not to build a presidio at Cuartelejo, in the Arkansas Valley, to protect them, led many Jicarillas south and west, where they were allowed to establish improvised settlements near Pecos and Galisteo, and by 1733, at Trampas de Taos. Trampas (Ranchos) was already the location of the Cristóbal de la Serna land grant, one of the first in the Taos area. When Serna could not settle it successfully, he sold it in 1724 to a group of Genízaros from the village of El Quemado (now Córdova), led by José Diego Romero, whose extended family populated the valley. The largest settlement was the extensive, fortified Villalpando hacienda, where families gathered when danger threatened. Despite its four *torreones,* or defensive towers, and its cache of firearms, it was overrun in the Numunuh revenge attack of August 1760, and all of its defenders were killed or taken captive (Adams and Chávez 1956:217, Grant 1934:202, Gregg 1926:139, Noyes 1993:55, Parkhill 1965:13–14).

During the entire eighteenth century, Taos was the northernmost center of Numunuh commerce in New Mexico, and everyone in the valley had contact with the goods exchanged, including the captives, many of whom were adopted and raised as *criados* (those reared by a family, but as their servants). After the Treaty of 1786, it was possible for local Comanchero traders to go to the Plains to carry their goods to the Numunuh, instead of waiting for them to come west over the mountains (Haley 1934–35, Levine 1991:155–69, Simmons 1961). In addition to these contacts, it is recalled in local oral histories that a group of marooned Numunuh settled with friends and family in the Taos Valley when the U.S. government banished them to Fort Sill and their reservation in Oklahoma (L. Harris 2002).[2] The links are many and complex. Whether or not they directly descend from the Numunuh or from Genízaros is not as important as the identification with Genízaro culture that the Comanches of Ranchos de Taos affirm. They are aware of their history and claim it as part of their identity.

❧ Being and Becoming "Comanche"

Genuine affective links with Native cultures were made when the Spanish-Mexicans, by choice or necessity, came to identify with the Indians that surrounded them on all sides. This identification was hardest earned with Pueblo neighbors, because it had to grow out of the respect the Pueblos had won for themselves through an act of resistance and religious affirmation—the 1680 Pueblo Rebellion. New alliances and cultural bonds followed after the reestablishment of the colony, but the two cultures coexisted rather than fused; hence the appropriateness of the dated but still useful anthropological concept of "compartmentalization" (G. Barker 1931:450–53, Dozier 1954:681, Spicer 1958:434).

The Hispanic identification with non-Pueblo Indian cultures developed more easily, in part because of the more intimate social relations they experienced with nomadic Indian captives that joined Spanish households and families as criados. Pueblo Indians were allies and trusted neighbors, but a Genízaro with Navajo, Apache, Ute, or Comanche roots could be living under the same roof, taking care of the children and singing them native lullabies. The word *chichigua* is still used to mean wet nurse or Indian nanny (Cobos 1983:45). Before the arrival of modern medical services, every community had to have a lactating woman available to raise infants whose mothers died in childbirth; many chichiguas were criadas.

The cultural exchanges of those troubled times of warfare were often spent under the involuntary and stressful conditions of captivity, servitude, and what amounts to involuntary transculturation. It is precisely this personal and cultural trauma of the cautivos that is reenacted in Comanches ritual dance. Many youthful Spanish-Mexican captives were taken into Numunuh families and raised in the culture before making their way back to their original homes. Others were satisfied with their adopted Numunuh culture and identity. The inverse process was just as common and caused the emergence of the class of Genízaros. The last generation of criados in the Ranchos area survived into the 1920s and 1930s, and the current generation of octogenarians in the community remembers them (Rael y Gálvez 2000). These elders are also familiar with the repertoire of Comanche music and dance (Durán 1994). Individual families know "if they are Comanches or not" (F. Gonzales 1992). That is to say, previous ethnic boundaries are still recognized, even though the present population as a whole is legally considered to be "Hispanic."

The most prominent Comanche families include the Archuleta, Casías, Durán, Frézquez, Gonzales, Martínez, Montoya, Mondragón, and Valerio clans. Singers and dancers gather into loosely organized groups such as Los Comanches de la Serna, Los Comanches del Río Chiquito, and others, according to family alliances and friendships, and singers as well as dancers often join those of other groups and perform together (Valerio and Valerio 2002). Despite the exodus to urban areas during and following World War II, Hispano still Comanches return to Taos to observe their celebrations. Some permanently relocated families, such as those of Jake Aragón, Clodoveo Herrera, and others have transplanted their traditions as far away as Utah, where in towns such as Tooele, for instance, the complete cycle of music and dance may be found (F. Gonzales 1992).

For the current survey, three generations of the Gonzales family were interviewed to address basic questions about the origins, transmission, and repertoire associated with this tradition. The late Nelson Gonzales, the patriarch, was a retired schoolteacher who was dedicated to the Comanche traditions in his family and community. He compiled a personal archive of musical recordings dating back to the 1950s.[3] He recalled his early fascination with Comanche traditions, at a time when young children were "captured" and made to dance during the celebrations (N. Gonzales 1993). They were called *Pecas,* as they are in the eighteenth-century equestrian play *Los comanches de castillo.* Nelson Gonzales was tutored in Comanche ways by an uncle and by community elders (notably David Frésquez and Frank Durán), rather than by his father. It must be remembered that many families with a Genízaro background will tend to suppress it, since this stigmatized group occupied the bottom rungs of colonial society. However, there have always been certain families and individuals who have taken pride in their non-Hispanic origins.

Francisco "El Comanche" Gonzales, Nelson's son, has also dedicated much of his energy to the celebration of the Genízaro heritage. The repertoire he recorded for this survey includes more than two dozen songs and eighteen dances, along with explanations of their meanings and recollections of the neighbors and family members he learned them from. He began as a Peca captive and child dancer, who, with his younger brother Charlie, was given instruction when the men gathered on weekend afternoons to sing.

6.1. (opposite) El Patriarca y su Gente (Talpa). A lifelong educator, Nelson Gonzales learned Hispano-Comanche traditions from an uncle and passed them down to his family and community.

6.2. (above) Peca a Caballo (Ranchos de Taos). As a child, Francisco "El Comanche" Gonzales participated as a peca, or captive, in the staging of Los Comanches de Castillo in Ranchos de Taos. Courtesy of the Gonzales family.

    With the disappearance of the equestrian play in the Taos area, the principal initiation into the Comanches tradition is by dancing. Through the years, dancers participate more and more in the singing until gaining status as an elder in the tradition and becoming a full-fledged singer.

    "El Comanche" is an insurance counselor and former state senator. He has been shunned in some political circles, an all-too-familiar scenario for Genízaros in New Mexican society.[4] He is, however, one of the major carriers of the Hispano-Comanche tradition. Over the years he has recruited young people to dance as Comanches, especially those from Genízaro families in the area. He takes great pride in the fact that many of these young people have decided to pursue higher education and careers, due in part to the discipline associated with being Comanche dancers. The first group he taught was composed of his children and

6.3. Tres Generaciones Cantando (Ranchos de Taos). Three of four generations of Comanches in the Gonzales clan. Dancers start young, and singers never retire.

neighbors and was invited to perform in Washington, D.C., as part of the bicentennial celebration, in 1976. This group also toured the powwow circuit as far as Calgary, Alberta (F. Gonzales, Jr., 1991). Another generation of dancers returned to the Smithsonian Folklife Festival in 1992, when New Mexico was honored and the "American Encounters" exhibit was inaugurated at the Museum of American History (Lamadrid 1992a, 1992b).[5]

Francisco "Cisco" Gonzales, Jr., is a person who has come of age into the Comanche performance tradition. He has danced since he could walk, and with his brothers Estevan and David and sister Corina, is a prodigious dancer. He is also a fine singer, although his repertoire is still growing and does not yet approach that of his father. Cisco is an attorney and officer in the Air National Guard. His own children have also been dancing since they could walk. A second Gonzales sister, the late Frankietta, was also a fine dancer. Through their example, about half of the dancers who now participate in the New Year's celebration are female. However, I have only heard women sing on a few informal occasions. All the principal singers are elder males, only occasionally joined by younger men.

The main ritual context for Comanche dancing in Ranchos de Taos is New Year's Day, which is the patronal feast of Manuel (Emmanuel), another aspect of the long-awaited person of the Christ, who comes to fulfill the Old Testament prophesy of the Messiah. The underlying theme of the ritual is Christian conversion, the recognition by the "barbarian" non-Christian Comanche that the divine redeemer has indeed arrived. When Comanches dance on Christmas Eve, as in Bernalillo, the focus of their attention is the person of the Holy Child. In the New Year's celebration, "Comanche Christmas," homage is paid to the Emmanuel by dancing for everyone in the community who is named Manuel or Manuela, the namesakes of the Messiah. The theological implications of this ritual frame and practice surpass the boundaries of conventional Nativity devotions.

The ritual setting for other Ranchos de Taos Comanche celebrations in the past has been January 25, the feast of San Pablo. Upon closer examination, this is actually the feast of the Conversion of Saint Paul. The theme of the pagan finding Christianity through an intense personal experience while traveling has deep resonance with the circumstances of the Numunuh or fictive Comanche encounter with Western religion and subsequent political alliance with the same powers. In colonial times, the custodio, or Franciscan missionary province, that comprised New Mexico was named in honor of *La conversión de San Pablo,* since Christianization of the Indians was its main purpose. Now that the stage is set, a description of feast-day performances will be drawn, followed by a closer analysis of each dance and its accompanying song.

Los Comanches Bailan al Niño Manuel: *New Year's Day Dances*

Talpa. Ranchos de Taos. Llano Quemado. Cordillera. Los Córdovas. The first sun of the New Year rises to the beating of single-headed hand drums. Troupes of Hispano-Comanche dancers enter the graceful Santuario de San Francisco de Assís and the Capilla de Nuestra Señora de Talpa for prayers, followed by a *Redondo,* or round dance, outside in the plaza. So begins the feast of Emmanuel in these villages of Taos Valley, a celebration of a holy promise fulfilled. Divinity and humanity become one, and so the people dance. Like their neighbors at Taos Pueblo, the people in these Hispano villages dress in buckskin, velvet, fringe, and feathers to sing their oldest songs, a tribute to their indigenous, mestizo heritage.

Unlike the scene at the Pueblo, there is not a single tourist in sight, despite efforts to attract them to Indo-Hispano celebrations dating to the 1920s and 1930s, on the specially featured "Tour 3" in the *WPA Guide to 1930s New Mexico* (WPA 1989:287).[6]

From sunrise to sunset, from house to house, they sing and dance to honor Manueles and Manuelas, the namesakes of Emmanuel, the Holy Child, on his blessed day. The elders recall that at the turn of the century, visits were made on horseback (Durán 1994). Singers sang mounted on their ponies, while the dancers circled below. On their rounds, they would attract and carry off the Pecas, or captive children. They learned to dance by following in the footsteps of older dancers

6.4. (opposite, top) Mañanitas del Niño Manuel (Ranchos de Taos). At New Year's first light, Comanche dancers gather at the San Francisco de Asís Church in Ranchos de Taos, to pray to the Holy Child Emmanuel.

6.5. (opposite, bottom) Una Trocada de Comanches (Talpa). Truckloads of Comanches travel all over Talpa, Ranchos de Taos, and Llano Quemado, to dance for the Holy Child Emmanuel at the homes of his namesakes, Manuel and Manuela.

6.6. (above) Nevada del Año Nuevo (Talpa). Hispano-Comanche dances are an offering and a sacrifice fulfilled in any type of weather. Snow is a great blessing.

(N. Gonzales 1993). Today old and young pile into pickups that crisscross the Ranchos de Taos Valley to make the same rounds.

The itinerary of houses visited is based on a number of factors besides the presence of a Manuel or Manuela. Relatives are visited and brought into the circle of honor. Families of dancers returning from faraway cities for the fiesta make elaborate preparations to lure the group into lingering for extra dances and songs. The dance also comes to pay homage to those Comanche elders no longer able to make the rounds with the group. Important singers are always remembered. Special requests are also accepted from non-Comanche neighbors, eager for the colorful spectacle to grace and bless their homes. Singers also perform at the bedside of the sick, to raise their spirits. By the day's end, a single group may have performed at as many as twenty houses if the weather is right. Singers are hoarse and dancers are exhausted and cold, in sweat-soaked buckskins. If there is snow or mud, moccasins (and tennis shoes) do not stay dry for long.

As the Comanches ride around, then walk between houses, the *llanero* (plainsman) and *paseado* (traveling) songs can be heard. When the people in the house come outside to the yard or driveway, the dancing begins. Every set begins with the redondo, which can be danced to several different songs, all of which have the characteristic heartbeat, round-dance rhythm. Every set concludes with a performance of "La Rueda," the ring, or captive, dance, which features a pantomime taking of captives and has its own distinct song. The selection of the other three or four dances in a set is negotiated and determined by the singers and dancers. In the words of a dancer (F. Gonzales, Jr., 1998):

> We have a traditional round dance and then *La Rueda* and we'll throw in an *Espantao* (Frightened One). It's what we feel like dancing. The other dancers can request to have one that they watched before. The structure is very informal and dynamic and individualistic. Very individualistic, each person has a role they can play if they want to. They can go and ask to request one or sit out if they want to, or talk to somebody while the dance is going on, then throw their heart into it on the next song. What's going through their minds is the whole repertoire of songs that they have. They'll go to somebody's house and remember that this guy liked this song, and what was that song. Different things will trigger the songs. They'll flat out remember one and start in.

After a set of dances are completed, the honored family ransoms its captives by offering the *rescate* (rescue price) or *desempeño* (redemption price), usually in the form of cash for gasoline and costumes, or shots of whiskey or *vino de capulín* (chokecherry wine) for the singers. Refreshments are offered to everyone and consist of sweets, sodas, coffee, and the omnipresent *biscochito,* or anise-flavored cookie typical of the season. A light midday meal is usually offered in one of the houses. The dancing is so strenuous that dancers do not eat a big meal until they return home, exhausted.

Hispano-Comanche dancing typically lasts from sunrise to sunset. As they make their visits across the valley and its five villages, dancers from as many as four different troupes cross paths during the day. On the years when New Year's Day falls on a Sunday, the local parish holds a potluck, and all of the Comanche troupes converge. As many as a dozen singers and several dozen dancers can be seen on these occasions. As night falls, the celebrations of "Comanche Christmas" come to an end until the following year. Before World War II, Hispano-Comanche celebrations were observed on the January 25 feast day of the *Conversión de San Pablo* (Conversion of Saint Paul), but work schedules have since interfered and made the New Year's feast more important, since it is accessible to all (F. Gonzales 1992).

6.7. Dulces y Tragos (Talpa). The captives' ransom is paid in part with sweets and anise biscochitos, washed down with Gatorade, whiskey, and chokecherry wine.

In addition to feast-day performances, Los Comanches de la Serna dance in festival settings as well as the annual Taos Fiesta parade. Before further examining the Comanche dance repertoire, the musical tradition must be highlighted.

Cantos Comanches: *Texts and Origins*
As with most forms of dance, movement is driven by song. The Hispano-Comanches of Ranchos de Taos perform a sizable repertoire of songs that comprise a synthesis of old and new Pueblo, Southern Plains, and Navajo styles and sources (Wapp 1998, Williams 2000). The existence of this repertoire in the maroon and mestizo Comanche settlements in the Taos valley is a tribute to the persistence and adaptability of Genízaro culture. Most Genízaros, assimilating first to Hispano and then American culture, were only too eager to leave behind the customs and cultural expressions of their indigenous past. On the other hand, the Hispano-Comanches of Taos clung to them as emblems of the pride that provided them with the inspiration and strength to face the challenges of the present.

It is difficult to appraise the antiquity of the Hispano-Comanche music of Taos. Some songs have been in the community for generations, others are newer. Stylistic elements and the ear of an ethnomusicologist will provide the best clues, since the vast majority of the repertoire is composed of vocable songs, the syllable singing characteristic of North American indigenous music (Powers 1987). Some of the paseados, or traveling songs, are closely related to the Pan-Indian Powwow songs from Oklahoma (Wapp 1998). Much of this more recent late-nineteenth- and twentieth-century repertoire came to the Río Grande Valley through Taos Pueblo, which is undoubtedly how it got to Ranchos de Taos. Other Hispano-Comanche songs are much older.

It is the use of Spanish and even English in a few songs that give some more tantalizing clues as to the provenance and antiquity of this music. The Comanches of Ranchos de Taos sing a number of Spanish verses that are clustered together in only two or three songs. Some vocable songs are still remembered from the last performances of *Los Comanches de Castillo* in Ranchos in the 1950s, especially a wardance song associated with Cuerno Verde and a captive song associated with the Pecas, or captive children, from the play (Gonzales 1992).

On the special occasions when singers gather to sing without the dancers, the Cuerno Verde song is sung as a chorus, alternating with verses recalled from the

Arengas para Cuerno Verde

Sung by Comanches de la Serna of Ranchos de Taos

play and others improvised on the spot, which honor the Yamparica war chief. All are delivered in the heroic *arenga*, or war harangue, style.

Del oriente al poniente,	From east to west
del sur al norte frío,	from south to frigid north
suenen pífanos y tambores,	may trumpets and drums sound,
¡que viva el acero mío!	may my steel live long!
Yo soy aquel Cuerno Verde	I am that Cuerno Verde
el más feroz de todos,	the most ferocious of all,
vengo aquí a saludarles	I come here to salute you
de este modo y otros modos.	in this and other ways.
Cuerno Verde montado	Cuerno Verde on his horse,
no hay quién lo pueda alcanzar,	no one can ever catch him,
norte, sur, oriente o poniente,	north, south, east, or west,
el guerrero más afamado.	the most famous warrior.

The other verses of the *cantos comanches* are sung rather than recited. The main melody is recognized in Taos Pueblo as a gambling song, although it also resembles Plains round-dance music (F. Gonzales 1992, T. Isaacs 1991, Wapp 1998).

Many verses are filled with references to warfare, some of which can be attributed to definite historical periods. The following quatrain sung in Ranchos de Taos features a combat scene between the Numunuh and Apaches in which each has equal footing and prowess.

El comanche y el apache	The Comanche and the Apache
se citaron una guerra,	made a date for war,
el comanche no se raja	the Comanche doesn't give up,
y el apache se le aferra.	the Apache bears down hard.[7]

The key concepts here are the equal portrayal of the combatants and the verb *citar*, which indicates that their war was somehow scheduled or agreed upon. These elements point to the era after the great Comanche Peace was negotiated in 1786, between the government of Don Juan Bautista de Anza and Ecueracapa, the heroic Comanche leader who unified the many independent bands of his people. Part of the treaty agreement stipulated that every spring Comanche warriors would come to the presidio of Santa Fe to join the militia and travel south and west to engage their common enemy, the yet-undefeated Apaches of those regions (Kavanagh 1996:110–21, Noyes 1993:74–81).

At the turn of the twentieth century, the folklorist Aurelio M. Espinosa collected a slightly different variant of the same quatrain that suggests an even earlier origin. Here the Apache is ridiculed as a coward.

El Apache y el Comanche / The Apache and the Comanche
Se citaron pa' la guerra, / Made a date for battle,
Se citaron pa' la guerra, / Made a date for battle,
El Apache gime y llora, / The Apache groans and cries,
Y el Comanche se le aferra, / And the Comanche closes in,
Y el Comanche se le aferra. / And the Comanche closes in.

El Apache y el Comanche
Se citaron pa' la guerra,
Se citaron pa' la guerra,
El Apache gime y llora,
Y el Comanche se le aferra,
Y el Comanche se le aferra.

The Apache and the Comanche
Made a date for battle,
Made a date for battle,
The Apache groans and cries,
And the Comanche closes in,
And the Comanche closes in.

—A. Espinosa 1907:20–21

The most likely historical referent for suffering or crying Apaches would not be the fierce bands of the south, but rather the peaceable northern band of Jicarilla Apaches, who suffered grievously earlier in the eighteenth century. In 1724, the

Coplas Comanches

Sung by Comanches de la Serna of Ranchos de Taos

El co- man-che y el a- pa-che se ci- ta-ron

u- na gue- rra el a- pa- che no se ra- ja

el co- man-che se le a- fe- rra. A pa ya ya

a pa yo yo sa- ca na- va- jó je yo o

ya yo je ne ya je yo yo ya yo je yo

je je yo.

Comanches decimated the Jicarillas, carrying off half of their women and children and killing everyone else except for sixty-nine men, two women, and three boys (Bancroft 1889:239). Contingents of Jicarillas made desperate complaints to colonial authorities about their suffering at the hands of the Comanches.

Other verses sung in Ranchos de Taos refer to warfare with the Navajo, those formidable northern cousins of the Apaches. Oral histories brim with accounts of Navajo visits to Taos Valley, both friendly and warlike (Vásquez 1975).

Si tu andas en combate	*If you are in combat*
y tu tropa no ganó,	*and your troop didn't win,*
pide a Dios que te rescate,	*ask God to rescue you,*
si el enemigo es navajó.	*if your enemy is Navajo.*

Coro/Chorus
Epa nava, ene yo,
saca navajó, jeyó,
ya yo jene ya jeyó,
ya yo jeyo jaiaio.

Cuando vayas pa' navajó,	*When you go to Navajo land,*
aprevente del mortal,	*prepare for mortal trouble,*
porque la muerte de allá,	*because death awaits there,*
es firme y no se rebaja.	*firm and without compromise*

Coro/Chorus
Epa nava, ene yo,
saca navajó, jeyó,
ya yo jene ya jeyó,
ya yo jeyo jaiaio.

The musicologist John D. Robb also recorded this "Navajo dance song" in 1950, as sung by David Frésquez, an elder who taught many of today's elders (Robb 1980:459).

Other lyrics from the cantos comanches come directly from the regional oral repertoire of lyric quatrains, known by the people as *coplas* or *versos*. Of the two thousand or so collected in New Mexico, many are centuries old, and others can be found in the pages of *Don Quijote,* for Miguel de Cervantes also had a fine ear for folklore (A. Espinosa 1976:139–60). Still others are improvised on the spot. All float in and out of songs, even Comanche songs.

Anteanoche fui a tu casa	*Night before last I went to your house*
y vi luz en tu ventana,	*and saw a light in your window,*
tú siempre vas a ser	*you always will be*
el lucero de mi mañana.	*my morning star.*

Other love lyrics are raucous and burlesque, a characteristic aspect of the intercultural tradition of Nuevo Mexicano indita music:

Anteanoche fui a tu casa	*Night before last I went to your house*
y me dites de cenar,	*and you gave me to eat,*
tortillitas chamuscadas	*burned tortillas*
y frijoles sin guisar.	*and badly cooked beans.*

Unrequited or unreturned love takes on a new dimension when it occurs between cultures. Under- or overcooking is a sign that an appropriate cultural process has been bypassed or short-circuited.

Since the cantos comanches are sung to the tune of a gambling song, it is inevitable that gambling lyrics would surface as well. *El cañute* is an Indo-Hispano gambling game that was played extensively in the Taos area in the nineteenth century and is still played in the Pueblos on special occasions.[8]

Allí vienen los cañuteros	*Here come the cañute players*
allí vienen por la cañada,	*there they come up the canyon,*
parece que se la llevan	*seems like they'll be winning*
pero no se llevan nada.	*but don't get away with anything.*
Allí vienen los cañuteros	*Here come the cañute players*
los que no conocen miedo,	*those who are without fear,*
pero de aquí llevarán	*but here they'll only get*
atolito con el dedo.	*corn porridge with their finger.*

Gamblers came from distant plains and mountains to play cañute at trade fairs and feast days. Many of the cañuteros verses have inordinately erotic allusions (Loeffler, Loeffler, and Lamadrid 1999:23–24).

Surprisingly enough, even English lyrics make their way into the Hispano-Comanche repertoire, through the tradition of the Forty-Niner songs and Round Dances popular across the valley in Taos Pueblo. As displaced Natives from across the emerging mid-nineteenth- and twentieth-century American nation encountered each other in mining camps, work crews, and the armed services, the forty-niner songs emerged, with English verses and vocable choruses (Gelo 1988, Wapp 1998). The following well-known forty-niner is sung by the Hispano-Comanches as well as at the powwows of Taos Pueblo (and in the rest of North America).

I don't care if you're
married sixteen times
I'll get you yet.
Weya ja, weya jo . . .

Both the English and the Spanish lyrics alternate with vocable choruses. The Spanish burlesque and historical verses above are sung in the same section of the performance as the forty-niners, and are also considered "social or party songs"

(F. Gonzales 1992). One of the most popular Spanish-language forty-niners has very simple but hilariously ambiguous lyrics:

Dime sí, dime no.	*Tell me yes, tell me no.*
Dime sí, dime no.	*Tell me yes, tell me no.*
Yo jeyana jo . . .	

Although unmarked for gender, the lyrics can fit into any number of personal or intimate scenarios, and singers usually provoke much laughter with this simple song. With these few Spanish and English lyrics and the clues they provide, it can be concluded that the origins of the Hispano-Comanche repertoire stretch from the late eighteenth to the mid-twentieth century and on up to the present.

Besides the coplas cited above, Campa published another in 1946 that is notable for its level of reflexivity. It is not part of the Comanches dance tradition but rather comments about it. "El Comanchito" refers in jest to a visit of little Comanche dancers that is first mistaken for an ambush. Just as in Ranchos de Taos, the obligatory refreshments for dancers include sweets and wine. Like the *coplas comanches,* the verses are in Spanish, with refrains in vocable syllables.

"El Comanchito"	***"The Little Comanche"***
Ai vienen los indios	*Here come the Indians*
Por el chaparral;	*Through the chaparral;*
Ai vienen los indios	*Here come the Indians*
Por el chaparral.	*Through the chaparral.*
Ay nanita, ay nanita,	*Oh granny, oh granny,*
Me quieren matar.	*They want to kill me.*
Ay nanita, ay nanita	*Oh granny, oh granny,*
Me quieren matar.	*They want to kill me.*
Jeya, jeya, jeya,	*Heya, heya, heya,*
Jeya, jeya, jeya,	*Heya, heya, heya,*
Jeya, jeya, jeyaaaaah!	*Heya, heya, heyaaaah!*
Baila el comanchito,	*The little Comanche dances,*
Toca la tambor;	*He plays his drum;*
Baila por buñuelos,	*He dances for sweetbreads,*
Baila por licor.	*He dances for alcohol.*
Ay nanita, ay nanita,	*Oh, granny, oh granny,*
Me quieren matar.	*They want to kill me.*
Ay nanita, ay nanita	*Oh, granny, oh granny,*
Me quieren matar.	*They want to kill me.*
Jeya, jeya, jeya,	*Heya, heya, heya,*

Jeya, jeya, jeya,
Jeya, jeya, jeyaaaaah!

Heya, heya, heya,
Heya, heya, heyaaaah!

—*Campa 1946:220*

In his analysis, Campa claims that this lyric is a New Mexican adaptation of a lyric from the indita tradition of central Mexico, a genre of satirical songs about Mexicano Indian social and cultural relations. In Jalisco and Michoacán, a well-known song with the same tune and nearly identical lyrics warns against the Indians from Tepic, Nayarit. Characteristically aboriginal, it has been considered a New Mexican Indian song originating from some Comanche chant. Guerrero Galván, the Mexican painter, claims to have known it in Michoacán and Jalisco, where it is very popular. The opening lines are "Ai vienen los indios, vienen de Tepic."

Cantos Comanches: *Percussion, Voice, and Origins*

The drum is the heartbeat of Hispano-Comanche music. The tombé, a hand-held, single-headed drum, is made from rawhide stretched over a round or hexagonal wooden frame, similar to the Ute drum (Williams 2000). It is grasped by means of rawhide strings behind the head and held chest-high, in the manner of

6.8.   Cantantes y Tombés (Ranchos de Taos). Hispano-Comanches sing and play single-headed tombés in unison. Listeners recognize influences from Kiowa, Pueblo, and Navajo sources, as well as a few songs still known to the Numunuh.

the *chimal,* or battle shield. Some singers insist that the tombé evolved from the chimal, and that it served a dual purpose suited to a nomadic way of life (F. Gonzales 1992). *Chimal* is a Spanish adaptation of the Nahuatl *chimalli,* "shield" (Cobos 1983:46). The Spanish-Mexican militia early on discarded the *rodela,* a heavy wood and iron shield designed to repel crossbow darts. The much lighter rawhide *adarga* was modeled after the chimal, and could easily deflect arrows and even bullets. An implement of war, it also became an instrument of music (F. Gonzales 1992).

Comanche drumming style is distinctive, with each singer playing his own drum. In Southern Plains musical tradition, multiple singers beat a single drum, while Pueblo music is sung to the beat of one drum (on occasion two or more), each played by a single drummer (Williams 2000). In the far Northern Plains, another tradition of multiple hand drums and drummers can be heard. Hispano-Comanche songs use a single steady rhythm with none of the rests, feints, and metric shifts found in Pueblo and Navajo drumming.

The singing itself is characterized by the large percentage of vocables, an additional feature that links it to other Southern Plains styles. These vocables are euphonic, nonlexical, seed syllables that carry more implied emotional charge and association than specific linguistic meaning (Powers 1987). Sung to pentatonic as well as modal and chromatic scales, typical sequences of vocables found throughout the repertoire include the following (these transcriptions use Spanish vowels, consonants, and accents).

Yo-je-ya-na-e-ya-jó.
Je-ya-na-o-o-o-je-yá.
E-ne-yo-je-yá-je-yó.

The characteristic resonant sounds of vocables are the predominant open [a] and the mid [e] and [o] vowels, and the consonants [y], [n], and [x] (indicated here by the Spanish letter "j").

A vocal feature linking Hispano-Comanche singing to Navajo tradition is the extended vocal range. In the songs about Navajos, an allusion to Navajo singing style is made by adding deep velar consonants to the vocables—yang, ang, a . . . (Vennum 2001). More formal musicological analysis promises to reveal phrasing patterns that can link the repertoire to other regional traditions.

In the analysis of hybrid musical traditions, the intuition of traditional singers is as important as that of trained musicologists, and both sources were consulted in this study. Generalizations are as valuable as specific observations. For example, a Tewa Pueblo singer claims that the Hispano-Comanche music "sounds very much like Kiowa singing" (A. García 1999). Discernible Comanche musical elements, turns of phrase, and syllable sequences surface in several songs, according to a Numunuh–Sac and Fox ethnomusicologist (Wapp 1998). One of the most notable, "El Cautivo" (the captive), is recognizable as a Numunuh scalp dance song, although the Hispano-Comanches sing it slower than it is sung on the reservations of Oklahoma. In Pueblo and some Plains cultures, enemy scalps are fed, cared for, and "adopted" as powerful fetishes (Gutiérrez 1991:19–20).

The Numunuh also regularly adopted their captives. Eighteenth- and nineteenth-century testimonials describe a circle dance that new captives were forced to do for hours on end, repeating words that roughly translated "I am a captive." Participants claim that the ceremony had the effect of detraumatizing the recent captives, and giving them an opportunity to bond and sympathize with each other (G. Anderson 1999:222). "El Cautivo" has a melancholy melody and a round-dance or "heartbeat" rhythm that moves some listeners to tears. Many families in Ranchos de Taos still recount captivity narratives about long-departed relatives remembered for enduring the travails of captivity (N. Gonzales 1993). Appropriate to its rhythm, "El Cautivo" is danced as a redondo, with dancers facing inward in a circle.

In their interviews, Hispano-Comanche singers are confident in their knowledge of songs and attribute their origins to particular individuals and communities where the songs are especially popular. The diverse origins of the songs are acknowledged, but Hispano-Comanche singers take ownership of their repertoire and insist that for many generations, none of the songs were ever borrowed from local Indian groups, and certainly none from the powwow circuit (F. Gonzales 1991, F. Gonzales, Jr. 1991). Comanche songs have been around long enough to have developed notable melodic and rhythmic variations between groups performing the same songs in the same valley. The style of elder singer Juan Archuleta, from Los Comanches del Río Chiquito, is markedly distinct from that of the elders in Los Comanches de la Serna.

Cantos y Bailes Comanches: *Song Becomes Dance*

At this point, the music must be linked to the dance, since both are aspects of a whole. Stylistically, the Hispano-Comanche dances may be grouped into four categories: round dances, line dances, animal dances, and enemy dances.

Since there is apparently no particular formal distinction between sacred and social dances, the symbolic meanings of the dances are to be found in the performance contexts and sequences.[9] The following table identifies and links the Hispano-Comanche songs and dances.

Table 6.1

Bailes Comanches (Dances)	Cantos Comanches (Songs)
Processional Dances	
"El paseo" (The Stroll)	"Paseados" (Travelers)
	"Llaneros" (Plainsmen)
"La estrellita" (Little Star)	"Estrellita del Norte" (Little Star North)

Round Dances

"El redondo" (Round Dance)	"Paseados," "Llaneros," "Coplas"
"La amistad" (Friendship)	(verses), Forty-Niners
"La rueda" (The Circle)	"La rueda"
"La patita" (Little Foot)	"La patita"

Line Dances

"La fila brincada" (The Jump Line)	"La fila brincada"
"La fila bailada" (The Dance Line)	"La fila bailada"
"Cuadrillas" (Quadrilles)	"Cuadrillas"
"El cortejo" (Courtship)	

Animal Dances

"El águila" (The Eagle)	"El águila"
"El coyote" (The Coyote)	"El coyote"
"La tortuga" (The Turtle)	"La tortuga"
"El torito" (The Little Bull)	"El torito"

Enemy Dances

"El espantao" (The Frightened One)	"El espantao"
"El guerrero" (The Warrior)	"Danza guerrera" (War Dance)
"El cautivo" (The Captive)	"El cautivo"

A repertoire of several paseados and llaneros is used during travel and for processions. Some traveling songs have descriptive names concerning how or when they are sung, such as "La Estrellita," or Little Star, which is used for travel at night.

Round dances include "El redondo," or Round Dance, "La amistad," or Friendship dance, "La rueda," or Ring dance for captives, and "La patita," or Little-Foot dance. The symbolism and unity of the circle gives special significance and prominence to these dances.

Line dances include "La fila brincada," or Jump Line dance, "La fila bailada," or Danced Line dance, and "El cortejo," or the Courtship dance. Converging lines of dancers symbolize the concepts of separateness, confrontation, and merging.

Animal Dances include "El águila," or the Eagle dance, "El torito," or the Little Bull dance, "El Coyote," or the Coyote dance, and "La tortuga," or the Turtle dance. Animal spirits and their special associations come alive in these remarkable dances.

The principal enemy dance is "El espantao," or the Frightened One, which is recognizable as a Plains shield dance, along with its distinctive music. Although aspects of struggle, warfare, and captives are themes in the other dances, "El

El Paseado

Sung by Comanches de la Serna of Ranchos de Taos

o ya na oh   oh   o je e je ya ya

wo je yo   ay yo je o   oh   oh   o ya na

oh   oh   oh je e je   ya ya   wo je yo

e e we yo   e e e e   yo   e ne   e je je je yo

ja ya e no   ja ya ya ya   ja e ne yo a e ne

rit.   no meter

yo   o   oh

a ah e ne ya   ya   ya ne ya a yo   ya ne yo   oh

accelerando

o ya na   oh   oh   o je je na

ya ya ya yo   je yo a yo   je yo a ya ya yo

o e ne je e je we yo ja ya je yo

ja ya ya ya a e ne yo o ya na yo

oh ah a e ne ya ya ya ne yo je yo

a ya ya ya yo

espantao" is the most aggressive, as it demonstrates that victory is an attitude as well as a strategy. The dance also honors warriors clever enough to enter the enemy's encampment without being detected.

Cantos y Bailes Comanches: *Performance Sequences*

As the elders in charge, the singers monitor and direct the energies of time and place, responding as much to the reaction of the crowd as to the demeanor and strength of the dancers. With a resounding tremolo, the voices of multiple drums become one, as the order and length of songs are negotiated.

Paseados y Llaneros ∾ The first order of business is travel to the houses of the families being honored, and traveling songs are sung during processions as well as when walking, riding, or driving to the host houses. Most songs in the Comanche repertoire are uniquely named and specifically associated with dances. Only two, "El paseado" and "El llanero" can be considered types, since there are numerous examples of each. All are composed exclusively of vocables in familiar combinations. What distinguishes them are their tunes. Llaneros are sung on longer trips and are distinguished by a steady and more constant beat, be it slow or fast.

Paseados typically start with a slow tempo, then break suddenly to the frantic tempo of a war dance, the Danza guerrera.

"La estrellita" is a night-traveling song that honors either *el lucero de la noche o mañana* (the planet of the night or morning, that is, Venus) or *la estrella del norte* (the north star) for showing the way. The higher than normal pitch of "La estrellita" matches its celestial references as well as showing off the range of singers.

Los comanches de la serna

In the days before the coming of the railroad and the automobile, Hispano-Comanche traders and *fleteros* (freightmen) sang traveling songs as they drove their mules and wagons. The late Alfredo Martínez, a Comanche, used to tell a young Francisco Gonzales that his muleteers chanted llaneros and paseados on their journeys from Taos north to the San Luis Valley, east to Mora, and south to Carson at the turn of the twentieth century. Besides setting the heartbeat of the songs, the sound of the single-headed tombé was an announcement to would-be highwaymen that

El Llanero

Sung by Noberto Ledoux of Ranchos de Taos

Yo jo wi i yo o yo yo e

yo e yo Yo jo

wi i yo o yo jo e o e yo

e ne ya ya e je e ya yo ya je

yo je yo je yo ya ya je yo je yo

ya ya ya ya yo je yo a yo je yo

je ye yo.

6.9. Los Comanchitos Paseando (Ranchos de Taos). After each set of dances ends, the dancers march or truck off to the next house, to the rhythm of the paseados and llaneros, or traveling songs.

the fleteros were Comanches and that to bother them "traiba malas consecuencias," brought swift reprisal and bad consequences (F. Gonzales 1992).

In contemporary times, traveling songs are sung to pace the journey between houses visited on Comanche feast days. Dancers use straight walking steps and sometimes skipping steps, especially in the beginning of the day, when they are full of energy. After arrival at a house, a redondo usually begins a set and is danced to the music of other paseados and llaneros.

"El Redondo" ౿ The round dance is a sign of friendship and an invitation that is extended to the family being visited. The circle is the most inclusive symbol of the heavens and earth, along with the community of life and human beings upon it. To dance in a circle is to honor all these beings and forces (F. Gonzales 1992). The tempo starts out slow, which also serves to warm up the dancers, as their forward steps and bounce steps become more energetic.

When the spirit moves them, spectators who know the dance steps join the ranks of costumed dancers in the circle. A gesture that further incorporates the improviser is removing a hat and holding it in front of the chest, in the same position as that of the chimal.

In the rare case in which the honored family is not at home or not yet awake, an abbreviated set consisting of a single redondo is performed. If nobody comes out of the house to meet the Comanches, they move on. The rueda that usually marks the end of the set is omitted, because there are no captives to honor or ransom.

"Danza Guerrera" ∽ As the redondo progresses and the rhythm of the paseado gains momentum and breaks into a war dance song, the circle likewise is scattered. Heads nod forward and back, and dancers break into crouching spins, some clockwise and some counterclockwise, as the larger circle still turns. If the time and place are propitious and the right people are watching, the drums begin

Estrellita del Norte

Sung by Comanches de la Serna of Ranchos de Taos

ya ne ya ya e yo   je ya ya   we no je ya yo

yo je o eo   ya je ya ya   je yo   je ya ya   je

yo   o   je yo   yo   je yo we e   e   e   yo

ya je ya ya   e   jo je   ya ya   je

yo   yo je yo   yo   je yo   je ye ye ye

yo

El Águila

Sung by Comanches de la Serna of Ranchos de Taos

Dancers have split up so they can watch and learn. They're resting as well. The dancers will also stand by the singers to sing with them. With arms outstretched, they spin clockwise and counterclockwise. You stop, then you go to your left again. When the song pauses, then you stop and go to the right. He still travels the same circle. My brother Estevan dances with straight legs, but it's an individual style. The pattern is the same, the arms are horizontal, you stop and rotate, you stop and rotate. Then you go into the regular eagle fast dance. That's what birds of prey do, they'll turn to rotate, following a rabbit or whatever. They're going to turn rapidly one way or another, spinning to catch their prey. (F. Gonzales, Jr. 1991)

"El Torito" ∽ The little bull dance is done "to honor all the male animals, buffalo, deer, antelope, and bull, for their bravery and their quest to defend their families" (F. Gonzales 1992). Like the "Espantado" dance, opposing pairs square off and position themselves before engaging each other in a contest of locking horns. Several

El Torito

Sung by Comanches de la Serna of Ranchos de Taos

ya yaya e eh   ya e eh   ya e eh   ya yo e o   a ya

a ya yo   je yo je   je   a ya yo je ya ya yo   je yo   a   oh

a   ya   ya   ya   ya   yoje   e   yoje   e

ya   je e   ya   yo e yo   ya   ya   ya   ya   ja ya   yo je yo

je   ya   ya   ya   ja   ya   yo je yo   ya   yo je yo

ya   ya   ya   ya   yo

Numunuh dances use similar choreography, where dancers mill around during an introductory tremolo before engaging each other (Wapp 1998). Chimales are discarded for this dance, and arms are held out in an arc, to imitate horns. Dancers charge each other, lock their horns in a test of strength, and back off.

The music of "El torito" has a distinctive blend of Pueblo and Navajo elements (Wapp 1998). Its vocables are quite unique and resemble words. As happens with other North American indigenous musical traditions, words also find their way into song texts, but over the generations and between the cultures, specific meanings can be obscured. The following "words" signal the "Torito" dance, and dancers position themselves immediately upon hearing them.

6.14. El Torito (Ranchos de Taos). The dance of the little bull honors the bravery of the buffalo as well as the domestic bull. Dancers lock outstretched arms in this combat dance.

*Iroque, iroque, iroquestreee,
iroque, iroque, iroquestreee,
o eneyó, o eneyó . . .*

Since the Comanche word for buffalo is *kotso,* if these are words, they may be referring to some other aspect of the duels of the rutting bulls that are portrayed in the dance. Of all the animal dances, the "Aguila" and "Torito" are by far the most

La Tortuga

Sung by Comanches de la Serna of Ranchos de Taos

6.15. La Fila (Talpa). Line dances are known in the Hispano-Comanche tradition as filas. Since dancers often face each other, these dances are associated with courtship.

common, but the "Tortuga" and "Coyote" must be mentioned as well, since they are so distinctive.

"La Tortuga" ॐ One of the lines in "La tortuga," the turtle song, is also quite particular and unlike the vocables that float among most of the songs:

> *Ayo, o eyo . . .*
> *Chopa ene, huezti ga, eyaya,*
> *aya oweyo ei ei ei ei,*
> *eyo, ayo, ayo, jeyo . . .*

Further linguistic analysis is needed to determine what these enigmatic utterances may mean. Since they do not occur in any other song, and since they are so phonologically distinct from the vocable sequences, they may yet be deciphered. Dancers regard "La tortuga" as a great test of strength, since so many squats and hops are required. In several northern pueblos, New Year's Day is celebrated with the turtle dance, which has sacred qualities evidently lacking in the Hispano-Comanche dance of the same name. In Talpa, the dance is referred to as "El sapito," the little toad.

"El coyote" ∽ "El coyote" is a dance that dramatizes the ironies of the hunt with elaborate and evocative choreography. Three dancers separate in a line from the group. The outside dancers crouch and lurk like coyotes, while the middle one stands erect, like a man. As he hunts the first coyote with measured stealth, from north to south, he is unknowingly hunted by the other. The first dancer crouches and lurks like a coyote, while the other follows behind with measured stealth. Then the dancers turn, hunters become hunted, and vice versa. Pauses between repetitions of this vocable stanza indicate the shifts.

> *Ya, ya, ya, ya,*
> *yo jeyó, yo jeyó,*
> *ya jeyó, ya jeyó*
> *eo, ai, ai, ai, ai . . .*

The irony of the hunt is that the hunter is also the hunted, the man is also the coyote. A dancer reflects on this unusual dance:

> When to stop and when to turn is the key. I'm the coyote and Estevan is follow-ing me and he doesn't know he's being followed. The hunter sees the coyote and is going after the coyote. He's the guy in the middle. All of a sudden he sees one behind him and he turns around and goes after him and the other one turns around and follows. The question is not really who is the hunter. The man in the middle is. Whichever way the man thinks he's hunting the coyote, he is actually being hunted himself. The other coyote is tricking him into following him . . . (F. Gonzales, Jr. 1991)

"El coyote" is danced in extended sets that are performed at the houses of eld-ers and Comanche families.

"La Patita" ∽ Whereas other round dances focus on captives and group solidar-ity, "La patita," the little foot dance, has special symbolic significance in reference to the passage of time. According to singers, this tight circle dance marks the change from day to night. To signify the coming of night, the dancers close ranks facing in, and point their outstretched right arms to the center, moving them in with an up-and-down chopping motion. When the song repeats, the dancers squat with hands touching the ground, then pivot around and resume the dance facing outward, to signify the coming of day. Outside is day and inside is night.

"La patita" is infrequently performed, perhaps once in an entire day of danc-ing, usually toward the middle of the day.

"La fila brincada," "La fila bailada" ∽ Hispano-Comanche line dances are per-formed in extended sets and on social occasions, when onlookers join in the dancing, not as captives, but as guests. Dancers face each other in two rows,

which close in to meet each other and then move back out again. In "La fila brincada," or the hopping line dance, opposing dancers approach each other in a series of vigorous short hops. In "La fila bailada," the danced line dance, the approach is made with continuous dancing steps.

Since they are performed to the same song, singers will announce which variant is to be done by naming it at the beginning of the song. When dancers are face to face as the lines close in, there is no particular interaction between them, as each is self-absorbed.

Curiously enough, line dances are performed to the singing of *cuadrillas,* a term usually applied to the formal square dances (quadrilles) of the courts of Europe. Although they are sung with vocables, the hybrid melodies of the cuadrillas sound less Native than other songs and are deserving of a thorough musicological analysis.

"El Cortejo" ∾ The courtship dance is another type of line dance. The two lines of dancers face each other, men in one and women in the other. With the beat of the music, the lines approach each other, as the dancers advance in two-footed hops. When the lines meet, individual couples face each other, hands down, and thrust their faces forward over their partner's shoulder, first one, then the other, then one, then the other.

La Cuadrilla

Sung by Comanches de la Serna of Ranchos de Taos

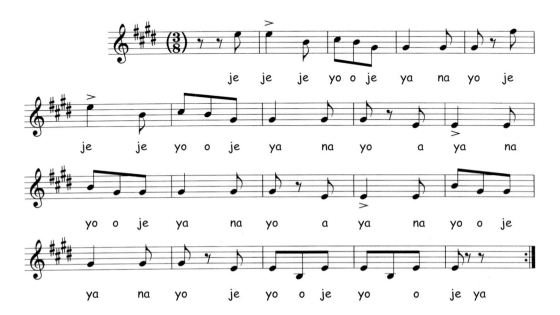

je   je   je   yo o je   ya   na   yo   je

je   je   yo o je   ya   na   yo   a   ya   na

yo o je   ya   na   yo   a   ya   na   yo o je

ya   na   yo   je   yo o je   yo   o   je ya

Los comanches de la serna

173

6.16. Memorias del Cautivo (Talpa). The pain of captivity is still a living memory in many Indo-Hispano families, and emotions run high as they are honored.

Facial expressions range from friendly or flirting smiles to serious, stern looks. Then the dancers hop backward, maintaining the same line until they reach their starting positions. Then the dance is repeated.

"El Cautivo" ∾ After a selection of round, animal, and line dances, an emotional climax is reached with the sad and plaintive tone of the first slow vocables of "El cautivo," the song sung by captives when warriors brought them to their new home. As noted in the discussion of origins, this is one Comanche song recognizable by the Numunuh as a scalp dance song. According to local tradition, the song could be heard at the *rescates* or slave markets, of the great trade fairs at Taos and Pecos (F. Gonzales 1991).

O-yana-jó-o-o-oo-oe-ee-ee-ya-jeyó

Even an ear attuned to Western music can hear the moans of the captives and musically perceive the pathos. Many of the *o* sounds are sung with falsetto breaks or sobs, known in Spanish as the *quebranto,* a sign of lamentation. "El cautivo" is sung as a kind of processional, as dancers walk alongside their captives, to show them off. They hold the captive tight with the right arm. With the free left arm, which holds the chimal, the dancer sometimes makes threatening gestures, as if to hit the captive, in a display of dominance.

"La Rueda" ॐ At the end of the set, after the initial redondo and other dances are finished, a distinctive vocable refrain signals the impending emotional climax and release of "La rueda," the ring dance done to honor rather than humiliate captives (in contrast to the previous example). Sung to a loud, slow tremolo on the tombé, dancers break into the crowd and return with their prisoners to the circle of honor. Sometimes they abduct an elder, sometimes a child, and occasionally a whole family, then the ring of dancers surrounds them, facing inward, as the dance begins.

Ayana yoooo, je je yaya,
jene yayo, ane yaya,
ene yoyo, ene yayo,
ene yayo . . .

In a gesture said to be a kind of blessing, the dancers lift their arms skyward,

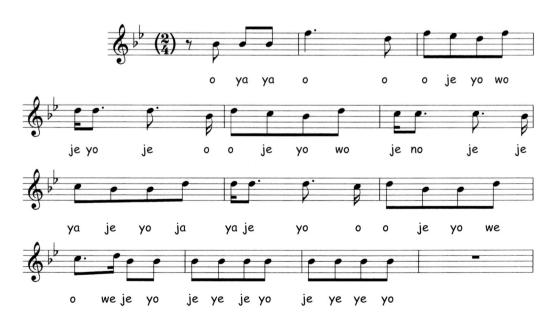

El Cautivo

Sung by Comanches de la Serna of Ranchos de Taos

o   ya   ya   o   o   o   je   yo   wo

je yo   je   o   o   je   yo   wo   je no   je   je

ya   je   yo   ja   ya je   yo   o   o   je   yo   we

o   we je   yo   je   ye   je yo   je   ye   ye   yo

Los comanches de la serna

La Rueda

Sung by Comanches de la Serna of Ranchos de Taos

to direct their energy into the circle and into their captives. The outstretched arms of the dancers "symbolically pull spiritual blessings and the goodness of the universe through the dancers to the circle and their cautivos" (F. Gonzales 1992). Responses to this symbolic captivity and blessing range from elation to tears of remembrance, for virtually every extended family in Ranchos de Taos can recount stories of captivity and redemption.

Even though slavery was formally abolished with Mexican Independence, in 1821, the trade in cautivos in New Mexico continued well into the nineteenth century. One of the most famous captives was Rosario "Ma-ya-yo" Martínez, a young Navajo woman who joined the household of the famous liberal priest, Padre Antonio José Martínez. After her repeated attempts to escape, the padre found, purchased, and reunited her with one of her lost children. In gratitude, she stayed in Taos, even after word of Lincoln's Emancipation Proclamation reached New Mexico. A beloved grandmother figure in the extended Martínez clan, she lived well into the twentieth century and is still remembered fondly (Vásquez 1975).

In the middle 1860s, after Navajos and Apaches had been defeated and interned in Fort Sumner, and as the military campaigns against the Kiowa and Numunuh continued in Oklahoma, the American government placed orphaned children with Hispano families all over the state (Márez 2001:275–77). Again, a significant number came to the Taos area. As already noted, criados often spent their entire lives with their adoptive families, especially in the case of women who bore children out of wedlock and became chichiguas, or wet nurses. The last generation of criados lived into the 1920s, well within living memory of the elders of today.

Although there is no specific documentation to prove it, numerous Numunuh individuals chose exile in New Mexico over internment in Fort Sill, after 1875. They stayed in familiar places and with people they were already knew, such as Ranchos de Taos and some of the pueblos. Like the Genízaros of the previous century, they blended with the general population, especially since the Americans did not distinguish Hispanicized Natives from other mestizos (Márez 2001:279).

6.17. La Rueda (Ranchos de Taos). Making their rounds on New Year's Day, Hispano-Comanches stop at each house to take captives into the round dance.

The musical legacy of the Numunuh, Kiowas, Navajos and Apaches, as well as of the Pueblos, may be heard in the Hispano-Comanche repertoire, which is a synthesis of them all.

In the symbolic space of "La rueda," captors face their captives and bow to them in the breaks of the song. If there are more than a few cautivos, they form a ring and turn counter to the movement of the dancers. The dance ends with handshakes and hugs all around, as the captives are released. *El desempeño,* or the captive's ransom, is not a condition of release, but rather a courtesy, a simple offering of thanks, of sweets, of drink.

Unlike the other Hispano-Comanche celebrations across New Mexico, in Ranchos de Taos there are no texts of redemption or prayer songs to the Virgin of Guadalupe or the Santo Niño de Atocha. As in the pueblos, all is encoded in gesture, movement, and choreography. The central drama of captivity and deliverance, transculturation and atonement is enacted over and over again, with every family, year after year. Captors and captives are reconciled and become one. The lost children all come home to dance and sing and teach their children. Being and becoming "Comanche" is enacted in the circle of honor, the circle of culture and family, the circle of history.

7

Desire, Mimesis, and Atonement

cultural Legacies of the pax comanche

Españoles y cumanches	Spaniards and Comanches
todos en armonía,	all in harmony,
se juntaban a cantar	would come together to sing
y a bailar con alegría,	and dance with gladness,
jeya, jeya, jeya, ja.	heya, heya, heya, ha.

—Cleofes Vigil (1992[1976])

The cultural legacy of the *Pax Comanche* is ritualized in the Pueblo and Hispano celebrations illustrated in the previous chapters. Pueblo Indians "dance with the enemy" to honor both the struggle and the peace that was forged from it. In festivals, secular and sacred drama, and ritual dance, all christened *Los comanches,* Hispanos celebrate the ancient festival paradigm of conflict, victory, reconciliation, and conversion. Curiously, by the mid-nineteenth century, the repertoire even extended into the realm of social dance. "La comancha" (the Comanche woman) is a stately couples dance, part processional and part waltz, documented in the dance halls of Taos (Sedillo 1945:30).

To understand the myriad facets and perseverance of the Comanche legacy, a series of key scenes in its development must be revisited, beginning with the ceremonial ratification of the Spanish-Numunuh Treaty of 1786, then proceeding through four seminal periods of twentieth-century cultural history in New Mexico:

1. The territorial era from 1848 to statehood in 1912, with programs of emerging cultural nationalism.
2. The era between the two World Wars with the Anglo-mediated artistic and cultural revivals promoted by the art colony and the folklore surveys of the New Mexico

179

Writers' Project of the Works Progress Administration, the famous and devilish expeditions of the "Diablo a pie."[1]

3. The university-based Chicano movement of the 1960s and 1970s and its neo-indigenist cultural activism.
4. And the great cultural and historical commemorations of the last quarter of the twentieth century and the cultural soul-searching and skirmishes inspired variously by the 1976 American Bicentennial, the 1980 Tricentennial of the Pueblo Revolt, the 1992 Quinto Centenario of the Euro-American Encounter, and the 1998 Cuarto Centenario of the founding of New Mexico.

From the end of the Spanish colonial period through the Spanish American War and the entire twentieth century, "Comanches" traditions continued to generate significant cultural meaning, identity, and pride for the Indo-Hispano peoples of New Mexico, long after the Numunuh themselves were banished to their Oklahoma reservation, in 1875. The foundation and symbolic origin of "Comanche" traditions can be traced to an extraordinary encounter on the mountain pass that still links New Mexico to the Great Plains.

༄ De Anza and Ecueracapa at Pecos

On the afternoon of February 28, 1786, at a diplomatic summit hosted by Pecos Pueblo, Governor Juan Bautista de Anza and his staff gathered with the great chief and newly appointed "General" Ecueracapa and eleven western Kotsoteca leaders, who signed a treaty as they ceremoniously "buried" eight decades of warfare between the Numunuh and the Españoles mexicanos.[2] A number symbolic objects, probably weapons broken for the occasion, including gunpowder and cartridges, were placed in a specially dug hole, which was filled in as oaths to the sun and the earth were recited.[3] Ecueracapa was also presented with a saber, a Spanish flag, and a staff of office emblematic of the authority that the Spanish government invested in him (Thomas 1932:76). More importantly, he had earned his authority among his own people, who recognized these objects as emblems of power as well. Six and a half years had passed since the defeat of Cuerno Verde and only several months since the assassination of the last major hostile chief, Toro Blanco. Many doubts still lingered, since abundant winter snows prevented the attendance of the eastern Kotsotecas, the Yamparicas, and the Jupes. The prospect of uniting autonomous bands dispersed over a huge geographical area was daunting indeed. But hopes for a lasting peace shone brightly with the visit of over six thousand Numunuh leaders to New Mexico over the following spring and summer (Kavanagh 1996:112).

The extraordinary diplomacy of De Anza and Ecueracapa had produced one of the most durable treaties ever negotiated between Euro- and Native Americans. More than just paper, power objects, and ceremony, it was built on a real desire for peace, trade, and productive alliance. With an eye toward the indomitable Apaches in the south and the ambitious Anglo Americans in the east, the Spanish government welcomed the buffer zone that Numunuh military strength could provide. Past hostilities were forgotten. Captives were exchanged. An alliance against the Apaches was forged, and regular seasonal campaigns were waged. Salaries were assigned to Numunuh leaders and warriors, and regular installments of gift goods were promised and delivered to their people. Trade relations were guaranteed, along with free access to Santa Fe. Beginning with Ecueracapa himself, Numunuh leaders sent their sons to Santa Fe and other cities for instruction in the Spanish language and religion (Kavanagh 1996:160).

The political and economic fortunes of the Spanish-Mexicans waxed and waned, as New Spain became Mexico in 1821 and then passed into the sphere of Anglo-American influence in 1846. But the peace held in New Mexico, and the seasonal visits of the Numunuh into the Río Grande Valley were always cause for celebration. In the territorial period, this historic legacy was drawn on as a source of cultural pride. An idealized and heroic past became an important component of the discourse of emerging statehood and the basis for intercultural respect and cooperation. Even the bitterest episodes of warfare became infused with emulation and yearning, the expression of a profound desire for peace and atonement. After the war with Spain, Anglo-Americans were also attracted to the symbolism of Comanche celebrations, in a kind of imperial nostalgia for the empire they now controlled (Márez 2002).

⤳ "They Thought They Were Comanches": Cultural Mimesis and Warfare

The *Pax Comanche* is widely celebrated, although only a few of its protagonists are recalled. In popular memory, it is the antagonists who still loom larger than life. The name and boasts of Cuerno Verde still resound across the region, and Carlos Fernández is remembered in the villages where his descendants still reside. What remains of the Numunuh themselves is an iconic memory as adversaries, then allies, and finally kin.[4] The memory is ritualized in cross-cultural mimesis. Pueblo Indians still don Plains regalia to dance and sing with the voice of their former enemies. Beyond the ritual enactments, oral history and legend complete the picture with narrative.

Hispanos memorialize the last great military campaign against the Numunuh in the equestrian play *Los comanches,* where a strong mimetic impulse can be perceived as well. The ancient theme resonates deeply: "the nobility of the enemy is the measure of our own." Mimetic qualities can be found even in battle tactics. The enemy is defeated on his own terms by his own maneuvers.

The first modern revival of the equestrian play *Los comanches,* in 1907, was the fruit of the collaboration of a folklorist, Aurelio M. Espinosa, and Amado Chaves, a community scholar, historian, and son of a prominent military leader, who provided not only the source manuscript but the community traditions and oral histories in which it was embedded. Publication of a critical, annotated edition of the play in the *Bulletin of the University of New Mexico* created a sensation.

The historical context for this phenomenon was the final push for New Mexico statehood, characterized by a Hispanophile cultural agenda that promoted an idealized identification with the heroic past. "Spanish Colonial" culture was the favorite pursuit of later territorial governors, such as L. Bradford Prince, as well as of the fledgling art colony, led by luminaries such as Mary Austin, Frank Applegate, Mabel Dodge Luhan, and friends. Their modernist interest in "primitivist" art and literature found fertile ground in New Mexico. Austin's personal papers contain at least five manuscript copies of *Los comanches,* which she acquired over the years.[5]

In the same way that Anglo-American preservationists and cultural activists encouraged santeros to emulate colonial artistic styles, they also urged communities and museums to stage the ancient cycle of "Spanish Colonial" secular and religious plays, including *Los comanches.* History buff Frank Cheetham in Taos, provided copies of Espinosa and Chaves's version of the play and promoted productions such as the fabled Comanche extravaganza in the summer of 1929 in Taos, promoted by the local Lions Club and heavily "boosted" for tourism.[6] To their credit, these promoters successfully identified the authentic Comanche groups in their communities. However, these productions did not survive, because not only did they remove the celebrations from their customary winter feast venues, but they also encouraged the use of the full colonial text, replete with obligatory homages to Crown, Church, and imperial power. The productions that did manage to survive on their own, without such well meaning Anglo "encouragement," use scripts that have evolved to fit the changing cultural landscape. The "discourse of power" articulated by the 1779 text in the hands of the community evolved into a "discourse of resistance," as in the 1963 Alcalde text (Lamadrid 2000:173).

Recognition of the importance of Espinosa and Chaves's collaboration was echoed in the Spanish-language press. Scenes from the play were published in several Spanish newspapers, from the turn of the century into the 1950s.[7] An unsigned editorial in the January 3, 1908, *El Labrador* hailed the play as the foundation of a true "literatura nacional," worthy of being part of the curriculum of regional grammar and high schools. The underlying question would be, for which nation? The irony was that the sense of cultural and literary nationhood for New Mexico was compromised and complicated by its actual subordinated status as a U.S. territory.

Interestingly, the academic prestige of Dr. Espinosa was fully matched by the community prestige of his collaborator. Amado Chaves was not only the conservator of valuable manuscripts but was also a repository of folk knowledge and tradition. He was extensively interviewed and quoted by historians, journalists, and folklorists alike, and served the territorial government as superintendent of public instruction in the 1890s. But it is in the writings of the community scholar where the impulses toward cross-cultural mimesis can be detected. Chaves published what can be termed a "folk historical" account of the military campaigns on which *Los comanches* is based. Entitled *The Defeat of the Comanches in the Year 1717* [*sic*], it provides a fascinating counterpart to the more objectivized commentary of the academic scholar, Espinosa.

Chaves writes what he calls his "letter" in Los Luceros, the eighteenth-century colonial home of Capitán Sebastián Martín, at La Villita, near Alcalde, New Mexico, the last village where the play is still regularly performed. This setting for the writing of the letter lends cultural authority to his claims, since Don Carlos Fernández himself was the son-in-law of Martín. The 1717 date he ascribes to the actions is corrected by Espinosa to 1777 and by later historians to 1774. But chronological accuracy is not as significant as the cross-cultural mimesis that surfaces in the account of the battle. He goes so far as to claim that the victory of the Spanish-Mexicans was based on their close resemblance to the Numunuh enemy, both physically and tactically.

> In those days the Spaniards wore their hair long similar to the Indians, but tied in the back. Before starting all the men painted their faces red with almagre and let their hair down *in order to look as much like Indians as possible.* At break of day, they were close to the Comanche camp and hundreds of tepees were in sight. A charge was ordered and with the war cry of Santiago, the men charged and surprised the enemy. *Many of the Comanches thought when they first saw the Spaniards that they were bands of their own tribe returning from a victorious campaign....* (Chaves 1906:7, emphasis added)

It is true that the armaments, military tactics, and leather armor of both the Numunuh and the colonial militia were similar enough for warriors and militiamen to resemble each other in the field (Kavanagh 1996:73). But what of the scores of presidial soldiers in the expedition, their distinctive felted headgear (not sixteenth-century steel helmets), regulation lances, and uniforms, tattered as they might be? Chaves makes quite clear that imitation was the formula for victory, becoming like the enemy in order to defeat him. After defeat, he will in turn be obliged to resemble his foe, to acquire his values, language, and lifestyle. In the play based in part on the 1774 expedition, this process of wishful or imagined transculturation is already in evidence linguistically. The verbal virtuosity of the Numunuh warriors already matches the rhetorical display of their Spanish-Mexican antagonists. The poetics of cross-cultural mimesis have a predictable grammar and syntax: "My enemy is my equal, I share in his power and his glory."

However, other more historically objective texts indicate that the phenomenon of Hispano-Comanche cultural mimesis is a reality that goes beyond wishful thinking. After the peace of 1786, trade fairs were no longer necessary and Comanchero traders ventured from New Mexico east to the Plains, to deal directly with the Numunuh (Haley 1934–35, Levine 1991:155–69, Simmons 1961).

They became so closely allied with their partners that by the mid-nineteenth century, American observers had difficulty telling them apart (Kavanagh 1996:177–79, Kenner 1966:78–97). Anglo authorities also had similar problems in distinguishing Numunuh children from the Mexican captive children raised in the same families. Mexican captive children were preferred over Anglo-American children by the Numunuh, for this very reason (Márez 2001:279).

Cultural mimesis, emulation, and identification are all produced by desire (Young 1995). Strangely, even the most appalling episodes from the worst years of the Comanche wars are seen through the wishful lens of desire, the desire for peace, which lends a romantic dimension to the most unimaginable scenes of human suffering in New Mexico, the tragic massacres of the late eighteenth century.

✑ Homicide, Honor, and Romance: Tragedy and Cross-Cultural Desire

As nationalism emerged across the Americas in the nineteenth century, and regional cultural and economic centers developed into nations, the historical romance became a favorite mode of storytelling. People make sense of their trials and social contradictions by using narrative as a way to posit imaginary resolutions to cultural and political dilemmas. Literature, both inscribed and oral, becomes a socially symbolic act, "a symbolic resolution to a concrete historical situation" (Jameson 1981:117). With typecast characters and conflicts viewed in direct relation to social and historical phenomena, the romance is a quest for the transformation of reality. The protagonists, usually a star-crossed couple, are allegorical emblems of the social or ethnic strata to which they belong. In the most hopeful scenarios, resolution is symbolized and consummated by marriage. In the romance, the tribulations of reality are obstacles blocking the progress of a romantic couple on the pathway to felicitous union, or so the story goes.

In tune with the times, territorial New Mexico also produced its share of allegorical novels, in which the emerging sense of region and nation was complicated by ethnic conflict and the reality of annexation to the United States (E. Chacón 1982). Journalism also plays a crucial role in the formation of group consciousness (B. Anderson 1983[1991]), and the Spanish-language press flourished in the second half of the territorial period, satisfying the narrative appetites of the Nuevo Mexicanos (Meléndez 1997).

After statehood, in 1912, a number of romantic historical legends were collected and published, beginning with the work of Charles Lummis, in 1916, and continuing with the New Mexico Writers' Project and the projects of the New Mexico Folklore Society. In the historical record, the massacre of Tomé is grimly recorded without embellishment by Fray Andrés García, who traveled from Albuquerque's San Felipe parish to Tomé to bury the twenty-one victims of the Comanches, on May 26, 1777.

Todos los muertos murieron sin resebir los últimos sacramentos, por la biolencia de sus muertes que fué a manos de los enemigos Cumanches, aunque acaeció que el día anterior se avían confesado y comulgado en cumplimiento de Nuestra Sta. Madre Yglesia, y para qe conste lo firmé en dicho día, mes y año ut supra. (A. Espinosa 1907:11–12)

(All the dead died without receiving last rites, through the violence suffered at the hands of the enemy Comanches, although it happened that the day before they had confessed and taken communion in compliance with our Holy Mother Church, and to wit, I have signed on the aforesaid day, month, and year. [author's translation])

No speculation is offered concerning the motivation for the attack, beyond the common knowledge that Tomé had regular contact, both friendly and hostile, with Comanches, Apaches, and Navajos, given its southern location and proximity to Cañón del Comanche and Abó Pass, two major routes to the Plains.

Survivors and neighbors were left with the almost inconceivable task of explaining or justifying such a devastating tragedy. The response is captured in the oral histories told by people such as Edwin (Baca) Berry about his ancestor Don Ignacio Baca (chapter 3). The only explanation plausible to the Hispano imagination was an offense of family honor and the vengeance wreaked by an unnamed Comanche chief. The hope for peace was embodied in the solemn promise of alliance by marriage between his unnamed son and "María," the beautiful daughter of Don Ignacio. The genre of historical romance, whether oral or literary, fulfills its paradigm when the opposing forces embodied by the romantic couple are reconciled in marriage. This promise of personal fulfillment and cultural harmony is rent asunder, just as in the case of the auto de entrada, when Cuerno Verde faces death rather than conversion and forgiveness.

The Tomé parable circulated widely in the twentieth century. Berry (1993) credited family history for the legend. Lummis (1912) offered no particular source. New Mexico Writers' Project field-worker Allen A. Carter (1936) collected the story from Rev. Alberto Castanes, pastor of the Immaculate Conception Church in Tomé. Erna Fergusson (1946–47) recalled hearing an Apache version of it from Amado Chaves. In his biography of famed military leader Manuel Antonio Chaves, Marc Simmons recounted and embellished the story, with footnotes and the imprimatur of "history," although he still admitted that it was a tale. "The tale still forms part of the oral tradition of the Tomé district, and although some details show that history and legend merged, the main outline is amply documented by Church and Spanish archival records" (Simmons 1973:18).

In their book, Gilberto Espinosa and Tibo Chávez (1967?:93) chose the path of historical objectivity that the Espinosa's brother Aurelio took, in reporting only the "cold facts"—that several Comanche and Apache massacres had indeed taken place in Tomé.

What none of these writers reflect upon is the meaning of the legend and how the people have imagined complications of love and honor to try to comprehend the catastrophe. The romance genre imagines and invents the possibility of peace and resolution by adding the element of cross-cultural desire. When the consummation of the union of Numunuh and Hispano is rendered impossible, the depth of the tragedy can be felt, even if it is not understood.

Although the most notorious episode of death and captivity suffered by Hispanos in the Comanche wars in amply documented in historical sources, the legends surrounding the Villalpando incident at Taos in the summer of 1760 somehow escaped the WPA surveys and did not appear in written form until the 1960s (Parkhill 1965). Even in the late twentieth century, when I first heard them, these oral histories were still tinged with romance, yet another illustration of the power of cross-cultural desire and mimesis in the folk tradition.

According to the historical record, the tragedy of 1760 ended a decade of peace that Governor Tomás Vélez Cachupín had achieved with the Numunuh through attention to state hospitality and careful regulation of trade. Not long after he left office, unfair advantages were taken by local Hispanos at an early spring trade fair in Taos. Insult was added to injury when at a dance at Taos Pueblo, a pole with over a dozen identifiably Numunuh scalps was displayed to the horrified visitors. Word had it that a campaign of vengeance would come later in the summer. A force of several thousand Numunuh warriors in fact attacked and were repulsed at the walled and fortified Taos Pueblo. When they went south to Ranchos, all of the local Hispano families gathered in the protective fortifications of the Villalpando hacienda, with its four torreones. Frightened by the approaching army of warriors, the defenders opened fire prematurely, eliminating any possibility of negotiation. After a day of furious fighting, with losses of forty-nine warriors, the fortress was breached. All of its defenders were put to death, and fifty-six children and women were taken captive. In its detail (and despite conflicting numbers of victims), the historical record supplies ample motivation, but stops there.[8]

The oral tradition in Ranchos de Taos supplies an affective dimension that goes beyond the story of the scalps. The narrative elements closely parallel the Tomé legend from 1777. In all the versions, careful genealogical connections are traced to negotiate credibility for the tale, a characteristic of legend performance (Briggs and Vigil 1990:224). The legend may be summarized as follows.

In the mid eighteenth century at Ranchos de Taos, a long and peaceful alliance was forged between Onacama, a Numunuh chief, and a local ranchero, Don Pablo Villalpando, who promised him his little granddaughter in marriage. The commitment of marriage was broken years later, when the girl, now fourteen, was taken away to Abiquiú. The Numunuh chief followed her there, only to be told that she had died of the plague. He discovered the subterfuge and took vengeance by attacking the Villalpando hacienda in August of 1760, killing both the grandparents. The girl's mother, María Rosalía Villalpando de Jácquez, was taken captive and later sold to the Pawnees, who in turn sold her to a French trapper, who abandoned her with two daughters. One daughter returned to her mother's family in Ranchos de Taos, married a Frenchman, and became the mother of the famous mountain man Antoine Leroux (Parkhill 1965:12–30).

Forbes Parkhill, Leroux's biographer, insists that Chief Onacama was responsible for the Villalpando massacre. Local oral tradition, however, attributes the raid to none other than Cuerno Verde himself (M. Martínez 2001, J. Padilla 1998).

As in the legend of the Tomé massacre, cross-cultural desire is frustrated by the decades of warfare prior to the Treaty of 1786. A romance plot that could have pacified the indomitable Cuerno Verde (or Onacama?) was unconsummated, resulting in twenty-six more years of warfare and a victory play where the great chief would figure as the main character and sacrificial victim.

By 1940, many high-school history students in New Mexico could recognize the name Cuerno Verde and had studied or seen *Los comanches.* Before World War II, it was required reading for every graduate student of Spanish literature at the University of New Mexico. Several modified productions were organized by high-school drama departments in the late 1930s (P. G. Martínez n.d.). Productions to attract summer tourists were promoted in Taos and Galisteo. The complete equestrian production was a highlight of The First American pageant in Albuquerque in 1930 (Cassidy 1934). The high point of this era of interest in regional culture came in 1940, with the celebration of the Coronado Cuarto Centennial, included pageants, folk theater, and presentations of music and dance throughout the state (Campa 1979:10–17). With World War II and the geopolitical reorientation and era of prosperity that followed, interest waned in the cultural traditions of New Mexico through the 1950s. The social and political activism of the 1960s and 1970s began a new chapter in the cultural history of New Mexico, however. The legacy of Indo-Hispano traditions would be reconfigured prominently in the collective search for roots and cultural identity.

ᕲᕵ Cross-Cultural Desire Fulfilled: Hispano-Comanche Songs of Peace and Love

The names of the protagonists of the struggle for peace in colonial New Mexico have been forgotten, except in the annals of history and an occasional verse. Not surprisingly, the most specific praise poems to the *Pax Comanche* come from the Taos area. Each of the two were composed in traditional style in the late twentieth century, when all the forms of Hispano-Comanche celebrations were revitalized, as part of the general "Chicano Renaissance" throughout the Southwest.

Groups such as Los Comanches de la Serna have long identified as Chicanos.[9] One of the Chicano youth groups in northern New Mexico associated with the Alianza Federal de Mercedes and the land-grant activism of the 1960s and 1970s called themselves Los Comancheros del Norte. In their manifesto, they emulated the defiance of nineteenth-century Comancheros and characterized themselves as "the militant vanguard of the New Breed—the Indo-Hispano people of the Southwest" (Steiner and Valdez 1972:307–10). In other areas of the Southwest, such as California and Texas, a "neoindigenist" exploration of Aztec culture was part of the Chicano renaissance (Márez 2001). In New Mexico there was no need to look to such exotic sources, since native traditions were closer at hand and already part of the cultural landscape. The cultural revivals of the 1960s and 1970s continued through the end of the century, as many New Mexico communities faced urbanization and an unprecedented influx of newcomers.

In the 1990s, the following verse was composed by Jerry Padilla, one of the singers of Los Comanches de la Serna.[10] It became part of their repertoire of historic and burlesque coplas comanches, sung to the beat of the round dance and danced as a redondo, as described in the chapter 5. In a recording made of Comanche elders and singers in September 2001, this and a number of other versos were sung in honor of Cuerno Verde:

Versos de la Paz	*Verses of Peace*
Cuerno Verde con su guerra	*Cuerno Verde with his war*
nunca pudo conquistar	*could never conquer*
lo que De Anza y Ecueracapa	*what De Anza and Ecueracapa*
consiguieron con la paz,	*achieved with peace,*
comanches y mexicanos	*Comanches and New Mexicans*
bailando su amistad.	*dancing in friendship.*
Epa yaya, epa yo,	*Epa yaya, epa yo,*
yo jeyana ajeyó . . .	*yo heyana aheyo . . .*

The contributions of the leaders of the eighteenth century are finally entering popular consciousness. On the occasion of the bicentennial of the treaty of 1786, Don Juan Bautista de Anza was honored for his leadership and diplomacy with a bronze bust installed at the Old Ciénega Museum at Rancho de las Golondrinas Museum.[11] A similar bust is being proposed to honor Ecueracapa, although there is no known likeness of him to model it on.

In a similar commemorative vein, famed traditional singer Cleofes Vigil composed an indita song, complete with traditional vocable choruses, for the occasion of the American bicentennial celebrations in 1976.[12] Vigil was a collaborator of La Academia de la Nueva Raza, a group of Chicano activists and intellectuals based in northern New Mexico who conducted cultural and oral history surveys in the 1970s.[13] The main theme of Vigil's indita is idealized and fully consummated cross-cultural desire, in a hymn of praise to the mestizo heritage and people of New Mexico. Pueblo Indians and Genízaros, as well as Comanches, are part of the mix. The Españoles seek and find their *querencia,* a folk concept that designates a deeply rooted sense of belonging to a homeland, further sanctified and personified as Santa Madre Tierra, Holy Mother Earth. The geographical mestizaje completes and reflects the cultural mestizaje through the term Sangre de Cristo,

Himno a la Nacioncita de la Sangre de Cristo

Composed and sung by Cleofes Vigil of San Cristóbal

Vi- nie-ron los es-pa-ño- le-

-es de la Es-pa-ña a es- ta tie- rra,

don-de ha- lla -ron sus que- ren- cias, her- mo- sas in

-dias mo- re- nas je ya, je ya je

ya ja.

Blood of Christ, the Spanish toponym for the southern spur of the Rocky Mountains that dominates the landscapes of northern New Mexico. This Holy Land is further sanctified by the sacrificial blood of its children.[14]

Himno del Pueblo de las Montañas de la Sangre de Cristo	***Anthem of the People of the Blood of Christ Mountains***
Vinieron los españoles	*The Spaniards came*
de la España a esta tierra,	*from Spain to this land, where*
donde hallaron sus querencias,	*they found their heart's desire,*
hermosas indias morenas,	*beautiful dark Indian women,*
jeya, jeya, jeya, ja.	*heya, heya, heya, ha.*
Aquellas indias hermosas	*Those beautiful Indian women*
virtuosas y llenas de gracia,	*virtuous and full of grace,*

escogieron para esposas	were chosen as wives
donde nació linda raza,	and bore a new handsome race,
jeya, jeya, jeya, ja.	heya, heya, heya, ha.
Raza buena y amorosa	A good and loving race
color bronce de mestizo,	bronze-colored people,
mezcla del indio del pueblo	mixture of the Pueblo Indian
donde salió un genízaro,	from whence came the Genízaro,
jeya, jeya, jeya, ja.	heya, heya, heya, ha.
Con sus cantos penetrantes	With their penetrating songs
y sus cuadros espirituales,	and spiritual pictures,
alaban la Santa Tierra	they praise the Holy Earth
que para todos es la madre,	a mother to us all,
jeya, jeya, jeya, ja.	heya, heya, heya, ha.
Ya se oía en los campos	In the countryside could be heard
aquel canto aquella danza,	that song that dance,
retumbaba en la montaña	echoing in the mountains
que Sangre de Cristo llamaban,	they called the Blood of Christ,
jeya, jeya, jeya, ja.	heya, heya, heya, ha.
Españoles y cumanches	Spaniards and Comanches
todos en armonía,	all in harmony,
se juntaban a cantar	would come together to sing
y a bailar con alegría,	and dance with gladness,
jeya, jeya, jeya, ja.	heya, heya, heya, ha.
Comiendo elotes tostados	Eating roast corn
que la tierra producía,	that the earth produced,
machucando carne seca	pounding dried meat
de cíbolo que había,	from the buffalo,
jeya, jeya, jeya, ja.	heya, heya, heya, ha.

The final bucolic scenes of dancing and feasting recall historical descriptions of Comanche trade fairs, as well as the contemporary celebrations to be found in the Taos Valley, such as the annual feast of San Gerónimo at Taos Pueblo, on September 29.

The desire for cultural harmony is as intense as the yearning for peace and the excruciating process by which it was won. A strong sense of Indo-Hispano identity emerged in the late twentieth century, which is expressed in the renaissance of these intercultural traditions. As in postrevolutionary Mexico, mestizo identity began to take on a positive value; cultural hybridity began to be appreciated for the rich and complex phenomenon that it is. The efforts of institutions to recognize and interpret the mestizo traditions of New Mexico would present the next challenge.

✑ From Village Plaza to National Mall: Crisis and Challenge in Cultural Representation

Since the cultural agenda of the statehood movement promoted Spanish Colonial culture, including *Los comanches (de castillo),* an examination of the Indo-Hispano tradition was successfully avoided and deferred. At the time, it was more politically expedient to emphasize Spanish-European rather than Mexican or mestizo traditions, and the work of folklorists such as Aurelio M. Espinosa reflected their times. Nuevo Mexicano elites embraced Hispanophile discourse for its social and class distinctions, the motivation for the emergent *criollo* discourse all across Spanish America. Curiously, there is ample evidence to suggest that the Hispanophile cultural agenda was promoted, even initiated, by Anglo elites, impatient with the endless national deliberations concerning New Mexico statehood. The writings and speeches of Governor L. Bradford Prince typify this process. He wrote with much sympathy on Spanish culture and history in New Mexico, but used his collection of documents to benefit his own ambitions as a member of the "Santa Fe Ring" of politicians and lawyers, who amassed their enormous wealth and landholdings with many fraudulent methods (Nieto-Phillips 2000:116–23).

Perhaps inevitably, the antimiscegenationist sentiment of Anglo-American culture was articulated through cultural essentialism, the valorization and search for "authentic" or "pure" Spanish or Native cultural traditions, in research as well as public cultural policy. The critical gaze of folklorists, anthropologists, artists, activists, and documentary photographers such as Edward Curtis avoided any form of cultural hybridity.

These tendencies resulted in the idealization of Native culture and the denigration of Hispanic culture, along with the avoidance or repudiation of any hybrid between the two. This noble/ignoble savage paradigm is visible at all levels of cultural production, from dime novels and ethnographies to movies and museum policies (Lamadrid 1992c). The cultural revivals of the 1960s and 1970s are significant because they involved a fundamental reorientation of values and categories, a true paradigm shift.

Until recently, Hispano-Comanche celebrations could only be found in the original performance context of traditional feast days, attended only by local families and their friends. Only *Los comanches (de castillo)* was promoted by schools and museums beyond the village level, and then only to World War II. Beginning in the mid 1970s and through the 1990s, however, the Hispano-Comanche dances from Ranchos de Taos traveled to perform in festival settings in the region and as far away as Washington, D.C. Nevertheless, the other forms of Comanche celebrations are still found only in community and devotional settings.

This "rediscovery" of Hispano-Comanches and their representation beyond the local plaza and into the more politicized spaces framed by museum exhibits and cultural festivals has some interesting implications. Whatever the degree of personal identification with and participation in indigenous traditions, cross-cultural mimesis can evoke deep feelings of ambivalence and aversion in many people. In the American imagination, the contemplation of cultural hybridity can be cause for anxiety and revulsion, factors that must be taken into account in doing cultural work, in any media or setting.

Cultural festivals are a good indicator of the shifting cultural agendas of institutions and community groups; a brief survey reveals a growing public awareness and interest in mestizo traditions.

From Coronado to Popay

The 1940 Coronado Cuarto Centennial, true to its times, emphasized the Iberian legacy in New Mexico, exemplified by the explorer Francisco Vásquez de Coronado and his rapacious explorations of New Mexico in 1540. The main voice of reason and moderation in this year-long celebration was that of the folklorist Arthur L. Campa, who reflected deeply about the legacy of conquest in his newspaper columns, while reminding readers not to lose sight of the important contributions of Native and Mexican cultures in the midst of all the emphasis on Spain and its conquistadors (Arellano and Vigil 1980).

The 1976 American Bicentennial Celebration featured an extended, three-month Smithsonian folklife festival that honored regional folk traditions from all over the country. Indo-Hispano traditions of New Mexico were featured for the first time in a national forum, by the participation of folk poet and singer Cleofes Vigil, from San Cristóbal (who sang the indita discussed above), and the Comanches de la Serna dance group, from Ranchos de Taos. The great theme of the American Bicentennial was *E pluribus unum,* and the representation of mestizo culture was received positively, as one of the parts of the great national whole.

The 1980 Tricentennial of the Great Pueblo Revolt was a celebration initiated by a carefully considered alliance of Natives and Hispanos. It was initially greeted with suspicion by groups such as the Santa Fe Fiesta Council, which criticized the event for "celebrating warfare and violence." In the symposia and events that followed, the 1680 Revolt was portrayed not so much as a war but rather as a cultural and religious restoration movement that set the stage for intercultural respect and cooperation in the future. An interesting result of this public reflection was the revision of the historical role of Popay, the spiritual leader of the revolt. His transformation from villain to culture hero has led to the proposal to install a bronze statue of him in the rotunda of the national Capitol, in Washington, D.C. A key document of the Tricentennial is *Ceremony of Brotherhood* (Anaya and Atencio 1981), an anthology of Native and Hispano literature and art that served as a groundbreaking forum for creative reflection on Indo-Hispano traditions and cultural hybridity.

Contested "Comanches" at the 1992 Smithsonian Folklife Festival

The 1992 Columbian quincentennial celebrations at the national level were contested by Native groups, then reconstrued as the Great American Encounter by the Smithsonian, with two important exhibits. "Seeds of Change," in the National Natural History Museum, featured the plants and animals of the Columbian exchange, which forever changed culture and agriculture in both Old and "New" Worlds. The "American Encounters" exhibit, in the National History Museum, featured a case study of the cultural history of New Mexico over four centuries of Native and Hispano cultural relations. The year 1992 was a banner year for New Mexico, because in addition, the state was honored in that year's Smithsonian folklife festival, and two Smithsonian-Folkways CDs featured both Hispanic and Native musical traditions. In the tense and rarified atmosphere of 1992, the appearance of Los Comanches de la Serna at the festival created a fascinating controversy that merits closer attention.

After a week of "cultural conversations" on the National Mall, threats of both internal and external boycotts of the festival arose from both individuals and groups disturbed by issues of "cultural representation" in the inclusion and presentation of Hispano-Comanche culture to a national audience (Carrillo 1993). Mestizo culture was deemed as "too complex and confusing" to portray properly without offending Native groups. The use of feathers, buckskins, vocable singing, and dance was just too suggestive of Native culture and was therefore totally inappropriate for use by a non-Native group in a national showcase. After considerable negotiation and mediation, the boycott was called off, with the stipulation that the "Comanches" events be removed from the central plaza area of the adobe village that had been specially built on the Mall (Parker 2001). The performances were moved past the edge of the exhibit area, to the center lawn of the Mall. The controversy and its resolution provided excellent topics for discussion by participant panels on the narrative stages and provided provocative material for the presenter, Enrique Lamadrid, in a recording made on the National Mall. "In colonial times, Indo-Hispano or genízaro occupied the bottom rung of society and were often settled in marginal or unprotected areas far from the main centers of population. Our location on the Mall is an interesting and appropriate parallel" (Lamadrid 1992b).

Presenters and participants were also cautioned not to make any claims to Native cultural heritage or identity. The Hispano-Comanches have never made any tribal claims and are quite closely aligned to what they term "Chicano" identity, since they identify as cultural activists. The topic of federal recognition of indigenous groups and how these groups are identified and entitled also provided fascinating topics for the panel discussions on narrative stages. Participants measured their words carefully and came up with quite stunning and sensitive statements, such as these by the Abiquiú singer Floyd Trujillo.

> First of all I want to say that we do not pretend to be Indians. But yes, our ways
> of celebrating the great feast of our parish, which is St. Thomas, shows the blood

in our veins in action. We normally dress two little girls in Indian costumes and in war paint on their face. These little girls dance in front of the statue of Santo Tomás, and at the same time we also have another little song that we play where we capture those that have come into the village.

Normally it'll be somebody that comes to visit from the outside, it might be one of you one of these days, that visits the village on such an occasion. You will be captured, danced with, and then you will be put up for ransom. And somebody has to know you in order to pay the ransom for you. Once they pay the ransom, you are acknowledged as one of the members that can come at any time to our feasts in Abiquiú . . .[15]

One of the songs that we play is called "El Coyote," it is very popular, it is sung, it is danced. Normally these two little Indian girls are the ones that lead the dancing. They are the ones that go out there in the crowd and start hauling people to dance these dances. And like I say, we do not pretend to be Indians, because we know that we're not. (F. Trujillo 1992)

There is a clear understanding that *Indian* refers to status under the law, rather than to cultural heritage, because Abiquiú is historically a Genízaro village with

7.1. Floyd y su Tombé (Abiquiú). Some listeners hear strains of Towa eagle captivity songs in the Nanillé music. The meaning of "nanillé" has been lost in a community in which many indigenous languages were spoken.

multitribal roots (Córdova 1973). The mention of "El coyote" is also quite revealing, because *coyote* is the old caste term for the mixed blood or half-breed.

There was understandably a great sensitivity to issues of cultural misrepresentation in the quincentennial year.[16] The low tolerance for cross-cultural imitation of any kind is explained by real concern for issues of cultural appropriation and cultural property. The charge of being a cultural "wannabe" or having a recently constructed cultural identity was a grave insult in 1992, and those persons delivering such a slur were fully cognizant of it.

Wisely, the curators of the New Mexico festival called for a full accounting of fieldwork and a seminar to discuss the consequences. The field-worker (again, Enrique Lamadrid) delivered the following statement.

> To the best of my knowledge, and using archival, oral historical, and ethnographic methodology, the Indo-Hispano traditions being represented in the Festival originated in late eighteenth century New Mexico. The lyrics in "Comanche" songs directly allude to political struggles and cultural relations between 1740 and 1786. The musical tradition is transmitted by elders who learned it from their elders. (Lamadrid 1992b)

With a tough call to make, the Smithsonian festival directors were able to forge the compromise that simultaneously supported their own curatorial team while responding positively to the critiques that were voiced. Inclusion of certain groups in a cultural landscape may cause controversy and tension, but excluding them is tantamount to social erasure, a practice with dangerous antecedents and nefarious results (Kurin 2001). In the end, Smithsonian's "dialogic approach to cultural interpretation" and their inclusion of community scholars and tradition bearers in the "cultural conversation" proved to be invaluable. The festival by-line that "cultural identity is negotiated on the Mall" comes from long experience and many trials (Parker 2001).[17]

"Comanches" and "Kwítara" Share the Cuarto Centenario

The 1998 Nuevo México Cuarto Centenario observances were scheduled all over the state, but many were altered or canceled due to controversies about the human rights record of Don Juan de Oñate, who led the colonizing expedition to the upper Río Grande in 1598. In January of 1599, a rebellion in Acoma Pueblo was suppressed with great loss of life and the humiliating trial and punishment of survivors, including servitude and the amputation of the right foot of the men. The commemorative year of 1998 began on the morning of January 1, with the discovery that the right foot of the equestrian bronze statue at the Oñate Cultural Center in Alcalde, New Mexico, had been removed, an act whose ironic symbolism attracted a headline from the *New York Times* (Brooke 1998). In the midst of the continuing controversies, the only successful Cuarto Centenario observance in central New Mexico was mounted in Albuquerque, by the University of New

7.2. Comanches en la Plaza, 1930s (Taos). The earliest photographs of Hispano-Comanche dancers date to the 1920s and 1930s in Taos. The distinctive plumero, or single-row feather headdress, is a longstanding tradition. Courtesy of Taos Historic Museums, accession no. 79.29.52 G7/991.

Mexico. The festival and symposium avoided controversy by directly addressing its causes and celebrating what unifies the traditional peoples of New Mexico—the traditional celebrations of their Indo-Hispano culture. The festival press release outlines justifications and goals:

> From El Paso and the Río Abajo to Santa Fe and the Río Arriba, numerous communities are observing the New Mexico Cuarto Centenario by staging elaborate pageants and costumed *entradas* to honor the first Spanish Mexican colonists of the northlands. By recalling the triumphs of the spring and summer of 1598, attention and historical conscience is inevitably drawn to the tragedies of the winter of 1598–99. There has been much soul searching in the Hispano and Native American communities over these divisive issues.
>
> To fulfill our mission of education and multi-culturalism, UNM proposes to observe the Cuarto Centenario by emphasizing the other 398 years of New Mexico's hstory which encompasses two layers of Conquest, Resistance, Accommodation, and Transculturation. No mere pageant script or film treatment could possibly encompass or do justice to this vast human drama.
>
> It is our belief that in their own folk dramas and ritual celebrations, the people themselves have developed answers to their own historical dilemmas. They express themselves collectively in the Matachines, Comanches, Moros y Cristianos and other traditional celebrations in Hispano and Native American communities across the entire region. These scripts have evolved over four centuries and provide a profound insight into ongoing cultural relations. Performed by Native Americans and Hispanos all up and down the Río Grande from Taos to Laredo and well into northern Mexico, the Matachines dance drama is the best known intercultural Indo-Hispano celebration of the region. Inscribed in a rich texture of symbols and choreography is the cultural process of conquest, resistance, and reconciliation. Jémez Pueblo is known for its beautiful rendition of the Matachines and will present it on Saturday, September 26, 1998.
>
> Moros y Cristianos was the first play of European origin ever performed in New Mexico. To witness it is to gain insight into the explosion of exploration and colonization that followed the Reconquest of Spain in 1492. Oñate and his colonists celebrated it when they first crossed the Río Grande in El Paso del Norte and later in San Juan Pueblo. The play has been performed continuously ever since in communities all over the region. The plot is simple. A Christian army faces a Moorish army on the field of battle. The Moors steal the Holy Cross and after several battles, it is recaptured. The defeated Moors are forgiven and become Christians in the last scene. The ideological message is that enemies of the Spanish are not annihilated, but rather included as fellow subjects of the empire. The famous Chimayó Moros y Cristianos will also perform on Saturday, September 26, 1998.
>
> The second great inter-cultural tradition in the region which expresses the

7.3a (opposite) El Comanche Luis Girón (Talpa) & **7.3b.** (above) El Comanche David (Talpa).

Since cultural hybridity has negative value in American culture, Indo-Hispano traditions are scorned as being tainted or impure.

relations and aspirations of Hispanos, Pueblos, and plains Indians are the "Comanche" celebrations of the Upper Río Grande. In the 1770's, the mighty Comanche chief, Cuerno Verde, boasted of his power to completely destroy New Mexico, but stopped short because he "needed the Mexicans and Pueblos to raise his horses for him." By 1779, after a terrible war, much of New Mexico lay in ruins. When Cuerno Verde was defeated and the great Comanche Peace was forged in 1786 by Governor De Anza and the great chief Ecueracapa, all of New Mexico rejoiced. The celebration has continued to the present day in the Indian Pueblos and Hispano Villages of New Mexico. The Hispano Comanche dances of Taos are a part of this tradition.

Since folk plays occur mostly in village settings, urban dwellers do not get the opportunity to observe and participate in these age-old spectacles. UNM will remedy that by bringing them to New Mexico's largest metropolis where they will be celebrated within an educational framework. Complete translated scripts of the folk plays and essays on their historical importance and modern relevance will be presented to the public. (Lamadrid 1998)

7.4a. (opposite) La Comancha Corina; & **7.4b.** (above) Un Comanchito (Ranchos de Taos).

Hispano-Comanche regalia can range from the finest buckskins to rough-cut flannel, but the tradition began in the eighteenth century.

The event achieved the goal of bringing together in a festival setting for the first time scholars of and participants in the Indo-Hispano cultures of New Mexico.

An integral part of the festival was an exposition of the documentary photographs of Miguel Gandert, entitled "400 Years of Indo-Hispano Culture," which grew and became the inaugural exhibit in the National Hispanic Cultural Center in 2000. Entitled "Nuevo México Profundo: Rituals of an Indo-Hispano Homeland," and accompanied by a book with the same title, it is a document of the long collaboration of Miguel Gandert and Enrique Lamadrid.[18] It took nearly a century for the Hispanophile cultural discourse to be revised and amplified by the mestizo heritage it eclipsed for so long. In a key series of Hispano-Comanche portraits made with a large-format camera in the style of Edward Curtis, Gandert engaged and contested Curtis, who visited the Taos Valley in search of noble Natives, averting his gaze from the "European contamination" that mestizos represented to him.

✑ *Los Comanches* in the Twenty-First Century

The traditions of ritual dance and drama seen in this survey are an indication of how broad and diverse the cultural category of "Comanche" is. Although the point of departure is the Numunuh tradition, many other peoples have identified with it as a source of wealth, strength, individualism, and spirituality. The boundaries between cultural self and Other are constantly shifting in this tradition. Pueblo "Comanche" dances offer a deep sense of joy and well-being to their participants. *Kwítara,* the name Tewas give to them, reveals a burlesque scatological-erotic aspect of cross-cultural emulation.[19] Despite this charade, Pueblo identity remains constant. The Comanches of Ranchos de Taos move past emulation to identification, but the content is hybrid. The Ranchos Comanche music is a synthesis of Pueblo, Navajo, Kiowa, and Numunuh sources. The choreography is likewise diverse and related to the much more recent powwow tradition, also a pan-Indian phenomenon (Evans 1931).

The Comanche celebrations to be found all across New Mexico are the legacy of the *Pax Comanche,* the Treaty of 1786, and a lasting tribute to the perseverance and vision of Spanish-Mexican and Numunuh leaders, who understood that the future of the province was in their hands. They had already suffered the tragedy of warfare and had proven that the cycles of violence and retribution could last decades. Despite the demise of Cuerno Verde, the Numunuh were still strong and negotiated from a position of strength. Their descendants still believe that the treaty represented not defeat, but victory, and a new relationship with the Spanish-Mexicans (Bigby 1998). To this day, they regard New Mexico with nostalgia and regret, a kind of lost homeland (Wapp 1998). Most Numunuh families know about Spanish-Mexican bloodlines and recognize the mixture in their own kin (L. Harris 2002). Each year they renew friendships and memories at the feast of San Gerónimo at Taos Pueblo, the same grounds their ancestors returned to year after year in colonial times.

Through their rituals, Nuevo Mexicano communities also recognize their historic and cultural relations with the Numunuh, although today there is little social contact with them. In the military play, the historical struggle is revisited, and the victory is redefined to include both Spanish and Comanche. In the dances, the captives are remembered and honored. Parents dress their children as Comanchitos and pray to the Santo Niño to remember them all. The spiritual dimension of the Comanches goes even further than commemoration, however. There is a spiritual power in cultural transformation that inspires the faithful and heals the sick. *Los Comanches* is a testament to survival and adaptation. The willingness to cross cultural boundaries to affirm a new sense of self is an exercise in humility and faith. The cultural legacy of the Comanche wars of the eighteenth century in New Mexico holds lessons for a globalized world where hybridity is no longer the exception but the rule, and where identity is rooted in the past and negotiated for the future. The historical struggle of Hispanos, Pueblos, and Numunuh is one of many episodes of conflict, resistance, accommodation, and transformation. But the celebrations left in its wake are spectacular and deeply resonant for all who participate and all who have the good fortune to observe them.

7.5. La Fe de los Hijos (Tomé). Now that Edwin Berry, the guardian of Cerro de Tomé, has passed away, his sons have taken up his hymns, to fulfill their father's promise.

⌁ Epilogue

The Indo-Hispano fiestas celebrated in New Mexico are dynamic and responsive to change and challenge. For the first time ever, in December 2001, Los Comanches de la Serna paid a *visita* to the Comanches de Castillo, in Alcalde, on December 27. A new location west of the church was chosen to accommodate all the dancers and singers from Taos and to incorporate them into the performance. In the script, the *juntas de guerra,* or war councils, are signaled by calls for *"¡música!"* and musical accompaniment. Previously, Alcalde used a measured *marcha,* played on violin and guitar for both Spanish and Comanche councils. Singers from Taos remembered the music that accompanied the Comanche juntas in the performances of the 1950s and sang it for Cuerno Verde's council. Comanche dancers used paseados and llaneros in their procession to the battlefield and incorporated war dances, including "El espantado" into the performance. Nobody in the audience could recall having seen anything like it for fifty years!

On New Year's Day of 2002, the Alcalde Comanches reciprocated, traveling to Ranchos de Taos and viewing the dances. As usual, no tourists or outsiders know about or attended these events. Interestingly, these extraordinary developments only attracted the attention of the New Mexico State Police.

7.6. Comanches Amenazados (Talpa). Since colonial times in New Mexico, Genízaro identity and culture have always been questioned and contested.

Most officers were on duty north of the town of Taos, to patrol the traffic due to the many hundreds of tourists visiting Taos Pueblo for the famous turtle dance of New Year's Day. A young, inexperienced Anglo state policeman, happening to drive south through Ranchos, noticed fully costumed Comanche dancers riding, as they always do, in the backs of pickup trucks and in open trailers. A group of dancers and singers were stopped, questioned, and threatened with hefty fines for each person without a seat belt. The Comanches explained that there have been dancers riding in trucks on New Year's Day since the first trucks came to the Taos Valley, in the 1920s. An altercation developed and a singer and dancer were arrested, but Hispano officers showed up in the nick of time to prevent an even larger problem (Valerio and Valerio 2002). Although the Taos Chamber of Commerce would not be contacted, the authorities were advised by the author to pay proper respect in the future to some of the oldest celebrations in the valley.

One of the tendencies of ethnographic work is to assume that festivals are somehow more constant and static than they really are. The only observable constant is that the Indo-Hispano fiestas of the Upper Río Grande continue now, as they have for centuries, as the dynamic expressions of the cultural values and persistent historical memory of a proud mestizo people.

appendix 1

"Los Comanches"/"The Comanches"

"Los Comanches"

Manuscrito de El Pino (Campa 1942; nonstandard spellings are original in the manuscript)

Barriga Duce:
Vengo a avisaros de prisa
Fernández, mi capitán,
Que allá al pie de aquella mesa
Vi un indio con chimal.
Ellos me querían llevar,
Pero yo con mi honda y maza
Los hice pronto arrancar;
Y fué tan buena mi traza
Que os he venido a avisar.

Capitán:
Si es ciertos lo que dices
Pronto me pondré en campana,
Y triunfantes y felices
Nos reuniremos manana.
El clarín que toque Diana,
Y que venga el general,
Y con mi espada en la vaina
Los saldremos a encontrar.

"The Comanches"

El Pino Manuscript (Campa 1942)
Verse translation—Larry Torres

Sweet Belly:
I have come with haste to warn thee,
Don Fernández, on this field,
That I saw close to that mesa
A bold Indian with a shield.
They did really want to seize me
But I, with my sling and mace,
Quickly caused them to forsake me;
So effective was my pace
That I've come hither to tell thee.

Captain:
If 'tis true what you are telling,
I in full campaign shall fight,
And triumphant, with joy swelling,
Shall tomorrow each unite.
Let the morning reveille herald.
Let each general attend,
And shall I, with sword still sheathed,
Lead all to that crucial end.

(Toca el clarín)

Don Carlos:
¿Qué toque llamado es ese,
Que me tiene sorprendido?

Capitán:
Qye allá al pie de aquella mesa
Los Comanches han salido.

Don Carlos:
Pronto pues, mi capitán,
Prepare vuestros soldados,
Y al indio hostil encontrar
Cuando estéis bien preparado.
Aquí tenéis la bandera
Que el sargento llevará
Porque de cualquier manera
La religíon triunfara.

Capitán:
(Agarrando la bandera)

Bandera entre mil banderas,
Hermoso emblema español.
De nubes se pone el sol
Del mundo señor, empero.
Yo te adoro porque eras
La gloria que en suenos vía
Mi entusiasta fantasía,
Y hora que quisiera ufano
Enarborlarte en mi mano.
Te dejo, bandera mía.

(Al sargento)

Tomar sargento y cuidar
Del pabellón estrellado,
y a los comanches matar
¡En gloria de este reinado!

(Los indios hacen escaramuzas y se adelantan al castillo mientras suena el clarín.)

(The trumpet sounds.)

Don Carlos:
What trumpet am I hearing
Which surprised me with its surge?

Captain:
Near that mesa, I am fearing,
The Comanches have emerged.

Don Carlos:
Hasten please, my captain, quicken,
Hold your soldiers readily.
To meet those hostile Indians
When you well-prepared shall be.
Here you hold the solemn banner
Which the sergeant shall unveil,
Since, in all regard and manner
Our religion shall prevail.

Captain:
(Seizing the banner)

Oh, thou flag amongst all pennants;
Spanish emblem passing fair,
The clouds hide the sun in tenants
From the world, sire, ruling there.
I adore thee for thou wert here
All the glory of my dreams.
My unbridled fantasy near,
And now with delightful schemes
I shall leave thee, banner dear,
With my hand to hoist thy gleams.

(To the sergeant)

Sergeant, take and guard securely
The bespangled pennant,
And kill the Comanches surely
For glory of this kingdom spent.

(The Indians make a slight skirmish and advance toward the fortress while the trumpet sounds.)

Cuerno Verde:

Desde el oriente al poniente,
Desde el sur al norte frío
Suena el brillante clarín
Y reina el acero mío.
Entre todas las naciones
Campeo osado, atrevido,
Y es tanta la valentía
Que reina en el pecho mío.
Se levantan más banderas
Por el viento giro a giro
Que de las que he atributado.
Refreno al más atrevido,
Devoro al más arrojado;
Pues con mi bravura admiro
Al oso más arrogante,
Al fiero tigre rindo.
Que no hay roca ni montaña
Que de éste no haiga rendido,
Que de ella no haga registro.
Al más despreciado joven,
Aquel que más abatido
Se ve porque su fortuna
A tal desdicha lo ha tráido
Pues no hay villa ni lugar
Que no se vea combatido
De mi nación arrogante
Que hoy con el tiempo se ha visto,
Y como ahora lo veréis.
Este soberbio castillo
Hoy lo he de ver en pavezas.
Lo he de postrar y abatirlo
Con sus rocas y baluartes
Aunque se hallen prevenidos,
Y con la incomodidad
De un repentino descuido,
Será más osado el brío
Que tienen nuestras personas
Que certifico y he visto,
Como lo canta la fama,
Y un cuartelejo de gritos.
Diga la nación Caslana,
Díganlo tantas naciones

Green Horn:

From the east to west horizons
From the south to northern cold
Rings the blast of that bright trumpet
Where doth reign my steel so bold.
Among all the varied nations
I do battle daring, last,
And such is the valor reigning
Here within my breast held fast.
Unfurled flags in the wind rising
Wheeling round and round about,
Above all those in my tribute.
The most daring I restrain,
the most dauntless I devour;
And in my bravura admired
The most arrogant bear and
Fiercest tiger do I conquer.
There is no rock nor mountain
Which does not yield to my fervor
Or acclaim far and wide my fame.
Every youth scorned and rejected,
Everyone that's thus abased,
To this end is brought by fortune
To this wretched state effaced.
There be no township nor place
Yet undefeated verily
By my proud and haughty nation
At this time you all can see,
You shall see this all too shortly.
This imposing castle here
All this I'll reduce to rubble.
Full-abased and beaten clear.
Even with its stones and bulwarks
Although in preparedness,
And with all the inconvenience
Of a sudden heedlessness,
All the more stalwart the courage
Which our fighters do possess
I can certify and witness
As their own fame doth express,
In song and shouts from their quarters.
Let the Caslana Apaches,
As so many nations claim

A quien quité el señorío.	Whose own sovereignty I've taken
Hoy se ven desmoronados	Now, by slow degrees the same
Sus pueblos dando gemidos,	Pueblos whine at my prowess,
Como se ven combatidos	When they find themselves engaged
Huyendo de mi furor.	And then fleeing from my fury.
Se les ha acabado el brío	Their dwindling courage waged,
Se remontan de tal suerte	They withdraw from such a fortune
Que hasta hora no lo hemos visto.	Which 'til now we hadn't seen.
Pero, ¿para qué me canso	But, why should I be weary
En referir lo que han visto	Of recounting what has been
Que de este reino en sus lugares,	Since in their province I now reign,
Cuando todo el Cristianismo	And draw forth all Christianity
Traje de tantas naciones	After me from all these nations
Que no le alcanza el guarismo?	Whose numbers still can't touch me?
Y sólo los españoles	And only the Spanish refrain
Refrenan el valor mío,	My valor which doth shine.
Pero hoy ha de correr sangre	But today blood shall flow
Del corazón vengativo.	From this vengeful heart of mine.
Me recuerda la memoria	It recalls to mind and memory
De un español atrevido	A daring Spanish soldier
Que, ufano y con valentía,	Who, full-proud and filled with valor,
Y con tanto osado brío	And with unsurpassing furor
El campo vistío de flores	Dressed the battlefield as with flowers
En sangre de colorido,	Crimson and with scarlet red,
De los muertos la distancia	Of the men, women and children
Hombres, mujeres y ninos	Killed at distance, fully-dead.
No pudiendo numerarse	We could not begin to number
Ni contarse los cautivos.	Nor to count the captives claimed.
Ea, nobles capitanes,	Your attention, noble captains,
Genízaros valerosos,	*Valorous janissaries,*
Que se pregone mi edicto,	Let my edict be proclaimed.
Que yo como general	That I, as your general speaking
He de estar aprevenido;	Must be well-prepared and seize;
Que general que descanza	For a general who reposes
En vista de enemigo	Within sight of enemies
Bien puede ser arrogante,	Very well could be called haughty,
Bien puede ser atrevido.	And might daring be indeed.
Yo no me he de conformar	But I shall not be contented
Con estos vagos destinos	With those fickle destinies
Y así, comiencen un canto,	And so, begin the chant of war.
Que suene el tambor y pito.	Beat the drum and play the fife!
¡Al baile, y punto de guerra!	Start the dance and launch the battle!
Pasaremos al distrito	Through the district, full of spite

Para que en vista de todos
Estemos aprevenidos.
Y advierto que con la unión
Que me tienen prometida
Obraré como prudente,
Que tal renombre ha tenido
Todo nuestra descendencia.
Y así, como el más impío,
He de mostrar mi fiereza
Con esta lanza de vidrio.
Al oso más arrogante
Y al fiero tiguere rindo,
La más elevada Elena.
Este bruto saltó un brinco,
Pues ya no hallo a quién temer.
Es tanta mi fuerza y brío
Que entrando osado y altivo
Buscando a ese general
Que con locos disvaríos
Usó de tanta fierza,
Destruyó como he dicho.
Lo llamo en campal batalla,
Lo reto y lo desafío
¿Quién es, y cómo se llama?

Don Carlos:
Aguarda, detén, espera
Que soy de tan noble brillo
Que vengo sin que me llames
A cuidar este castillo.
Pues no memester carteles;
Ya tus valentías he oído.
Dime tu nombre, porque
Del todo quedo entendido.
Para ahorrarme de palabras
Basta con lo que me has dicho.

Cuerno Verde:
Yo soy aquel capitán
No capitán, poco he dicho.
De todos soy gran señor,
De todos soy conocido.
Yo soy, y por el turbante,

Let us march that all may see us
Armed and ready for a fight.
And I tell you, this allegiance
Which you've promised me so far
I shall safeguard well and prudent,
For such is the fame in war
Of our fathers and our offspring.
Since I, for impious pass,
I shall show my fierceness ever
With this black obsidian lance.
I defy the most disdainful
Bear or tiger as I do
Even the resplendent Helen,
And likewise, this brute shall too.
I find none to fear nor cower.
Such is my own strength and might
That I enter, bold and haughty,
Seek their general with my sight
Who, with senseless rant and raving
And his own ferociousness
Destroyed all, as I have stated.
Him, I summon with duress,
To the battlefield and challenge
Him to state his name, confess!

Don Carlos:
You must stop, desist, wait ever
For I am of noble heart,
That I come without your summons
To safeguard this fort apart.
No need to exchange agreements;
I've heard of your prowess here.
State your name for I would have it
Knowing all without that fear.
But I'll save us both discussion
What you've said's enough and clear.

Green Horn:
I am that selfsame, great captain.
No sire, few words I've devised.
Of all tribes I am the leader,
And by all am recognized.
I am, by this headdress, noticed,

Este cuerno que ha aplaudido
Verde y dorado que ves,
Hoy se me postran rendidos
No sólo de mi nacíon
Que emprende mi señoría,
Sino todas las naciones
Que coloca el norte frío.
Ciegos me dan la obediencia.
Caiguas, y Cuampis, Quichuas,
Panamas, Jumanes, Amparicas,
Y otras muchas infinitas.
Y por no cansarme callo;
Basta con lo que he dicho.

Don Carlos:
Aguarda, detén, espera
Que he de anular tu cerviz
Y quebrantar tu soberbia.
Sabrás que en la mejicana
El señor que nos gobierna
Es un señor soberano
Que a todo el mundo gobierna
Encumbró los cuatro polos
Que se encumbran en la tierra.
¿Qué no sabes que en la España
El señor soberano
De los cielos y la tierra
Y todos los cuatro polos
Que este gran círculo encierra?
Brilla su soberanía,
Y al oír su nombre tiemblan
Alemanes, portugueses,
Turquilla y la Inglaterra,
Porque en diciendo españoles
Todas las naciones tiemblan.
Tú no has topado el rigor,
No has visto lo que es fierza
De las católicas armas,
Por eso tanto bravas.
Si quieres saber quién soy,
Te lo diré porque sepas
Que no es la primera batalla
Esta que tú me demuestras.

And this horn which you did laud
Green and gold as now you see it.
All kneel to me as to God.
And not just by my own nation
Which my lordship undertakes,
But by every other nation
That the northern cold lays waste.
Blindly they pledge me obedience.
Kiowas, Arapahos, Quichuas too,
Pawnees, Jumanos, Yamparicas.
Countless others also do.
But so as to not belabor,
I'll cease talking now to you.

Don Carlos:
You must stop, desist, wait ever
For my chains around your craw
Shall soon crush your self-importance.
You will learn of that great lord
That rules from Mexican lands.
A sovereign lord above us all,
Who governs the entire world.
He has raised up those four poles
That give direction to this globe.
Don't you know, in Spain by law
The most Sovereign Lord of Heaven
And of all the earth right here
By the four poles thus enclosed
Within this unending sphere
Shines in majesty and splendor?
And when His name's heard withall,
Tremble Portuguese and Germans,
Turkey, as does England all,
At the mention of us Spaniards,
Every single nation quakes.
You have yet to face our rigor,
And the fury to partake,
Of our Catholic arms when brandished.
That is why you brave so much.
If you'd know my appellation,
I'll reveal it to you such.
This is not the first engagement
On the battlefield for us.

Las que he hecho son infinitas,	The campaigns I've fought are many,
Siempre he pisado tus tierras	I've always trodden your lands
Aunque ya avanzado en años,	Although now advanced in years,
Y me veas de esta manera	You still see me in the ready
Siempre soy Carlos Fernández	Carlos Fernández am I always.
Por el mar y por la tierra,	O'er the land and o'er the sea
Y para probar tu brío	I'll challenge your pride and mettle
Voy a hacer junta de guerra.	And now prepare to give you battle.

Cuerno Verde:

Pues yo voy a hacer lo mismo
El sol es quien nos gobierna.

(Toca el clarín a junta de guerra)

Don Carlos:

¡Guerra a muerte capitán!
A guerra mandé tocar
Para que con la destreza
De vuestra gran vigilancia
Use usted con gran presteza
De las católicas armas,
y concurran a la empreza
De los grandes corazones.
¡Ea, leales capitanes,
Cuyo vasallos del rey
Hacer que vuestra patria,
Y el Altísimo Patriarca
Que nos ha de dar victoria
Por su concepción divina,
Marche al campos y nos prevenga!
Si tú eres grande campeón
Te prepararás a la guerra.
Muestra, comanche, el valor.
Yo te hablo de esta manera,
Pues para que todos sepan
Cómo el comanche atrevido
Como una bárbara fiera
Se arroja despavorido.
¡Santiago! Y darle a esta infame
Canalla hasta que mueran.
Vamos a romper acero;
Hacer que muera esa fiera.

Green Horn:

I shall do the same outside.
The sun is our only sovereign.

(The trumpet sounds the call to battle.)

Don Carlos:

To the death, captain, with pride!
Have the battle cry be sounded
So that with dexterity
From your never ending vigil
You might, with agility
Make use of those catholic arms,
Hearten to the undertaking
Every great heart anxiously.
Let us witness, loyal captains,
Who be vassals of the king,
Cause each one in your own homeland,
And that Highest Ruler mine,
Who bestows on us the vict'ry
By His conception divine,
Take the field and shield us ever!
For if you, great champion be,
You'll prepare yourself for battle.
Show, Comanche, your bravery.
I address you in this manner,
So that all may come to know
How Comanches, ever-daring
Like wild beasts do throw
Themselves fearless into battle.
Saint James! Slayer of them all.
Smite to death this mob ignoble.
Let us break our swords withall;
Cause the death of this brute creature.

¡A destruirlos que son pocos,
Y a quebrantar su bravesa!
Preguntando con disfraz
Si yo era diestro en la guerra,
O si yo era el capitán
Que le pisaba sus tierras.
Y saliéndole al incuentro
Con claridad le di muestra
De aquel castillo sin par.
De decirlo el pecho tiembla,
Pero mejor es callar,
Y que enmudezca la lengua.
Pero vamos adelante,
Que hoy se trata de la guerra.
Dadme vuestro parecer
Como diestros en la guerra,
Usted Don Tomás Madril,
Y Don José de la Peña,
Soldados, cabos, sargentos,
Y don Salvador Ribera;
Y en vista de su presencia
Se procederá a la guerra,
Y estando todo concluido
Se verá lo que se ordena.

(Toca el clarín; sigue la marcha)

Don José De la Peña:
Respondo porque es preciso,
Porque tu valor me esfuerza.
Esforzado comandante
Así tu valor me alienta,
Viendo que esta vida es vuestra
Y que me podéis mandar,
Yo os prometo la obediencia
Y es para pronto pelear,
Y breve daré la prueba.
En un número crecido
Siendo cien hombres de guerra
No me daré por vencido
Pues tengo bien conocido
Y me late el corazón

Destroy all since few they be,
And break down their gallantry!
Asking thin disguisedly
If I were dexterous in battle,
Or the captain of the field
Who would trample down their lands,
Or to meet them I should yield,
Well, most clearly did I show them
Our great fortress with no peer.
My own breast heaves now with trembling,
But I'll say no more right here,
Let my tongue be stilled in silence.
Let us sally forthwith now
For this day be ruled by battle.
Tell me your thoughts anyhow
As those who are versed in battle.
Don Tomás Madril are you,
And Don José de la Peña,
Soldiers, chiefs, and sergeants too.
And Don Salvador Ribera,
In whose sight and presence shall
We proceed forthwith to battle.
Having brought an end to all,
We shall see what is ordained.

(The trumpet sounds. The march begins.)

Don José de la Peña:
I must answer for 'tis needed,
For your valor does compel.
Valiant commandant your courage
Bolsters me and heartens well,
For you see, my life is yours now
And command it, well you may.
I have promised you obedience
And I'm soon to join the fray,
And will shortly give credentials.
Though the number be dire high
Be they hundred men in battle
There, unvanquished shall be I
I have always known this truly
And my heart beats very fast

Que jamás seré cautivo	Knowing I shall not be captured
De este bárbara nación	By this savage nation cast.
A ganarles el terreno	To retake the ground is best now;
Es lo mejor que se puede	It's what we can do; 'tis fate
Para salvar nuestro reino	To safeguard our kingdom here
Que nuestra patria venera	Since our homeland venerates
Aquel príncipe Miguel,	Blessed Michael of nine choirs;
De las nueve jerarquías.	The hierarchies he allays
Será nuestro gran sostén.	He will be our intercessor
En la guerra de estos días,	In the war these dreary days,
Señor, ésta es mi verdad	Sire, this is the truth I've spoken
Esta es toda mi propuesta,	'Tis my proposition true,
Con nuestras armas tirar	That we should discharge our weapons
Para que así se arrepientan.	So that they repent and rue.

El Teniente:	*The Lieutenant:*
Pues yo con el parecer	*I in accord with the view*
De don José de la Peña	*Of don José de la Peña*
Hoy diré en una palabra,	*In one word will say to you,*
Y me conformo y que sea	*I agree and will act with*
Toda mi conformidad.	*Whole heart on my conviction.*
Y mi voluntad queda hecha;	*My will staunch and unyielding;*
Y luego, señor don Carlos,	*And then, noble don Carlos,*
Siendo mi lealtad tan cierta,	*My loyalty is unfailing,*
A quien pretendo servir	*You who I will serve gladly*
Es mi gloria haciendo fuerza.	*It's my glory in the making.*
Oh, ilustre general,	Oh, illustrious General Peña,
A quien toda la obediencia	To whom all obedience I
Debo dar, y se la doy	Must set forth and do so freely
Con mi lealtad dando muestras	My loyalty an example,
Del atributo gallardo	*Of gallant attributes and*
De cual con tan altas prendas,	*With such high endowment,*
No siendo mercedor,	*No doubt undeserving,*
Así mi fé lo confiesa	*In such my faith confessing*
De que en este empleo honoroso	*That in honorable service*
Huesa merced me pusiera;	*Your mercy would place me;*
Yo digo que me conformo,	*I declare I'm in agreement*
Y ésta es toda mi repuesta.	*And this is all my answer.*
Esa insigne capital	That distinguished seat of power
Que de por sí se demuestra	Which doth flout itself for thee,
¡Pólvora y balas con ellos	Now to reduce them with bullets
Para que así se arrepientan!	Until they repent verily.

Don Salvador Ribera:

Señor don Carlos Fernández,
Esa razón me hace fuerza
De ver que podéis mandar,
Y yo os daré la obediencia.
Me conformo con que sea
Como lo ha dicho el teniente,
Y don José de la Peña,
En rendir a Cuerno Verde
Que es el indio más valiente
Que se esfuerza en la pelea.
Así su valor me ensena,
Que todo el mundo lo vea.
Me parece que ya veo
Con todo el valor que medra
Al Comanche ¿qué desea
El indio Cabeza Negra?

Cabeza Negra:

Detente, insigne señor,
Porque es tanta mi fiereza,
Que quiero con mi destreza
Daros mi resolución.
Pues quiero que me conozcan,
Y que ustedes vean mis fuerzas,
Que sepas con quíen conversas
Y quíen te habla en la ocasion;
Y que sepas mi fiereza
Y mi valiente corazón.
Yo saqué de los Crisitanos
Dos ninos que cautivé
Y con mis fuerzas mostré
El valor a tus paisanos.
Sin hacerles ningún daño
Los mantuve con mis bienes,
Y son los dos que tú tienes
Hoy transitando esta tierra
Por quien el comanche viene
A formarte cruda guerra.
Yo soy aquel capitán,
Soy aque que nunca medra
En la guerra y en la paz;
Siempre soy Cabeza Negra.

Don Salvador Ribera:

My lord, Don Carlos Fernández
This, your reasoning gives to me
Strength to see that you can order
And I yield my will to thee.
I'm content to be as stated
Our lieutenant solemnly,
And Don José de la Peña,
To defeat Green Horn you see
Who's the most courageous Indian
In each combat and each strife.
Who does flout his valor ever
To the world and to my life.
Seems to me that I perceive him
With the courage that refines
The Comanche, but what is it
That Dark Hair wants at this time?

Dark Hair:

Desist now, most valiant lord,
For so much do me they fear,
That I would, in my vigilance
Tell thee my decree right here.
Well, I would that thou shouldst know me,
And witness all my strength that be,
So thou'd know whom thou'rt addressing
And who's speaking back to thee.
So that thou would know the courage
That my valiant heart has taught,
It was I who from the Christians
Took two children that caught,
And with all my might I showed thee
And thy countrymen quite fair
That I did not ever harm them
But sustained them with my wares.
They're the two youth which thou hast now
In this land where thou intrude
For which the Comanche hastens
To do battle ever crude.
And I am that selfsame captain,
Who does never budge right there
Be in war or be in peacetime;
Always known as Lord Dark Hair.

Mi fama jamás se quiebra,
Y con fuerte resistencia
Todo el mundo al verme tiembla,
Hoy verás tú mi defensa.

Oso Pardo:
No hay que detenerse un punto
Que como bárbara fiera
Con esta lanza animosa
Le he de cortar la cabeza
A aquel cristiano arrogante.
Al punto y con ligereza
Si alguno se propasare
Sin hacer reminiscencia
De que soy el sin segundo
En brío *y en fortaleza.*
Y si alguno en su arrogancia
Quisiera tocar mis fuerzas,
Lo reto a campal batalla
De cuerpo a cuerpo a la empresa.

Cuerno Verde:
Ea, nobles capitanes,
Aquello más animosos
Aseguren la defensa;
Todos preparen sus armas
Para que embistan furiosos
Estén todos prevenidos
A punto fijo y que sea
Con esfuerzo y con valor.
Advierto que con la unión
Que me tenéis prometida,
Obréis con grande prudencia,
Que por régimo ha tenido
Toda nuestra decendencia,
Así, como el más impío,
He de mostrar mi fierza,
He de postrar y abatirlos,
Que con esta lanza ó vidrio,
Al oso más arrogante,
Al fiero tigre rindo,
Díganlo vuestras personas,
Se testifica y es visto

My great fame remains unbroken,
And with strong resistance tense
Everyone who sees me, trembles,
Now, thou'll witness my defense.

Brown Bear:
There's no need to sue for favor
Since, like a barbarous beast
With my great, blood thirsty lancet
I would lop the head at least
Of that Christian who's so haughty,
Swift and with agility.
If one should transgress the limits;
Not remember who I be,
That I am without an equal
Both in valor *and in might,*
And if *one* be so foolhardy
As to test them, with delight
I would challenge to pitched battle,
Hand to hand we then would fight.

Green Horn:
Attention, noble captains,
See to it with all your strength
That assured be the defense;
That your arms be sharp and ready
So you may furiously charge
Prepare yourselves all at once,
From this very moment hence
Honed with courage and with valor.
I warn you that in this union
That you have surely promised
You will act with great caution,
For by this strict discipline
Have all our people prospered,
Thus as your outrageous leader
I will demonstrate my daring,
And will surely strike them down,
With this obsidian lance
As with the most arrogant bear
Or fierce mountain lion defeat,
Pronounce it well among yourselves,
I've testified to your witness.

"Los comanches" / "the comanches"

Cantos alegres, que ya
Se va a comenzar la guerra
Los pífanos y tambores
Suenen, que la hora se llega
Y si sale el capitán
No se admite más respuesta
Que poner mano a sus armas
Sin que tenga resistencia
Ninguno. No se detengan,
Yo haré que sosiegue la ira,
Y que use de prudencia,
Porque todo en un compás
Sean conjunto; la propuesta
Salga, porque ya es preciso
Un señor Zapato Cuenta.

Zapato Cuenta:
Respondo porque es preciso
Que aunque todas las prospuestas
Que había dado el capitán
Se cumplen con negligencia,
Quiero de conformidad
Que vayamos a la guerra
De la que así se platica
Que lo demás es quimera.
Y que salga un capitán
A destrozar esta fiera
Que horroriza la montaña
Y que hace sufrir las selvas.
El oso más arrogante
Se encoge de mi fierza
El tíguere en las montañas
Huye en la oculta sierra.
¿Quién se opone a mi valor?
¿Quién cautiva mi soberbia?
¿Quién habrá que desbarate
Tanta lealtad que se encierra
En lo altivo de mi pecho?
¿Quién hay que lo desvanezca?

Don José De la Peña:
Yo quebrantaré la furia,
Que soy la más alta peña

Sing gladly, for it is time
For the battle to commence.
Let our fifes and drums ring true
For the hour is fast upon us.
If their captain sounds alarms,
Your response on this occasion:
Place your hand upon your arms.
No uncertainty must ever
Hold you back for just a trace.
I shall calm all wrath and fury,
Putting prudence in its place.
Everything must be well-measured
Together, in harmony too,
As we hear the advisement
Of our lord, Beaded Shoe.

Beaded Shoe:
I must answer as it's needed,
For, although each offer be,
Which our captain did propose now,
Executed carelessly,
As one body move toward battle
Showing full conformity
Focus on the very subject;
For the rest is fantasy.
Let our leaders step forth boldly
To destroy the savage beast
Terrorizing all the mountain
Which, in forests, makes its feast.
Even the most arrogant bear
Shrinks from my vengeful rampage
Even the lion of the mountains
Can be made to hide and flee.
Who opposes my own valor?
Who'll entrap my pride that be?
Who'll undo the bonds that hold back
That unending loyalty
In my breast where it's enclosed?
Who'll divide it verily?

Don José de la Peña:
I shall shatter all his fury,
As my last name indicates.

Soy peñasco en valentía,	I am rock in might and valor,
En bríos y en fortaleza.	Which my strength ne'er moderates.
Esas locas valentías	Your exalted gallantries are
Son criadas de la soberbia	Born and bred of foolish pride.
Que tanto infunde el valor	Spurred and infused is your valor
En vosotros la manteca	From that lard you have inside
Que coméis con tanta gula	Gleaned from buffalo and eaten
Y con ella criáis la fuerza	With such healthy appetite
De vuestras disposiciones	To engender strength within you
Por vuestra industria compuestas.	By your labor made just right.
Nace el sol y luego muere,	The sun rises and it sets then,
Porque nunca cuerpo a cuerpo	And you've never, hand to hand,
Habéis hecho resistencia.	Fought with any force behind you.
En un choque que tuvimos	In a skirmish on this land,
Siendo cien hombres de guerra,	Although we were but a hundred,
Siendo el número crecido	And many more warriors had ye,
De tu bárbara nación,	With all your barbarous nation,
La victoria no fué vuestra.	You could not win victory.
Esa sí que es arrogancia	Yours are naught but boasts outstretching
De historia muy verdadera,	History as it should work,
Que exceden en valentía	Which outstrip by far the prowess
Al alemán y a Turquía.	Of the German and the Turk.
Los doces pares de Francia	Further still from being equal
Lejos quedan de tu tierra;	To those great Twelve Peers of France;
Yo te los pondré delante	I would place them far above you
Que te tiemble la corteza.	Just to watch you squirm and dance.

Don Toribio Ortiz:	***Don Toribio Ortiz:***
Yo soy don Toribio Ortiz	I am Don Toribio Ortiz
Que en todo soy general;	General like all the rest;
Al rey le sirvo a mi costa	At my cost the king I'm serving
Con un esmero especial.	With a special mindfulness.
De las tropas y milicia	Of both troops and the militia
Soy la base principal.	The core principal I be.
Vean si hay entre vosotros	See if there be one among you
Quien me pueda contestar.	Who does not answer to me.
¿Quién de éstos me cabe en suerte?	Which of one thinks he's my equal?
¡Salga luego, que al instante	Let him step forth instantly
Verá si le doy la muerte!	For I'll smite the life force from him!
El Cuerno Verde me dicen	Chief Green Horn, they're telling me
Que es el hombre más valiente;	Is the man of greatest courage;
No tengo para empezar	Please don't start that tale with me.
Con él y toda su gente.	I can't stand him and his people.

"Los comanches"/"the comanches"

De mis tropas arregladas,
Soldados, cabos, sargentos
Ninguno se descomponga.
Esténme todos atentos
Que hoy el sol en su carrera
Ha de ver algún portento,
En caso tan adecuado
Y lance tan oportuno.
Todos rendirán sus vidas
O de éstos no queda ni uno.
Santiago y la Virgen María
Serán nuestro norte y guía
Entre esta gente cobarde.

Don Carlos:
Viendo esas resoluciones,
Conozco bien que concuerdan
Con la mía, y así digo
Que toda nuestra propuesta
Queda ya en una palabra
Concluida de esta manera.
Y así esforzados leones,
Todos al arma, guerreros.
Suénese tambor y guerra
En el nombre de Santiago
Y de la Virgen María
Márchense pronto al campo
Atravesando esa selva,
A tomarles el torreón
A lo mejor que se queda.

(Se revuelven en batalla algunos sol-
dados y algunos indios. Los más de los
indios están tratando con Barriga Duce y
Tabaco. Después de algunos tiros, retroce-
den los españoles. Los indios se llevan los
dos indios que están en el castillo. Después
vuelve Tabaco con bandera de paz.)

Tabaco Chupa Janchi:
Como nobles capitanes
Han mandado disponer
Contra las Cristianas armas,

With my troops they all shall see,
Soldiers, chieftains, sergeants also
All in perfect harmony.
Be alert to what I'm saying:
As the sun shall run its course
All shall see a mighty portent
Of a satisfactory force
And an opportune, apt casting.
All shall render their lives here
Lest there not be one among them.
Saint James and the Virgin pure
Shall be our north star and compass
Among these people of fear.

Don Carlos:
As witness to your great resolve
I see you are of heart and mind
The same as mine, so I do behest
May all our purpose keep in kind
And resume in a single word
Concluding with our very best.
And so my indomitable lions,
To the fight my noble warriors.
Sound the drums of war
In the name of Saint James
And of the Virgin Mary
March forthwith to battle
Crossing this forest,
To take them in the tower
The very best we can.

(Some Indians and soldiers meet in bat-
tle. The other Indians are trading with Sweet
Belly and Tobacco Smoking Janchi. After a
few shots, the Spaniards turn back. The
Indians retake the two Indians that were
held in the fort. Afterwards, Tobacco
Smoking Janchi returns with a white flag.)

Tabaco Chupa Janchi:
All of you as noble chieftains
Have thus ordered things put straight
All against the Christian armour.

Ahora os hago saber
Que también soy capitán
Y falta mi parecer.
Mi valor es sin segundo
Porque ninguno me iguala;
Tiembla de pavor el mundo
Sólo de ver mi embajada
Yo a Taos fuí de embajador
A solicitar la paz,
Y ninguno me siguió
Porque no se halló capaz.
Se me concedió al momento,
En virtud de mi valor.
Porque toda la nobleza
Reina en el pecho español,
Y así mis armas están
Rendidas por la ocasión
No quiero ser enemigo,
Ya no quiero ser traidor.
Gozar quiero del empleo
Que tengo de embajador.
Suene el pífano y tambor
Y apercíbase la guerra
Con esfuerzo y con valor,
Y adquirir algún honor,
Que yo me voy a avisar
Al Capitán español.

(Se acerca al castillo de los españoles)

Paraos, valeroso martir,
Detente, insigne señor;
Verás cómo Cuerno Verde,
El y toda su nación
Han levantado bandera
En contra del español.
Yo de Napeiste he venido
Sólo a traerte esta razón
Sabrás cómo el Oso Pardo,
Y también Cabeza Negra,
Han compuesto esta campana
Para darte cruda guerra,
Y así vete apreviniendo,
Que yo me voy a mi tierra.

And now I am here to state
That I too am such a leader,
With no equal among peers.
For my valor knows no second,
Since no one can match my years;
The whole world does quake in terror
To behold my embassy.
I, to Taos, was emissary,
Sued for peace and as you see.
Not a single one dared follow
For they lacked my manliness.
All I sought for was then given
In attest of my success.
All nobility does truly
Reign within the Spanish breast,
And so I'll lay down my weapons
And surrender like the rest.
I don't want to be a rival,
Nor a traitor want to be.
I just want to relish ever
My own proper embassy.
Sound the fife, begin the drumbeat
And the war prepare to start
With great force and full of valor,
Winning honor in your heart.
I shall go and bring a message
To the Spanish Captain there.

(He approaches the Spanish fortress.)

Stand still, oh most worthy martyr!
Halt, commendable lord fair!
You shall hear what Green Horn's doing,
He, and all his men, of course.
They have raised the battle standard
All against the Spanish force.
From the great Arkansan River
I've come but to tell you this.
You shall learn how Brown Bear started
With Dark Hair, that friend of his,
A campaign against all Spaniards
To do battle close at hand,
So you must now start preparing,
I'm returning to my land.

"Los comanches"/"the comanches"

221

Don Carlos:

Anda y lleva la contesta
De que yo estoy preparado,
Y que acepto la propuesta
Como ellos me la han enviado.
Si a mis indios se han llevado,
Pronto me pondré vengar.
Se los volveré a quitar
O acabaré su nación,
Pues mi ambición es pelear
Desde el norte al sentirrón. [sic]

*(Se va el indio, y el capitán se dirige a
los suyos)*

Veréis nuestro parecer
Y conozco la contesta
Que le he dado por los míos,
Aceptando la propuesta
Que doy yo en una palabra.
Concluida de esta manera
De los leales corazones
Que siendo ilustre campeón
Nuestro esforzado valor
El hablar de esta manera.
¡Ea, nobles capitanes,
Obedientes a la grey!
Por Dios y por nuestra patria
Y la corona del rey,
Porque confío en María
Y en el patriarca José,
Que nos han de dar victoria
Piedad concesión divina,
Consebida sin pecado;
Tan limpia y de gracia llena.
El arcángel San Gabriel
De aquellas tropas exelsas.
Preciso es tocar el arma,
Marche el campo a la batalla
Y todo el campo aprevenga.
Yo haré que se desborone
La más elevada Elena.
Vamos a romper el cerco

Don Carlos:

Go back now and take this message
That I am fully-prepared
To accept their latest challenge
Such as they have sent me, scared.
If they're swayed my other Indians,
I shall quickly this avenge.
I shall win them back or finish
With their nation in revenge.
My ambition is for battle
From the north come sweeping down.

*(The Indian leaves and the Captain
addresses his men.)*

Our own state of things you'll witness
And my answer of renown
Which, on your behalf I've given,
By accepting the request
Wrapped up in a word I sent it.
Ending thus, I may attest
From your loyal heart it echoes
The illustrious champion who
Is but our own valiant courage
Speaking in this way for you.
Let us see now, noble captains,
Servile to our own homestead!
For our God and for our country
And the crown on our king's head,
For I put my trust in Mary
And in Joseph, master mine,
That they both will grant us victory.
Mercy, Conception divine.
Thou, conceived without a blemish;
Pure and clean and full of grace.
The archangel, blessed Gabriel
Leads the troops in Heaven's place,
We must put our hand to blade now.
We must take the battlefield
And prepare the field completely
Wearing down and letting yield
Even the resplendent Helen.
Let us break the fence at will

Y hacer que muera esta fiera.
A destruirlos, que son pocos,
Y a quebrantar su cabeza.
El apóstol Santiago
Y concepción de María
Contra esta gente cobarde
Me sirva de norte y guía.

(Toca el clarin y dan vuelta la castillo)

Cuerno Verde:
(A los suyos)

Ya vienen apercibidos,
Ya el encuentro me da muestra
De este indigno capitán
Que desahogar no me deja.

(Toca el tambor.)

Que suenen el instrumento
Para comenzar la guerra.
Genízaros valerosos
Hoy vuestro valor se muestra;
Canten para dar principio
Que no es la primera vez
Que con esta gente necia
Levantaré mis banderas.
Acometed valerosos,
Y quebrantad su soberbia,
Porque junto en un compás
Don Carlos en mi presencia.

(Toca el clarín Guerra Fuerte)

Capitán:
Mueren indios a mis manos,
Y cese vuestra osadía.
¡Seguir valientes paisanos,
Que Dios sea vuestra guía!

(Tiros)

Hastening the beast's own downfall.
By destroying those few still,
Splitting all their heads wide open
Saint James the apostle blessed
And Mary's Conception too
Serve as north star and as compass
'Gainst this faint and craven crew.

(The trumpet blasts and they return to the fort . . .)

Green Horn:
(Addressing his men)

They are coming wholly ready.
It bespeaks much, you can bet
For this vile, unworthy captain
Who won't let me rest just yet.

(He beats the drum.)

Sound the instrument of battle
To begin the war, I say!
My valiant janissaries
Valor shines from you today.
Sing the war chant to begin now
Since this be not the first time
That against a foolish people
I have raised my standard high.
Hasten all ye full of valor
And break down their baseless pride,
That I may gather Don Carlos
In one fell sweep to my side.

(The trumpet sounds the Attack.)

Captain:
Death to Indians at my hands now,
Ceasing all their valiantry.
Push on, countrymen of courage,
May God be a guide to thee!

(Shots)

"Los comanches"/"the comanches"

Barriga Duce:

Que mueran, que para mí
Todos los despojos quedan.
Tiendas, antas, y conchelles
Para que mis hijos duerman.
Y la carne, a mi mujer
He de hacer que me la cueza
Y me la guise con chile
Que es una comida buena.
¡Apriétenles compañeros!
Que de eso mi alma se alegra.
Hemos de llegar al trono
Donde está mi panadera.
Yo entraré por esta puerta,
No me ofenda una saeta
Que esto no gusta a mi cuerpo.
Vaya yo de animador
De esa prenda que me cuesta
Lo he de apropiar para mí,
Y lo he de hacer hasta que muera,
Pues me hallaba yo en la selva
Encima de la montaña
Puesto en la contigencia
De escapar o de pagarla.
¿No están dispuestos lo mismo
Los soldados y la caja?
¿No estaban libres las Pecas?
¿Por qué ahora estan amarradas?
No podemos estar zafos
Si venimos a buscarlos.
No saben que soy el dulce
La cajeta, la ensalada,
L'azúcar y el piloncillo
Los anices y la gracia.
Porque en todas mis funciones
Siempre se halla mi valor
Y mi nobleza en las armas.
Tengo siempre en mi cintura
Mi honda muy bien fajada,
Y si alguno me replica
Le convenceré con pruebas.
Piensan que el báculo mío
Y mi honda no valen nada.

Sweet Belly:

Let them all die, for to me then
All the spoils will then stay!
Store rooms, skins and bedrolls also
For my kids to sleep away.
And the meat, my wife, I'd ask her
To prepare it nice for me,
And to season it with chile
As a dish most heavenly.
Push on forward, dear companions,
For it warms my heart and soul!
We shall soon reach the great throne room
Where my baker wife doth rule.
I shall enter through that doorway,
Lest an arrow pierce me clean.
That is not good for my body.
I'll go vitalize the scene
Of that gem that costs me dearly.
I'll usurp it all for me,
And I'd do so 'til I perish.
As when in woods totally
I was lost upon the mountain
At great peril of my life
Having to escape or forfeit.
Are you not in that same strife,
Treasure box and all you soldiers?
Were not the Pecas, once free?
Why then, are their hands tied now?
We are not exempt, you see
If we still must come to seek them.
Don't you know that I'm the sweet,
Carameled milk, and tasty salad,
Sugar coned and sugar treat,
Tasty and gracious as the anise.
For in all I ever do,
You will always find my valor
And my honor in arms too.
Always at my waist I carry
My own sling securely tied.
And if one should argue with me
I'd convince his foolish pride.
Do you think my staff and slingshot
Really do not matter more?

¿Con qué vencí al pastorcillo
Y al moro que levantaba
Hasta el cielo su grandeza
De la gloria que llamaba?
Pues callo, porque ya es tiempo
De comenzar la batalla.
¡Apriéntenles compañeros!
¡Viva el señor don Carlos
Y don José de la Peña!
Y vivan los mayordomos
Que toda su alma le entriegan
A la santísima Virgen
Que es madre de gracia llena,
Que como prenda estimada
Es la que nos da valor.
¡Santiago! Jesús nos valga,
Ahora si voy a mi tierra
A ver mi Catalina,
Y a una gallina con pollos
Que dejé cuando me vine.
Apriéntenles, compañeros
Haciendo danzas y loas
Comanches y maricuetas
Al modo que se permite
La limitada rudeza.
¡Albricias, que se nos van!
Huyen y nínguno queda
El guarapé en el comanche
Cuerno Verde ya se va.

(Suena el clarín de guerra. Sale corriendo Barriga Duce a donde están las Pecas, y se las trae. Los indios salen huyendo con los españoles tras de ellos.)

Capitán:
Ya mi vista no te pierde,
Indio traidor, inhumano.
Serás muerto por mis manos;
¡Muera, muera Cuerno Verde!

(Le tiran y cae Cuerno Verde. Siguen a los demás y los traen prisioneros.)

With what do you think I vanquished
The vile shepherd and the Moor
Who would boast of his own greatness
Hammering at Heaven's door?
Well, for now I'll stop my yapping
For it's time to start the war.
Push on forward, bold companions!
Long live Don Carlos and too,
Long live José de la Peña,
And the mayordomos who
Dedicate their souls most surely
To the Virgin up above
Who is Mother full of graces
And the jewel of such love,
Who in us infuses valor.
Saint James! Jesus be right there
As I go back to my home to
See my Catalina fair
And an old hen with her chickens
Left there brooding when I came.
Push on forward, bold companions
Doing dance and songs of praise,
Comanches and somersaults
Try to do as best you can
With your churlishness and limits.
Good news, captains, off they ran!
All flee and not one is staying
Guarapé and Comanche,
And Green Horn is also leaving.

(The war trumpet sounds. Sweet Belly runs out to where Las Pecas are and returns with them. The Indians run off with the Spaniards behind them.)

Captain:
You cannot hide from my vision,
Traitorous Indian inhumane.
By my own hand you shall perish;
Death to Green Horn and his name!

(They shoot and Green Horn falls. They pursue the others and return with their prisoners.)

"Los comanches" / "the comanches"

Barriga Duce:

Muelan, muelan compañeros
¿Por qué se me habían ido?
Sigan, buenos panaderos
Que yo los dos pagos pido,
Para ustedes el chimal
Y para mí los guayabes.
Las semillas y el nopal,
La panocha y estos reales;
Tambien el chile y cebolla
Con toditas sdtas heirbas
Que consiéndolas en una olla
Haremos buenas conservas.
Anden ustedes mostrencos
Lloren a su capitán.
Si no tienen sentimientos
A golpes han de llorar.

(Les pega y lloran, y le bailan cabellera.)

Capitán:

Venid hermosa bandera,
Rota por cruda metralla.
Tú serás en la batalla
Mi constante compañera.

(Toca el clarín Retirado.)

Fin.

Sweet Belly:

Lash them, lash them, brave companions,
Because they had fled from me.
Follow ever, dear bread bakers
For I crave both debts form thee.
You shall have your shield most trusty
I shall have my sweet bread,
Pumpkin seeds and cactus candy,
And that sprouted flour treat;
Money, chile and sweet onions
Laced with aromatic herbs,
Marinated in a skillet
We shall make some fine preserves.
Run away, you sorry numskulls.
To your captain make your wail.
If you have no real feelings,
Knock your heads to no avail.

(He whips them and they cry and dance.)

Captain:

Come to me, my fairest banner,
Riddled crudely by grape-shot.
Ever you shall be in battle
My companion, constant sought.

(The trumpet sounds the Retreat.)

The End.

APPENDIX 2

Los Comanches Nativity Play

These are the complete texts of "Comanches" music sung on Víspera de los Reyes (Epiphany Eve), January 5, 1997, at Ida Salazar Segura's home in Los Griegos, NM. Vangie Salazar Armijo credits Doña Beneranda Romero and Don Evaristo Gonzales with initiating the Comanches tradition in San Mateo. They passed it down to her uncle and aunt, Delfinio and Senaida Salazar. In western New Mexico, many people devoted to the Santo Niño de Atocha have made the pilgrimage to Zuni Pueblo, where a local family has a very old image of the saint. Amidst the feasting and celebration of the Epiphany, the Comanche dance is set between two recitations of the rosary, with special prayers for the recently departed in the middle of the dance (Salazar Armijo 2003). Contextual features are indicated between [brackets].

Los Comanches de San Mateo   **The Comanches of San Mateo**

(Vangie Salazar Armijo, Rafaelita Salazar Baca, Eufemia Salazar Trujillo, Ida Salazar Segura, friends and families.)

[At about 8 P.M., after feasting and the first rosary, a group of "Comanches" knocks at the door outside and asks permission to enter the house.]

Ábranse esas puertas	*Open those doors*
esta noche de enero.	*on this January night.*
Ábranse esas puertas	*Open those doors*
esta noche de enero.	*on this January night.*
Y demos paso de entrada	*And with this step let us enter*
semos buenos caballeros.	*let us be fine and gentle.*
Y demos paso de entrada	*And with this step let us enter*
semos buenos caballeros.	*we are good horsemen.*

Ena jeyó, ena jeyó,
ena, je ayne, ayne yo.

Ena heyo, ena heyo,
ena, he aynay, aynay, yo.

[The people inside the house reluctantly grant permission for the Comanches to enter, if they promise to be faithful.]

Pasen, pasen, comanches,
y díganme cuántos son.
Pasen, pasen, comanches,
y díganme cuántos son.

Come in, come in, Comanches,
and tell me how many you are.
Come in, come in, Comanches,
and tell me how many you are.

Pasen a bailarle al Niño
si vienen con devoción.
Pasen a bailarle al Niño
si vienen con devoción.

Come in to dance for the Child
if you come with devotion.
Come in to dance for the Child
If you come with devotion.

[The Comanches line up in front of the Christmas altar, guarded on each side by vigilant "padrinos," or godparents. They dance back and forth and in circles, as they fall in love with the Santo Niño.]

Aquí estamos los Comanches,
bailando de dos en dos.
Aquí estamos los Comanches,
bailando de dos en dos.

Here we are the Comanches,
dancing two by two.
Here we are the Comanches,
dancing two by two.

A todita esta gente
buenas noches les dé Dios.
A todita esta gente
buenas noches les dé Dios.

To all of these people
may God give them a good night.
To all of these people
may God give them a good night.

De lejos tierras venemos,
Comanches de dos en dos.
De lejos tierras venemos,
Comanches de dos en dos.

From far lands we come,
Comanches two by two.
From far lands we come,
Comanches two by two.

A todita esta gente
buenas noches les dé Dios.
A todita esta gente
buenas noches les dé Dios.

To all of these people
may God give them a good night.
To all of these people
may God give them a good night.

Ena jeyó, ena jeyó,
ena, je ayne, ayne yo.

Ena heyo, ena heyo,
ena, he aynay, aynay, yo.

Aquí estamos en su altar
pa' que no estén con deseos.
Semos pobres Comanchitos
de la plaza de San Mateo.
Semos pobres Comanchitos
de la plaza de San Mateo.

Ena jeyó, ena jeyó,
ena, je ayne, ayne yo.

Con rodillas en tierra
diciendo lo que a Dios le valga.
La Virgen sea mi madrina
y el santo ángel de mi guardia.
La Virgen sea mi madrina
y el santo ángel de mi guardia.

Ena jeyó, ena jeyó,
ena, je ayne, ayne yo.

Santo Niñito de Atocha,
San José y también María,
gusto tenemos de verte
y estar en tu compañía.
Gusto tenemos de verte
y estar en tu compañía.

Cuando me robé al Niñito
yo le pedí por mis hijitos,
y yo le prometí
que lo iba a velar,
Y yo le prometí
que lo iba a velar.

Ena jeyó, ena jeyó,
ena, je ayne, ayne yo.

Desde San Mateo he venido
pa' apreciar este lugar.
Denme razón del Niñito
que le prometí bailar.
Denme razón del Niñito
que le prometí bailar.

Here we are at your altar
so that you be without want.
We are poor little Comanches
from the town of San Mateo.
We are poor little Comanches
from the town of San Mateo.

Ena heyo, ena heyo,
ena, he aynay, aynay, yo.

With knees upon the earth
telling what is pleasing to God.
May the Virgin be my godmother
and my holy guardian angel.
May the Virgin be my godmother
and my holy guardian angel.

Ena heyo, ena heyo,
ena, he aynay, aynay, yo.

Holy Child of Atocha,
Saint Joseph and also Mary,
we are joyous to see you
and be in your company.
We are joyous to see you
and be in your company.

When I stole the little Child
I implored him for my children,
and I promised him
that I would hold his vigil.
And I promised him
that I would hold his vigil.

Ena heyo, ena heyo,
ena, he aynay, aynay, yo.

From San Mateo I have come
to appreciate this place.
Inform me of the Child
since I promised him a dance.
Tell me about the Child
since I promised him a dance.

Ena jeyó, ena jeyó,
ena, je ayne, ayne yo.

Semos pobres Comanchitos,
nos falta la educación,
pero el Niño agradece
siendo de fe y corazón,
Pero el Niño agradece
siendo de fe y corazón.

Ena jeyó, ena jeyó,
ena, je ayne, ayne yo.

Del cielo viene bajando
un arco de flores,
y el medio del arco viene
mi Señor de los Dolores.
Y el medio del arco viene
mi Señor de los Dolores.

Ena jeyó, ena jeyó,
ena, je ayne, ayne yo.

Yo le canto a este Niñito
porque es Niño de a virtud
a toditos los enfermos
Dios les preste su salud.
A toditos los enfermos
Dios les preste su salud.

Ena jeyó, ena jeyó,
ena, je ayne, ayne yo.

Al Santo Niño le pido
porque es Niño de a virtud
que le preste a mi hijita
que le preste su salud.
Que le preste a mi hijita
que le preste su salud.

Ena jeyó, ena jeyó,
ena, je ayne, ayne yo.

Ena heyo, ena heyo,
ena, he aynay, aynay, yo.

We are poor little Comanches,
with few manners,
but the Child is grateful for
we come with faith and heart.
But the child is grateful, for
We come with faith and heart.

Ena heyo, ena heyo,
ena, he aynay, aynay, yo.

From heaven comes down
an arch with flowers
and in the middle of the arch
comes my Lord of Sorrows.
And in the middle of the arch
comes my Lord of Sorrows.

Ena heyo, ena heyo,
ena, he aynay, aynay, yo.

I sing to this little Child
for he is a Child of virtue,
to all of the sick
may God grant them their health.
To all of the sick
may God grant them their health.

Ena heyo, ena heyo,
ena, he aynay, aynay, yo.

I ask of the Holy Child
because he is a Child of virtue
that he grant to my daughter
that he grant her her health.
That he grant to my daughter
that he grant her her health.

Ena heyo, ena heyo,
ena, he aynay, aynay, yo.

¡Qué plumaje, pluma fina,
plumaje de pavorreal!
¡Qué plumaje, pluma fina,
plumaje de pavorreal!

De lejos tierras venemos,
te venemos a bailar.
De lejos tierras venemos,
te venemos a bailar.

Ena jeyó, ena jeyó,
ena, je ayne, ayne yo.

En el portal de Belén
hay estrella, sol y luna,
la Virgen y San José
y el Niño que está en la cuna,
La Virgen y San José
y el Niño que está en la cuna.

Ena jeyó, ena jeyó,
ena, je ayne, ayne yo.

Del cielo viene bajando
un arco lleno de flores,
en medio del arco viene
mi Señor de los Dolores.
En medio del arco viene
mi Señor de los Dolores.

Ena jeyó, ena jeyó,
ena, je ayne, ayne yo.

'Ora sí, Niño chiquito,
'ora sí, Niño divino,
mientras Dios me preste vida,
nunca te echaré en olvido.
Mientras Dios me preste vida,
nunca te echaré en el olvido.

Ena jeyó, ena jeyó,
ena, je ayne, ayne yo.

What plumage, fine feathers,
plumage of the peacock!
What plumage, fine feathers,
plumage of the peacock!

From faraway lands we come,
we come to dance for you.
From faraway lands we come,
we come to dance for you.

Ena heyo, ena heyo,
ena, he aynay, aynay, yo.

In the portal of Bethlehem
are the star, the sun and moon,
the Virgin and Saint Joseph
and the Child in the cradle.
The Virgin and Saint Joseph
and the Child in the cradle.

Ena heyo, ena heyo,
ena, he aynay, aynay, yo.

From heaven is descending
an arch full of flowers,
in the middle of the arch
my Lord of Sorrows.
In the middle of the arch
my Lord of Sorrows.

Ena heyo, ena heyo,
ena, he aynay, aynay, yo.

Now it is certain, little Child,
now it is certain, divine Child,
as long as God gives me life,
I will never forget you.
As long as God gives me life,
I will never forget you.

Ena heyo, ena heyo,
ena, he aynay, aynay, yo.

Los comanches nativity play

Cuando vine yo a bailar	When I came to dance
pues no estaba mucho frío,	it was not very cold,
y le pedí al Santo Niño	and I prayed to the Holy Child
por el ánima de Isabel Segura.	for the soul of Isabel Segura.
Yo le pedí al Santo Niño	I prayed to the Holy Child
por el ánima de Isabel Segura.	for the soul of Isabel Segura.
Ena jeyó, ena jeyó,	Ena heyo, ena heyo,
ena, je ayne, ayne yo.	ena, he aynay, aynay, yo.
Ya toditos te adoraron,	Now all have worshiped you,
todos te ofrecen un don.	all offer you a gift.
Ya toditos te adoraron,	Now all have worshiped you,
todos te ofrecen un don.	all offer you a gift.
Yo soy pobre y nada tengo	I am poor and have nothing
te ofrezco mi corazón.	I offer you my heart.
Yo soy pobre y nada tengo	I am poor and have nothing
te ofrezco mi corazón.	I offer you my heart.
Ena jeyó, ena jeyó,	Ena heyo, ena heyo,
ena, je ayne, ayne yo.	ena, he aynay, aynay, yo.
Cuando vine yo a bailar	When I came to dance
pues estaba mucho frío.	well it was very cold.
Cuando vine yo a bailar	When I came to dance
pues estaba mucho frío.	well it was very cold.
Rezaremos un sudario	We will pray the sudario
también pa' Dennis Trujillo.	also for Dennis Trujillo.
Rezaremos un sudario	We will pray the sudario
también pa' Dennis Trujillo.	also for Dennis Trujillo.
Ena jeyó, ena jeyó,	Ena heyo, ena heyo,
ena, je ayne, ayne yo.	ena, he aynay, aynay, yo.

[At this point, the singing and dancing pause for the solemn prayer for the dead, especially the most recently departed.]

Sudario	**Shroud Prayer**
Por el ánima de Isabel	For the souls of Isabel
y Dennis Trujillo.	and Dennis Trujillo.
Señor, Dios que nos	Lord, God who left us

dejastes la señal de tu
divina pasión y muerte,
la sábana santa,
tu cuerpo muerto
tu cuerpo santísimo,
cuando por José
fuistes bajado de la cruz.
Concédenos, Señor, oh
piadosísimo Señor y Salvador
que por muerte
y sepultura santa
te has llevado las ánimas
de Dennis Trujillo
e Isabel Segura
a descansar en la
gloria de la resurrección,
donde su Señor vive
con Dios padre en unidad
Dios por todos los siglos
de los siglos santos.
Amen.

the sign of thy divine
passion and death,
the holy shroud,
your lifeless body
your holiest body,
when by Joseph thou wert
lowered from the cross.
Grant us, Lord, oh most
compassionate Lord and savior
that through death
and holy burial
you have taken the souls
of Dennis Trujillo
and Isabel Segura
to rest in the glory
of the resurrection,
where their Lord lives with
God the Father in unity
God for all the centuries
of the blessed centuries.
Amen.

[Singing and dancing then resume with full intensity.]

A mí no me lleva el río
por más crecido que vaya,
yo sí me llevo al Niño
con una buena bailada.
Yo sí me llevo al Niño
con una buena bailada.

The river will not take me away
as high as it may be,
I will take the Child with me
with a good dance.
I will take the Child with me
with a good dance.

Ena jeyó, ena jeyó,
ena, je ayne, ayne yo.

Ena heyo, ena heyo,
ena, he aynay, aynay, yo.

Santo Niñito divino,
te pido de corazón,
con tus benditas manitas
échanos tu bendición.
Con tus benditas manitas
échanos tu bendición.

Divine Holy Child,
I ask you with all my heart,
with your holy little hands
give us your blessing.
With your holy little hands
give us your blessing.

Ena jeyó, ena jeyó,
ena, je ayne, ayne yo.

Ena heyo, ena heyo,
ena, he aynay, aynay, yo.

LOS COMANCHES NATIVITY PLAY

Óigame usted, doña Delia,
aquí le voy a decir,
que se pare a un ladito
que el Niño quiere bailar.
Que se pare a un ladito
que el Niño quiere bailar.

Hear me, Doña Delia,
here I will tell you,
to stand to one side
for the Child wants to dance.
Stand to one side
for the Child wants to dance.

Ena jeyó, ena jeyó,
ena, je ayne, ayne yo.

Ena heyo, ena heyo,
ena, he aynay, aynay, yo.

Óigame usted, doña Mary,
no se vaya a perdonar,
el Niño también quiere
que usted se venga a bailar.
El Niño también quiere
que usted se pare a bailar.

Hear me, doña Mary,
don't forgive yourself,
the Child also wants
for you to come and dance.
The Child also wants
for you to get up and dance.

Ena jeyó, ena jeyó,
ena, je ayne, ayne yo.

Ena heyo, ena heyo,
ena, he aynay, aynay, yo.

Se retiran los Comanches
ya con fe y con devoción,
San José y también María
nos echen su bendición.
San José y también María
nos echen su bendición.

The Comanches are leaving
with faith and devotion,
may Saint Joseph and also Mary
give us their blessing.
May Saint Joseph and also Mary
give us their blessing.

Soy de la Tierra Plateada   I Am from the Silvery Land

(Rafaelita Salazar Baca, Eufemia Salazar Trujillo, Vangie Salazar Armijo, and Ida Salazar Segura, friends and families.)

[The Comanches continue their loving dance before the altar of the Santo Niño, distracting the padrinos for the coming abduction.]

Soy de la tierra plateada,
soy de la tierra plateada,
donde está pintado el león,
donde está pintado el león.
También las inditas dicen,
también las inditas dicen,
—San Luis de mi corazón,
—San Luis de mi corazón.

I am from the silvery land,
I am from the silvery land,
where the lion is painted,
where the lion is painted.
The Indian girls also say,
the Indian girls also say,
—Saint Aloysius of my devotion,
—Saint Aloysius of my devotion.

Indita, indita, indita,
indita, indita, indita,
indita de Mogollón,
indita de Mogollón,
También las inditas dicen,
también las inditas dicen,
—San Luis de mi corazón,
—San Luis de mi corazón

Se robaron la cautiva,
se robaron la cautiva,
de la mesa del altar,
de la mesa del altar.

Caballo de navajó,
caballo de navajó,
todo se le va en correr,
todo se le va en correr.

Se robaron la cautiva,
se robaron la cautiva.
¿Cuándo la volveré a ver,
cuándo la volveré a ver?

Hermanita de mi vida,
hermanita de mi vida,
te pasaron por la lumbre,
te pasaron por la lumbre.

Esas manos navajoses,
esas manos navajoses.
¿Por qué venían alzados,
por qué venían alzados?
Indita, yo te daré,
indita, yo te daré
corales pa' tu garganta,
corales pa' tu garganta.

Una banda colorada,
una banda colorada,
pa' que te afajes tu manta,
pa' que te afajes tu manta,
y vayas a tu bailada,
y vayas a tu bailada,

Little Indian girl, little girl,
little Indian girl, little girl,
little Indian girl from Mogollón,
little Indian girl from Mogollón.
The Indian girls also say,
the Indian girls also say,
—Saint Aloysius of my heart,
—Saint Aloysius of my heart.

They have stolen the captive,
they have stolen the captive,
from the table of the altar,
from the table of the altar.

Horse of the Navajos,
horse of the Navajos,
all is spent in running,
all is spent in running.

They have stolen the captive,
they have stolen the captive.
When will I see her again,
when will I see her again.

Little sister of my life,
little sister of my life,
they passed you through the fire,
they passed you through the fire.

Those Navajo hands,
those Navajo hands.
Why have they risen up,
why have they risen up.
Little Indian girl, I will give you,
little Indian girl, I will give you,
corals for your throat,
corals for your throat.

A red sash,
a red sash,
for you to tie your shawl,
for you to tie your shawl,
and go to your dance,
and go to your dance.

Hermanitos comanchitos,
pues a mí me habían robado,
pues a mí me habían robado,
estas manos navajoses
estas manos navajoses,
¿por qué venían alzados?
¿por qué venían alzados?

Hermanita de mi vida,
hermanita de mi vida,
no me quisiera acordar,
no me quisiera acordar,
se llevaron la cautiva,
se llevaron la cautiva,
de la mesa del altar,
de la mesa del altar.

ululación

Little Comanche brothers and sisters,
well they had taken me captive,
well they had taken me captive,
these Navajo hands
these Navajo hands,
why had they been raised up?
why had they been raised up?

Little sister of my life,
little sister of my life,
I would prefer not to remember,
I would prefer not to remember,
they took the captive,
they took the captive,
from the table of the altar,
from the table of the altar.

ululation

APPENDIX 3

Hermanitos Comanchitos

CD PLAYLIST AND NOTES

The musical transcriptions to be found throughout the text are a first tentative step towards understanding the contours and musical complexities of a mestizo tradition. What is offered are basic melodic outlines with a provisional reference to tempos. Although there is an ongoing debate over the value of such an exercise, especially given the availability of recordings, many ethnomusicologists continue to use transcription as a form of interpretation.

All of the examples of "Comanche" music collected here are learned and taught orally in cultural settings in which musical notation does not figure in the chain of transmission. Based as they are on European traditions, the protocols of musical transcription are often inadequate to capture the subtleties of other musics. But sure enough, in the Indo-Hispano hybrid, the Hispano elements such as conventional melodies and regular tempos do emerge more clearly in transcription.

Fortunately, what is most difficult to analyze in Indo-Hispano music is easily intuited in simply listening to it. One cultural tradition is musically evoking and referencing another. Tewa "Comanche" songs may contain Numunuh words, but in the end they are still Tewa songs. Likewise, Hispano "Comanche" songs with Spanish words and vocable choruses reference the Native by transmogrifying the European.

This anthology is offered as a musical feast which will require the ear of an ethnomusicologist to fully decipher and appraise. However all listeners are invited to visit and contemplate this inter-cultural contact zone, one of the most complex in North America.

1. *Santa Fe Americana*—Kwítara (Tewa Comanche) Song—Andy García and Vinton Lonnie, San Juan Pueblo. Often sung for the Tewa Comanche Dances. The Spanish lyrics and native vocables honor the "Anglo" women from Santa Fe who faithfully attend the San Juan feast day celebrations. Only the introduction is transcribed. (Loeffler Archive)

2. *La Jeyana*—Rosanna Otero, San Acacio, NM. Sung for the San Luis Gonzaga dances of San Acacio. Although there are many more lyrics sung for San Luis, the most

poignant for this young singer is the verse "Dicen que las golondrinas de un volido pasan el mar" (They say the swallows cross the ocean in one flight), a symbolic reference to the Iberian diaspora. In this contemporary performance the traditional melody is considerably modernized.

3. *El Llanero*—Noberto Ledoux, Ranchos de Taos. A traveling or "plainsman" song by the finest of the new generation of singers of Los Comanches de la Serna.

4. *Arengas para Cuerno Verde*—Abrán Casías, Francisco Gonzales, Jerry Padilla, Ranchos de Taos. Chief Cuerno Verde's famous opening speech or harangue from Los Comanches de Castillo is recited with other verses of praise for the famous war chief.

5. *Danza Guerrera*—Los Comanches de la Serna (which include Francisco and Nelson Gonzales, Abrán Casías, Nobert Ledoux, and Jerry Padilla), Ranchos de Taos. A fast war dance song.

6. *El Espantao*—Los Comanches de la Serna, Ranchos de Taos . "The Frightened One" battle dance song and shield dance. In combat, as much is accomplished by surprise and intimidation as by actual fighting.

7. *La Rueda*—Francisco Gonzales, Ranchos de Taos. This song is a signal for the Hispano Comanche dancers to take their captives into the circle of honor.

8. *La Cautiva Marcelina*—Virginia Bernal, Ratón. Often sung at the Comanches Nativity play on Christmas Eve and Epiphany Eve. This captive's lament is heard as far south as Coahuila, Mexico, where it is sung at Matachines dances. (Loeffler Archive)

9. *El Cautivo*—Francisco Gonzales, Ranchos de Taos. The mournful song of the captives sung in camp or at the Rescates or slave markets, held in Taos in the late eighteenth century.

10. *Arrullo Comanche*—Leota Frizzell, Santa Rosa. Lullaby in the tragic mode about Comanches trading their children for sugar and coffee. Singer was raised on a ranch in east central New Mexico.

11. *El Venado y la Venada*—Floyd Trujillo, Abiquiú. An almost identical lullaby about deer trading their children for food. "Deer" is a reference to natives in this genízaro village populated by natives from several cultural groups.

12. *El Águila*—Comanches de la Serna, Ranchos de Taos. The Hispano Comanche eagle dance song.

13. *El Torito*—Comanches de la Serna, Ranchos de Taos. The bull or buffalo dance song.

14. *La Tortuga*—Comanches de la Serna, Ranchos de Taos. The turtle dance song.

15. *Hermanito Comanchito*—Edwin Berry, Tomé. Lullaby about yearly visits of Comanches at harvest time and the attempt to interest them in agriculture and the peaceful life. (Loeffler Archive).

16. *El Nanillé*—Floyd Trujillo, Abiquiú. Dance honoring the return of the captive children, sung at the Santo Tomás feast day in late November.

17. *Comanches Guadalupanos*—Priscilla and Eduardo Chávez and friends, Los Ranchos de Alburquerque. Sung and danced in honor of the Virgen de Guadalupe on December 12.

18. *Los Comanches de San Mateo*—Rafaelita Salazar Baca, Eufemia Salazar Trujillo, Vangie Salazar Armijo, and Ida Salazar Segura, friends and families, San Mateo, Bernalillo and Albuquerque. Sung and danced for the Santo Niño in the San Mateo Comanches Nativity Play (see Appendix II).

19. *Los Comanchitos de Bernalillo*—Enrique Lamadrid, Brenda Romero, Jesús Armando Martínez, Alburquerque. Sung and danced for the Santo Niño as part of Las Posadas and on Christmas Eve in Bernalillo. (Loeffler Archive)

20. *Soy de la Sierra Plateada*—Rafaelita Salazar Baca, Eufemia Salazar Trujillo, Vangie Salazar Armijo, and Ida Salazar Segura, friends and families, San Mateo, Bernalillo and Albuquerque. Sung and danced for the Santo Niño in the San Mateo Nativity Play (see Appendix II).

21. *Si Fueras pa'Navajó*—David Frésquez (age 67) Ranchos de Taos (Robb Archive). Song from Taos Hispano Comanche celebrations, recorded in 1950 by John D. Robb as "Navajo Dance Song." Hispano Comanche music draws from many musical sources, including Navajo, Kiowa, and Pueblo. For musical transcription, see Robb 1980: 459-60).

Si fueras pa' Navajó	*If You Go to Navajo*
1 Jeyá, je weya, je yaja,	Heya, he weya, he yaha,
ena jeyana jeya ja.	ena heyana heya ha.
Si fueras pa' Navajó pa,	If you go to Navajoland,
si fueras pa' Navajó o.	if you go to Navajo, yes.
Si fueras pa' Navajó pa,	If you go to Navajoland,
lleva mortaja segura pa.	take your shroud for sure.
Porque la muerte de allá pa,	Because death over there,
es firme y no tiene duda.	is firm and without doubt.
Navajó, allá no.	Navajo, over there no.
Ena jeyana ja eya, eeeeya.	Ena heyana ha eya, eeeeya.

22. *Coplas Comanches*—Comanches de la Serna, Ranchos de Taos. Historical, satirical, and burlesque Comanche verses, which includes a late twentieth century rendition of the above Navajo song.

23. *El Paseado*—Comanches de la Serna, Ranchos de Taos. The passer by or traveler, one of many traveling songs, also called llaneros.

24. Estrellita del Norte—Comanches de la Serna, Ranchos de Taos. A night traveling song.

25. *La Cuadrilla*—Comanches de la Serna, Ranchos de Taos. Comanche "quadrille" sung for the fila or line dance.

26. *Himno a la Nacioncita de la Sangre de Cristo*—Cleofes Vigil, San Cristóbal. Indita celebrating the peaceful relations of Spanish and Comanches in the Taos area, composed for the United States Bicentennial of 1976. (Loeffler Archive).

Music courtesy of the Archives of Enrique R. Lamadrid, Jack Loeffler's Peregrine Arts Sound Archive, and the John D. Robb Archives of Southwest Music (Center for Southwest Research, Zimmerman Library, UNM). Mastering courtesy of Peregrine Arts Studio, Santa Fe, NM. All musical transcriptions in text except 21.

Notes

∾ Chapter 1

1. Many terms of ethnic and cultural designation and self designation have been used in New Mexico (A. Bustamante 1982). Especially useful in this study are the following:

Españoles mexicanos (Spanish-Mexicans) is used extensively in colonial documents and helps resolve the contemporary dilemma and controversy surrounding Spanish vs. Mexican origins.

Hispano (culturally and linguistically Hispanic) is commonly used by the turn of the twentieth century. Its long-time use as a term of self-designation in New Mexico made the English term "Hispanic" more acceptable there when it was imposed on "Latinos" by the U.S. Census Bureau.

Nuevo mexicano (New Mexican) distinguishes Hispanic from other New Mexicans. The shorter *Mexicano* is also commonly used by Nuevo Mexicanos to refer to themselves, but is ambiguous when Mexicans from Mexico are being referred to as well.

Chicano derives from the nahuatl term *mexicano,* pronounced *meshicano* (native Mexican), and is associated with the cultural and political activism of contemporary Mexican-Americans.

2. Pueblo Indian groups, despite linguistic and cultural differences, are associated with each other because they live in "pueblos," or villages, and share similar lifestyles and religious beliefs. Tanoan, Keresan, Zuni, and Hopi groups are included in this broad category and are divided geographically into Eastern (Tanoan, Keresan) and Western Pueblos (Zuni and Hopi). The Tanoan group includes three languages spoken in eleven pueblos—Tiwa in Taos, Picuris, Sandia, and Isleta; Tewa in San Juan, Santa Clara, San Ildefonso, Nambe, Pojoaque, and Tesuque; and Towa in Jemez. Keresan, or Queres, is spoken in six pueblos—Santo Domingo, Cochiti, San Felipe, Santa Ana, Laguna, and Acoma. Zuni and Hopi are spoken in the pueblos of the same names (A. Ortiz 1972).

3. Since the 1993 publication of *Reconstructing a Chicano/a Literary Heritage,* edited by María Herrera-Sobek, and the establishment of the wide-ranging "Reconstructing the U.S. Hispanic Literary Heritage Project," headed by Nicolás Kanellos and based at the University of Houston, Latino scholars across the country have embarked upon a massive recovery effort of a literary and cultural heritage neglected and obscured by the biases and priorities of mainstream American criticism and cultural history. My pioneer fieldwork on Hispano-Comanches was encouraged, funded, and published (Lamadrid 2000) by the Houston "Recovery Project."

✑ Chapter 2

1. In the vast range of the southern Plains of North America, from the forested headwaters of the Arkansas River into the Llano Estacado (staked plains) and woodlands of the south, numerous autonomous bands of Comanches established their territories, displacing and absorbing many other indigenous groups. At various times in history the Numunuh have been designated by as many as a dozen or more ethnonyms recorded in chronicles and ethnographies. Most agree on three general divisions: the Yamparicas, or "root eaters," of the north; the Kotsotecas, or "buffalo eaters," of the south; and the Jupes, or plains woodlands dwellers (Kavanagh 1996:1–27).

2. An exact chronology of the emergence of Indo-Hispano cultural practices in New Mexico is beyond the focus of this study. However, certain key dates are reference points for the allusions present in Comanche texts: the 1779 defeat of Cuerno Verde, the 1786 Comanche peace treaty, the 1821 War of Independence from Spain, the 1846 American invasion of New Mexico, the 1875 conclusion of the U.S.-Comanche wars, and the 1898 Spanish-American War.

3. Likewise, traditional Hispano-Comanche rituals take place during the winter feast cycle. As discussed in chapters 3 and 5, the promotion of tourism moved some celebrations to summer dates attractive to out-of-state visitors, but left on their own, they returned to the winter calendar.

4. An alternate etymology is suggested by Kurath and García (1970:233), who note that before the use of the term *kwítara* in San Juan Pueblo, the Comanche dances were referred to as *franse-share*, or the French Dance. No explanation of either term is offered.

5. In September of 1998, the University of New Mexico staged the only successful observance of the New Mexico Cuarto Centennial 1598–1998 in central New Mexico: "*Moros y Cristianos, Comanches y Matachines*: Four Centuries of Indo-Hispano Folk Celebrations in New Mexico." The program featured a symposium and a festival with an equestrian performance of *Moros y Cristianos,* the Jemez Pueblo *Matachines,* and contrasting Pueblo- and Hispano-style eagle, buffalo, and Comanche dances from San Juan Pueblo and Ranchos de Taos. Complete audio and video documentation is available from the Center for Southwest Research, Zimmerman Library, University of New Mexico.

6. Harris notes that performances of *Moros y Cristianos* in central Mexico in the years after the 1521 defeat of Tenochtitlán included as many as fifteen thousand actors. The 1531 performance staged in Tlaxcala featured Hernán Cortez himself as the Gran Sultán (M. Harris 2000:134–44).

7. Carey McWilliams first developed the notion of the Spanish "fantasy heritage" to describe how Anglo-American elites symbolically de-Mexicanized and dehistoricized California (McWilliams 1990). The mechanical application of the concept to the "hispanophile" cultural politics found in New Mexico oversimplifies, decontextualizes, and distorts a complex and ambivalent phenomenon.

✑ Chapter 3

1. Pueblo and Hispano reports of Comanche braggadocio about their dominance of New Mexico are widespread. In reference to central New Mexico, Gilberto Espinosa and Tibo Chávez (1967?:35) report that "It was a common boast among the Comanches that the only reason they did not completely destroy the Spanish was that they were needed to raise horses and sheep for them to steal."

2. As Kavanagh and Noyes have pointed out, the documents of European-Numunuh political relations do not carry the weight or authority that is usually ascribed to them. There is such a wide variation of reported ethnonyms and names of individuals, that it is difficult to surmise what is happening and who the participants are, beyond the Europeans. This summary of Numunuh history is clouded by these problems. Oral histories are even more significant under these circumstances, which is why this chapter concludes with two.

3. Most historians place this battle east of Santa Fe toward the Tucumcari area, as does community historian Amado Chaves. Upon close examination of several sets of documents,

Thomas Kavanagh places the battle well to the north, near the Huajatollas or Spanish peaks of Southern Colorado (Kavanagh 1996: 85).

4. In colonial and nineteenth-century documents, Spanish-Mexican settlers are often called *vecinos* (neighbors). Pueblo Indians are called *naturales* (native-born), while enemy Indians are called *gentiles* (gentiles) and *indios bárbaros* (barbarian Indians), to distinguish them from the nominally Christian Pueblos.

5. Interestingly enough, similar narratives were collected and recounted by Charles Lummis in the 1880s, in a collection of stories and sketches (1912:94–100), and by the parish priest of Tomé, as collected by the WPA fieldworker Allen A. Carter in 1936 and recounted by Erna Fergusson in 1947 (Fergusson 1947:37).

☙ Chapter 4

1. This verse is present in all of the manuscripts and versions of *Los Comanches*; complete translations by Larry Torres (2002), except for the Alcalde manuscript, are to be found in appendix I.

2. The most complete research and analysis of the historical references and characters of *Los Comanches* is an unpublished manuscript by Thomas W. Kavanagh, entitled "Comanches: Comments on the Historical Context of a New Mexico Folk Drama."

3. Campa obtained the 1864 manuscript from nonagenarian Don Rafael Lucero, of El Pino, New Mexico (near Questa), who said that it "has been used extensively in Southwestern Colorado and Northern New Mexico even before the Civil War" (Campa 1942:23).

4. Amado Chaves provided Aurelio M. Espinosa with the manuscript of *Los Comanches* that he published in 1907. He and other historians place this battle east of Santa Fe, toward the Tucumcari area. Upon close examination of documents and diaries, Thomas Kavanagh places the battle as far north as the Huajatollas, or Spanish Peaks, of Southern Colorado (Kavanagh 1996:85).

5. With such personal losses to avenge, Pedro Pino "certainly had sufficient motivation to dramatize a Spanish victory over the Comanches and the release of captives" (Ortiz y Pino Family Papers).

6. The Bond manuscript is especially useful in contrasting the Espinosa and Campa versions. Translations of *Los Comanches* include Mary Austin (n.d.), Gilberto Espinosa (1931), I. L. Chávez (1900), and Larry Torres (2002). See also Mary Austin (1934).

7. Curtis Márez (2001) analyses Brown's 1939 report in the full context of social and economic relations between El Rancho and the neighboring Tewa pueblo of San Ildefonso. Alfonso R. Sánchez recovered the El Rancho text from José Alvarado Roybal (1916–1993). His father, Martín Roybal, directed the production for many years, including the one that Loren Brown witnessed. José directed it until the 1950s, when he moved to southern New Mexico.

8. Information and opinions are drawn from personal interviews with Roberto Vialpando Lara, Tomás Sánchez, Galento Martínez, and Alfredo Montoya, all of Alcalde, New Mexico.

9. Other communities where performances have been witnessed include Taos, Ranchos de Taos, and Llano (Campa 1979, Jaramillo 1980[1941], Robb 1980); Chamisal (Domínguez 1985); Galisteo (Campa 1979, C. Chávez n.d., Roeder 1976); El Rancho (Brown 1939; Brown, Briggs, and Weigle 1978); Rainsville and Mora (Rivera 1987), and the villages of the Purgatoire Valley in southern Colorado (Taylor 1963). Verse fragments of the script have been recovered from many other northern communities, such as Leyva (Robb 1980:599).

10. All this information and all of these opinions are taken directly from a personal interview with Tomás Sánchez, Española, New Mexico, January 28, 1991. The chronology of performances dating to the beginning of this revival is currently being reconstructed from ongoing oral histories.

11. For his revival of *Los Comanches*, Dr. Roberto Vialpando had to recruit actors with superb equestrian skills. When Richard Bradford's novel *Red Sky at Morning* was made into a 1971 Universal movie starring Richard Thomas, the Sánchez brothers Juan, Leo, and Tomás, along with the rest of the Comanches cast, were engaged to stage a traditional *corrida de gallos,* or "rooster pull," in one of the scenes. In breakneck competition, teams of riders pull a buried

rooster out of the sand and struggle to retain possession of it. A similar level of skill is necessary for the Comanches play.

12. Also played on violin and guitar, Alcalde Comanches music closely resembles the matachines tunes, since the same musicians play them both. In contrast, Comanche music used in past performances of *Los Comanches de Castillo* in Ranchos de Taos is unaccompanied pentatonic, vocable singing, which results in a completely Native American sound, discussed in chapter 5.

13. Translations of the Alcalde *Comanches* are the author's.

✑ Chapter 5

1. The longest and most complete versions of *Los Comanches* were published by Aurelio M. Espinosa in 1907 and Arturo L. Campa in 1942. Campa's more complete manuscript ends with the death of Cuerno Verde, while Espinosa's contains no reference to it. None of the shorter, abridged manuscripts retrieved from observed twentieth-century performance traditions—Alcalde (Vialpando 1963), Galisteo (C. Chávez n.d.), or El Rancho (Roybal n.d., Brown 1939)—present the death of Cuerno Verde, either. Historians cite this as proof that the play was composed after 1774 and before De Anza's 1779 campaign, seeing the death scene as a codicil. As I argue in chapter 3, the actual death of Cuerno Verde becomes less and less relevant to contemporary New Mexicans.

2. One curious twist in the cross-cultural identification with Numunuh culture occurs among Anglo-Texans and their folklorists, who romanticize Comanches while still vilifying Texas Mexicans. Américo Paredes (1994[1958]:20–21) critically notes that "After the 1870's when the Indian danger was past, it was possible to idealize the Plains savage. But the 'Mexican problem' remained. A distinction was drawn between the noble Plains Indian and the degenerate ancestor of the Mexican." In the same breath, he adds: "The Comanche did not consider Mexican blood inferior. Mexican captives were often adopted into the tribe, as were captives of other races."

3. In Tortugas (near Las Cruces, New Mexico), two groups of southern, Chichimeca- or Azteca-style matachines dance for the feast of Guadalupe, on December 12. The "Chichimeca Azteca" group wears bright red costumes and reed aprons, with full Plains-style warbonnets. The "Guadalupano Azteca" group dresses identically, but all in yellow (Sklar 2001:60–61).

4. The Cochití/Peña Blanca text is so designated because it was recovered by Charlie Carrillo and Father Thomas Steele from the collection of Christino Tafoya, a brother of the Cochití Morada before it disbanded, in the 1940s, prior to World War II. The membership and archives of the penitente morada at Cochití Pueblo passed to the Peña Blanca Morada, in the Hispano village across the Río Grande to the east (Carrillo 1993).

5. The original decision to dedicate the of New Mexico to the Conversion of San Pablo was his divine intervention to help the colonists to prevail in the siege of Acoma Pueblo on January 25, 1599, the day of his feast (Kessell:103).

6. Although it only contains vocables and one verse, "Dicen que las golondrinas de un volido pasan el mar" (They say the swallows cross the ocean in a single flight), "La jeyana," sung by Rosanna Otero, is typical of the inditas sung for San Luis. The image of the swallows symbolizes the Iberian diaspora. (See "Hermanitos Comanchitos" CD, included in this book.) Other references to San Luis are common (see "Soy de la Sierra Nevada" in the same CD).

7. Because of strong historical and cultural ties to the Tewa world, in Abiquiú, the *pangshare*, *"danza de los cautivos"* or captive's dance, enjoyed strong popularity at the beginning of the century (Kurath: 284). This ritual tradition evolved into a social dance form that includes waltz and polka-like couple dancing, which can be seen today in Tewa Pueblos as well as in Abiquiú at the Santo Tomás feast day (Córdova).

8. The numerous examples of the sharply satirical "Comanche y Comancha" (the Comanche and his wife) verses are often softened and euphemized by replacing the Indian characters with a buck and a doe—"El venado y la venada" (Lamadrid archive; Floyd Trujillo, Abiquiú, 1992):

El venado y la venada	*The buck and the doe*
se fueron pa' Santa Fe,	*went to Santa Fe,*
a vender a sus hijitos	*to sell their little fawns*
por azúcar y café.	*for sugar and coffee.*

9. In the Ibero-American tradition, over the centuries, narrative ballads in the tragic mode have often evolved into children's ballads in the satirical or burlesque mode. These latter are known as *relaciones* (Loeffler, Loeffler, and Lamadrid 1999:1–2).

10. A musical transcription and recording of "Las Posadas" can be found in Loeffler, Loeffler, and Lamadrid (1999:117–19).

11. A recording of *Los Comanchitos* sung by the Coro de Bernalillo can be found in Loeffler, Loeffler, and Lamadrid (1999:191–93) and in the Smithsonian-Folkways (CD SF 40409) *Music of New Mexico: Hispanic Traditions,* 1992.

◦⌒◦ Chapter 6

1. The Comanches de la Serna have performed for more than half a century in the Taos area, both on their feast day, in the Taos fiestas, and in many dance programs. For several years, they were active on the powwow circuit. Controversies concerning their cultural legitimacy have erupted in curated settings such as the Museum of International Folk Art in Santa Fe (1986), a meeting of the National Association of Chicano Studies (1991), and the Smithsonian Festival of American Folklife (1992). See chapter 6 text, below, for an analysis.

2. In Francisco Gonzales's 1992 proposal to New Mexico's Quincentennial Commission (to support dance performances), Numunuh cultural activist LaDonna Harris is cited to corroborate the existence of a Hispano-Comanche maroon community in Ranchos de Taos. Although there is no written record of them, they are remembered in oral histories in both New Mexico and Oklahoma.

3. The Gonzales family archive is now located in the John D. Robb Archive of Southwestern Music, at the University of New Mexico.

4. After the 1837 Chimayó Tax Revolt, José González, a Genízaro from Ranchos de Taos, was installed as governor. Although his government swore loyalty to the Mexican Republic, he was executed by the Mexican Army in 1838 (Simmons 1988:113).

5. *1992 Festival of American Folklife,* the visitors' festival guide (see Lamadrid 1992a), gives a good idea of the diversity of the largest curated folk festival in the United States, mounted annually by the Smithsonian Center for Folklife and Cultural Heritage.

6. In Taos and the rest of New Mexico, cultural tourism is largely directed toward the Indian Pueblos. Indianism—the romantic exaltation and celebration of Native culture, and Hispanophobia—the shunning and devaluation of Hispanic culture, have been part of the cultural equation of New Mexico since the opening of the Santa Fe Trail (Lamadrid 1992c).

7. Except as indicated, all Comanche lyrics were recorded by the author and are to be found in the Lamadrid archive.

8. "This game involved the use of four hollow reeds about eight inches in length, which were assigned different values and which were distinguished by their hues or the marks carved on them. Each was given a name: *el uno, el dos, el mulato,* and *el cinchado* (one, two, dark one, and one with a string around it). *El mulato* was worth four points, *el cinchado* three points, *el dos* two, and *el uno* only one point. Each team had the same number of players. The team in current possession of *los cañutes* hid beneath a blanket in their corner of the room and inserted a slender stick or nail into one of the *cañutes,* then buried all four of the *cañutes* in a pile of sand. Then they emerged from beneath the blanket and signaled the opposing team to come over and guess in which *cañute* the stick had been placed. There were variations as to how the game was played, and sometimes the stakes were high" (Loeffler, Loeffler, and Lamadrid 1999:23).

9. In the dance cycles of the neighboring pueblos, dances can be secular, social, or religious. The matachines dance in the pueblos is considered to be secular, although participants may make

holy vows to perform it. The animal and enemy dances are considered to be social in character, although particular dances, such as the eagle and buffalo dances, have sacred qualities. The turtle dance, on the other hand, is religious in nature (Sweet 1985:30, 92).

⤳ Chapter 7

1. The initials "WPA," pronounced in English, sound like the words *diablo a pie,* or the "devil on foot," to a Spanish speaker. Nuevo Mexicanos felt fortunate to be beneficiaries of President Franklin Roosevelt's New Deal, which ended the Great Depression. When asked who your employer was in those times, the answer in jest was "el diablo" himself.

2. Since Ecueracapa's Numunuh name was never recorded, scholars have not been able to establish his identity with certainty. *Ecueracapa* refers to his distinctive leather cape, but many native men dressed with leather capes. In some documents he is also know as *Cota de malla,* or coat of mail. For a summary of discussions on the identity of this important leader, see Kavanagh 1996:500–501.

3. The 1786 documents indicate only that a hole was opened and filled. An account by Berlandier of a similar ceremony conducted in 1828 in Béxar (San Antonio, Texas) notes that first a circle was drawn, an oath to the sun and earth was taken, and a hole was dug in the middle of the circle, into which were placed "some of their gunpowder, several arrows (which they broke before placing them in the hole), some daggers, and a quantity of the standard ammunition issued to the troops" (Berlandier 1969:66). Then the hole was solemnly refilled.

4. Curtis Márez (2001:284–87) traces the coercive process by which Mexican captive children, "rescued" from their adoptive Numunuh parents by the American army in the 1870s, were "civilized" and re-Mexicanized, often against their will.

5. Mary Austin's papers are at the Hunting Library in Pasadena, California.

6. *Taos Valley News* 18(38) (Thursday, September 26, 1929) has a motto on its masthead that reads "Boosting for Taos and Vicinity." *Revista Popular de Nuevo México* 28(38) (miércoles 25 de septiembre de 1929) also covers the fiesta from a perspective expressed in its motto, "Semanario Dedicado a los Intereses del Pueblo Hispano-Americano" ("weekly dedicated to the interests of the Hispanic-American people"). Cheetham also promoted the San Gerónimo feast day in Taos Pueblo (Cheetham 1929).

7. Newspaper installments of *Los comanches* followed Aurelio M. Espinosa's 1907 critical edition, as well as Arthur L. Campa's critical edition of 1942. Excerpts were also published throughout the 1950s in the weekly columns of Rubén Cobos, in *El Nuevo Mexicano.*

8. Accounts of the Villalpando massacre include Adams 1953, Adams and Chávez 1956:251, Foreman 1934:114, Grant 1934:282, Gregg 1926:139, Kavanagh 1996:77, Noyes 1993:55, Woodward 1956:237, and others. Bernardo Miera y Pacheco's 1779 map of New Mexico contains references to the Villalpando massacre in its legend (Adams and Chávez 1956:4). An exemplary relation of the legend of the Villalpando massacre is articulated in the first chapter of Parkhill (1965:13–24).

9. Francisco Gonzales, one of the principle leaders of Los Comanches de la Serna, was a Chicano activist at New Mexico Highlands University (F. Gonzales 1992). His group has performed at many Chicano cultural events, including the 1991 National Association of Chicano Studies meeting in Albuquerque.

10. Jerry Padilla is an educator and columnist for "El Crepúsculo," the Spanish-language section of the *Taos News.* A descendant of Hispano homesteaders and buffalo hunters, he grew up at the edge of the Great Plains in Springer, New Mexico, listening to his family's Comanche captivity stories (J. Padilla 2001).

11. De Anza and his men often camped at Rancho de las Golondrinas, at La Ciénega, New Mexico, the first *paraje,* or camp, on the Camino Real south of Santa Fe. It is currently part of the Ciénega Village Museum, a living-history community museum founded by George Paloheimo.

12. Cleofes Vigil, from San Cristóbal, New Mexico, sang "Himno al pueblo de las montañas de la Sangre de Cristo" on the National Mall in the summer of 1976. He was honored with the

Smithsonian Heritage Award in 1985. The song is recorded on the 1992 Smithsonian-Folkways CD *Music of New Mexico, Hispanic Traditions* (CD SF 40409).

13. La Academia de la Nueva Raza in its early days was called La Academia de Aztlán, the first Chicano group to use the name of the mythical Aztec homeland. It published a magazine, *El Cuaderno,* and an anthology of literary folklore, *Entre Verde y Seco.* In the following decade, its principal founder, Tomás Atencio, began the Río Grande Institute, the first regional arts and culture organization dedicated to bringing together Hispanos and Indians and defining a common ground. Another offshoot of the same alliance of scholars and cultural workers is Academia/El Norte Publications.

14. Although Sangre de Cristo (Blood of Christ) is a toponym found in colonial times in northern New Mexico and what was to become southern Colorado, it referred to a small river near the San Luis Valley. The mountain range itself was simply called *la sierra,* or the mountain range, on Spanish maps. Ironically, it was an 1896 tourist publication of the Denver and Río Grande Railroad that first applied the name Sangre de Cristo to the southern spur of the Rockies (Wroth 1983:287). This extension of the name was immediately accepted by everyone.

15. For a testimonial account of the taking of captives at the Santo Tomás feast day in Abiquiú, see Romero (2002).

16. In the summer of 1993, the Comanches de la Serna were invited to perform at the Museum of International Folk Art, in Santa Fe. A controversy instantly erupted, when a Native visitor complained loudly to curators, questioning the "authenticity" of the performance. Curators responded immediately by terminating the presentation and canceling the event (Mauldin 2002).

17. The politics and poetics of cultural representation at festivals is the subject of an ongoing critical dialogue (Bauman and Sawin 1991; Bauman, Sawin, and Carpenter 1992; Cantwell 1991, 1992, 1993; and Price 1994).

18. *Nuevo México Profundo: Rituals of an Indo-Hispano Homeland* was granted the Southwest Book Award for 2000–2001.

19. As noted in chapter 2, unbeknownst to the Tewa speakers who use the term to refer to Comanche dances, *kwítara* in the Numunuh language refers to "that musky or excremental smell that human beings emit when sexually aroused" (Bigbee 1998).

Bibliography

Adams, Eleanor B. 1953. "Bishop Tamarón's Visitation of New Mexico, 1760." *New Mexico Historical Quarterly* 28:192–221.

Adams, Eleanor B., and Fray Angélico Chávez. 1956. *The Missions of New Mexico, 1776: A Description by Fray Francisco Atanasio Domínguez with Other Contemporary Documents.* Albuquerque: University of New Mexico Press.

Adorno, Rolena 1988. "Nuevas perspectivas en los estudios literarios coloniales hispanoamericanos." *Revista de Crítica Literaria Latinoamericana* 14(28):11–27.

Aguilar, Charles. 1991. Interview with author, Bernalillo, N.Mex., December 2.

Anaya, Rudolfo, and Tomás Atencio, eds. 1981. *A Ceremony of Brotherhood: Tricentennial Anthology.* Santa Fe, N.Mex.: Blue Feather Press.

Anderson, Benedict. 1983[1991]. *Imagined Communities: Reflections on the Origin and Spread of Nationalism.* London: Verso, 1991.

Anderson, Gary Clayton. 1991. *The Indian Southwest, 1580–1830: Ethnogenesis and Reinvention.* Norman: University of Oklahoma Press.

Anderson, Reed. 1989. "Early Secular Theater in New Mexico." In *Pasó por Aquí: Critical Essays on the New Mexican Literary Tradition,* ed. Erlinda Gonzales-Berry. Albuquerque: University of New Mexico Press.

Arellano, Anselmo F., and Julián J. Vigil. 1980. *Arthur L. Campa and the Coronado Cuarto Centennial.* Las Vegas, N.Mex.: Editorial Telaraña.

Austin, Mary. 1927. "Native Drama in Our Southwest." *The Nation* 124 (3224):437–40.

———. 1928. "A Drama Played on Horseback." *The Mentor* 16 (September):38–39.

———. 1933. "Folk Plays of the Southwest." *Theatre Arts Monthly* 17:299–606.

———. 1934. "Spanish Manuscripts in the Southwest." *Southwest Review* 19(4):402–9.

———. N.d. "Los Comanches" (one English and three Spanish typescripts, Mary Austin Collection). San Marino, Calif.: Huntington Library.

Bakhtin, Mikhail M. 1981. *The Dialogic Imagination: Four Essays by M. M. Bakhtin.* Trans. Caryl Emerson and Michael Holquist. Austin: University of Texas Press.

———. 1984. *Rabelais and His World.* Trans. Helen Iswolsky. Bloomington: University of Indiana Press.

Bancroft, Hubert Howe. 1889. *History of Arizona and New Mexico, 1530–1888.* San Francisco: The History Company.

Barker, George C. 1958. "Some Functions of Catholic Processions in Pueblo and Yaqui Culture Change." *American Anthropologist* 60:449–55.

Barker, Ruth Laughlin. 1931. *Caballeros*. New York: D. Appleton and Co.

Barth, Fredrik. 1969. *Ethnic Groups and Boundaries: The Social Organization of Cultural Difference*. Boston: Little Brown and Co.

Bartra, Roger. 1993. *Oficio mexicano*. México: Grijalbo.

Bauman, Richard. 1986. *Story, Performance, and Event: Contextual Studies of Oral Narrative*. Cambridge: Cambridge University Press.

Bauman, Richard, and Patricia Sawin. 1991. "The Politics of Participation in Folklife Festivals." In *Exhibiting Cultures: The Poetics and Politics of Museum Display*. Edited by Ivan Karp and Steven D. Lavine, 288–314. Washington and London: Smithsonian Institution Press.

Bauman, Richard, Patricia Sawin, and Inta Gail Carpenter. 1992. *Reflections on the Folklife Festival: An Ethnography of Participant Experience*. Bloomington, Ind.: Special Publications of the Folklore Institute, No. 2.

Berlandier, Jean Louis. 1969. *The Indians of Texas in 1830*. Edited by John C. Ewers, trans. Patricia Reading Leclercq. Washington, D.C.: Smithsonian Institution Press.

Berry, Edwin Baca. 1993. Interview with author, Tomé, N.Mex., March 12.

Bhabha, Homi K. 1986. "The Other Question: Difference, Discrimination, and the Discourse of Colonialism." In *Literature, Politics, and Theory: Papers from the Essex Conference, 1976–84*. Edited by Francis Baker, Peter Hulme, Margaret Iversen, and Diane Loxley, 148–72. London and New York: Methuen.

Bigbee, Walter. 1998. Interview with author, Albuquerque, N.Mex., October 19.

Bond, Frank M., ed. 1972. "Los Comanches." (Typescript and notes.) Santa Fe, N.Mex.: Museum of International Folk Art.

Boulris, Mark. 1983. "Images of the Comanche and the Effects of the Horse." In *Essays on the Ethnohistory of the North American Indian*. Edited by Ian W. Brown, 2:87-114.

Bourke, John G. 1894. "The American Congo." *Scribner's* 15:590–610.

Briggs, Charles L. 1988. *Competence in Performance: The Creativity of Tradition in Mexicano Verbal Art*. Philadelphia: University of Pennsylvania Press.

Briggs, Charles L., and Julián Josué Vigil. 1990. *The Lost Gold Mine of Juan Mondragón: A Legend from New Mexico Performed by Melaquías Romero*. Tucson: University of Arizona Press.

Brooke, James. 1998. "Conquistador Statue Stirs Hispanic Pride and Indian Rage." *New York Times* (February 9) section A:10.

Brooks, James F. 2002. *Captives and Cousins: Slavery, Kinship, and Community in the Southwest Borderlands*. Chapel Hill: University of North Carolina Press.

Brown, Lorin W. 1939. "Los Comanches" (Typescript). In W.P.A. Files, File 5, Drawer 5, Folder 45 #1. Santa Fe: New Mexico Historical Library.

Brown, Lorin W., with Charles L. Briggs and Marta Weigle. 1978. *Hispano Folklife of New Mexico: The Lorin W. Brown Federal Writers' Project Manuscripts*. Albuquerque: University of New Mexico Press.

Bustamante, Adrian H. 1982. "Los Hispanos : Ethnicity and Social Change in New Mexico." Ph.D. diss., University of New Mexico.

Bustamante, Herman. 1988. Interview with author, Albuquerque, N.Mex., November 12.

Campa, Arthur L. 1941. "The New Mexican Spanish Folktheater." *Southern Folklore Quarterly* 5(2):127–31.

————. 1942. "Los Comanches: A New Mexican Folk Drama." *University of New Mexico Bulletin, Modern Language Series 7, 1*.

————. 1946. *Spanish Folk Poetry in New Mexico*. Albuquerque: University of New Mexico Press.

————. 1979. *Hispanic Culture in the Southwest*. Norman: Oklahoma University Press.

Cantú, Norma E. 1995. "*Los Matachines de la Santa Cruz de la Ladrillera*: Notes Toward a Socio-literary Analysis." In *Feasts and Celebrations in North American Ethnic Communities*. Edited by Ramón A. Gutiérrez and Genevieve Fabre, 57–70. Albuquerque: University of New Mexico Press.

Cantwell, Robert. 1991. "Conjuring Culture: Ideology and Magic in the Festival of American Folklife." *Journal of American Folklore* 104:148–63.

———. 1992. "Feasts of Unnaming: Folk Festivals and the Representation of Folklife." In *Public Folklore*. Edited by Robert Baron and Nicholas R. Spitzer, 263–305. Washington, D.C.: Smithsonian Institution Press.

———. 1993. *Ethnomimesis: Folklife and the Representation of Culture*. Chapel Hill: University of North Carolina Press.

Carrillo, Charlie. 1993. Interview with author, Santa Fe, N.Mex., April 4.

Carter, Allen A. 1936. "The Legend of Tomé" (Typescript). In W.P.A. Files, File 5, Drawer 4, Folder 1 #2, in the files of the New Mexico Writer's Project, Museum of New Mexico, Santa Fe.

Cassidy, Ina Sizer. 1934. "New Mexico in the First National Folk Festival." *New Mexico* 12(4):24–25, 45.

Cavallo-Bosso, J. R. 1956. "Kumanche of the Zuñi Indians of New Mexico: An Analytical Study." BA Thesis, Wesleyan University, Middletown Connecticut.

Certeau, Michel de. 1986. *Heterologies: Discourse on the Other*. Trans. B. Massumi. Manchester: Manchester University Press.

Chacón, Eusebio. 1892. *Tras la tormenta la calma*. Santa Fe, N.Mex.: Tipografía "El Boletín Popular."

Chacón, Herminia B. 1932. "The Christ Child Comes to New Mexico." *New Mexico* 10(12):7–9, 45–56.

Chacón, Rafael, and Jacqueline Dorgan Meketa, eds. 1986. *Legacy of Honor: The Life of Rafael Chacón, a Nineteenth-Century New Mexican*. Albuquerque: University of New Mexico Press.

Chaves, Amado. 1906. *The Defeat of the Comanches in 1717*. Santa Fe: Historical Society of New Mexico, Publications in History, No. 8.

Chávez Bent, Pauline. 2000. "Los Comanches." *La Herencia del Norte* 28:15.

Chávez, Bernabé. 1988. Interview with author, Ranchos de Taos, N.Mex., February 2.

Chávez, Clemente. n.d. "1908 Guerra Entre los Comanches y los Españoles." (Notebook.) In John D. Robb Archive of Southwestern Music. Albuquerque: University of New Mexico, copied December 6, 1925, collected by Robb in 1963.

Chávez, Eduardo, and Priscilla Chávez. 1996. "Comanches Guadalupanos." Los Ranchos de Albuquerque. Lamadrid Archive.

Chávez, Fray Angélico. 1979. "Genízaros." In *Handbook of North American Indians*, gen. ed. William C. Sturtevant, *vol. 9 Southwest*, ed. Alfonso Ortiz, 198–200. Washington, D.C.: Smithsonian Institution:.

Chávez, I. L., trans. N.d. "Los Comanches." Translation of M. Celso E. Aragon manuscript, Ranchos de Taos, December 24, 1900. (Typescript.) In W.P.A. Files, File 5, Drawer 5, Folder 45 #2. Santa Fe: New Mexico Historical Library.

Chávez, Thomas Esteban. 1978. "The Trouble with Texans: Manuel Alvarez and the 1841 'Invasion.'" *New Mexico Historical Review* 53(2):133–44.

Cheetham, F. T. 1929. "San Gerónimo Fiesta." *New Mexico Highway Journal* 7:20–21, 34.

Chorpenning, Joseph F., O.S.F.S., ed. 1992. *Patron Saint of the New World: Spanish American Colonial Images of St. Joseph*. Philadelphia: St. Joseph's University Press.

Cobos, Rubén. 1983. *A Dictionary of New Mexico and Southern Colorado Spanish*. Santa Fe: Museum of New Mexico Press.

Córdova, Gilberto Benito. 1973. *Abiquiú and Don Cacahuate: A Folk History of a New Mexican Village*. Los Cerrillos, N.Mex.: San Marcos Press.

Cornejo Polar, Antonio. 1994. *Escribir en el aire: Ensayo sobre la heterogeneidad socio-cultural en las literaturas andinas*. Lima, Peru: Editorial Horizonte.

Cummings, Tom. 1998. Interview with author, Albuquerque, N.Mex., January 2.

Dahlberg, Sandra. 1996. "Having the Last Word: Recording the Cost of Conquest in *Los Comanches*." In *Recovering the U.S. Hispanic Literary Heritage*. Edited by Erlinda Gonzales-Berry and Chuch Tatum, 2: 133–47. Houston: Arte Público Press.

DeFlice, John. 1999. Interview with author, Albuquerque, N.Mex., 1999.

Dekker, George. 1990. *The American Historical Romance*. Cambridge: Cambridge University Press.

Deloria, Philip J. 1998. *Playing Indian*. New Haven: Yale University Press.

Domínguez, José Amado. 1988. Interview with author, Ranchos de Taos, N.Mex., February 2.

Dozier, Edward P. 1954. "Spanish-Indian Acculturation in the Southwest: Comments on Spicer." *American Anthropologist* 56 (): 680–83.

———. 1957. "Spanish-Catholic Influences on Río Grande Pueblo Religion." *American Anthropologist* n.s. 60(3)():441–48.

———. 1961. "Río Grande Pueblos." In *Perspectives in American Indian Culture Change.* Edited by Edward H. Spicer. Chicago: University of Chicago Press.

———. 1983. *The Pueblo Indians of North America.* Prospect Heights, Ill.: Waveland Press].

Durán, Franke. 1994. Interview with Francisco Gonzales, Jr., Taos, N.Mex., August 6.

Ellis, Florence Hawley. 1954. "Comments on Spanish-Indian Acculturation in the Southwest." *American Anthropologist* 56:678–80.

Englekirk, J. E. 1940. "Notes on the Repertoire of the New Mexico Spanish Folk Theatre." *Southern Folklore Quarterly* 4():227–37.

———. 1957. "The Source and Dating of New Mexico Spanish Folk Plays." *Western Folklore* 16:232–55.

Ercilla y Zúñiga, Alonso de. 1979[1590]. *La Araucana.* Madrid: Editorial Castalia.

Espinosa, Aurelio M. 1907. "Los Comanches, A Spanish Heroic Play of the Year Seventeen Hundred and Eighty." *Bulletin of the University of New Mexico* 1(1)).

———. 1976. *The Folklore of Spain in the American Southwest.* Edited by J. Manuel Espinosa. Norman: University of Oklahoma Press.

Espinosa, Aurelio M., and José M. Espinosa. 1944. "Los Tejanos: A New Mexican Spanish Popular Dramatic Composition of the Middle of the Nineteenth Century." *Hispania* 27:289–314.

Espinosa, Gilberto. 1931. "Los Comanches." *New Mexico Quarterly* 1(2):133–46.

Espinosa, Gilberto, and Tibo J. Chávez. 1967?. *El Río Abajo.* Portales, N.Mex.: Bishop Publishing Company.

Evans, Bessie, and May G. Evans. 1931. *American Indian Dance Steps.* New York: Barnes.

Ewers, John Canfield. 1955. *The Horse in Blackfoot Indian Culture, with Comparative Material from Other Western Tribes.* Bureau of American Ethnology Bulletin 159. Washington, D.C.: Smithsonian Institution.

Fergusson, Erna. 1946–47. "The Massacre of Tomé." *New Mexico Folklore Record* 1:37.

Fordyce, Kenneth. n.d. "Los Comanches" (Condensed from "Something Pretty for the Altar," by Lolita H. Pooler, in the Christmas 1936 edition of the *Raton Range.*) WPA #122, New Mexico State Records Center.

Foreman, Grant. 1934. *Pioneer Days in the Early Southwest.* Cleveland: Arthur H. Clark Co.

Frisbie, Charlotte Johnson, ed. 1980. *Southwestern Indian Ritual Drama.* Albuquerque: University of New Mexico Press.

Gandert, Miguel and Enrique R. Lamadrid et al. 2000. *Nuevo México Profundo: Rituals of an Indo-Hispano Homeland.* Santa Fe: Museum of New Mexico Press.

García, Andy. 1999. Interview with author, San Juan Pueblo, N.Mex., February 6.

García, Angela, and Georgia García. 1995. Interview with the author, Albuquerque, N.Mex., April 22.

———. N.d. "Indita" from *Los Comanches,* Atrisco, N.Mex.. Lamadrid archive.

García, Mario T. 1989. *Mexican Americans: Leadership, Ideology, and Identity, 1930–1960.* New Haven, Conn.: Yale University Press.

Geertz, Clifford. 1973. *The Interpretation of Cultures; Selected Essays.* New York: Basic Books.

Gelo, Daniel J. 1988. "Comanche Songs, English Lyrics, and Formal Continuity." *European Review of Native American Studies* (Budapest) 2(2)():2–7.

Gerald, Rex E. 1974. "Aboriginal Use and Occupation by Tigua, Manso, and Suma Indians." In *Apache Indians,* vol. 3. New York: Garland Publishing.

Gonzales, Francisco. 1992. Interview with author, Ranchos de Taos, N.Mex., January 28.

Gonzales, Francisco, Jr. 1991. Interview with author, Albuquerque, N.Mex., February 22.

———. 1998. Interview with author, Albuquerque, N.Mex., August 10.

Gonzales, Nelson. 1993. Interview with author, Ranchos de Taos, N.Mex., August 2.

Grant, Blanche C. 1925. *Taos Today.* Taos, N.Mex.: Author.

———. 1934. *When Old Trails Were New; The Story of Taos.* New York: Press of the Pioneers.

Gregg, Josiah. 1926. *Commerce of the Prairies.* Edited by Milo Milton Quaife. Chicago: R. R. Donnelly & Sons.

Grimes, Ronald L. 1992. *Symbol and Conquest: Public Ritual and Drama in Santa Fe.* Albuquerque: University of New Mexico Press.

Gutiérrez, Ramón. 1991. *When Jesus Came, the Corn Mothers Went Away: Marriage, Sexuality, and Power in New Mexico, 1500-1846.* Stanford: Stanford University Press.

———. 1993. "The Politics of Theater in Colonial New Mexico." *Reconstructing a Chicano/a Literary Heritage: Hispanic Colonial Literature of the Southwest.* Edited by María Herrera-Sobek. Tucson: University of Arizona Press.

Haley, J. Evetts. 1934–35. "The Comanchero Trade." *Southwestern Historical Quarterly* 38:157–76.

Harris, LaDonna. 2002. Interview with author, Corrales, N.Mex., March 1.

Harris, Max. 1993. *The Dialogical Theater: Dramatizations of the Conquest of Mexico and the Question of the Other.* New York: St. Martin's Press.

———. 2000. *Aztecs, Moors, and Christians: Festivals of Reconquest in Mexico and Spain.* Austin: University of Texas Press.

Hurt, Wesley R. 1940. "Shadows of the Past." *New Mexico* 18(5):21, 37–38.

———. 1966. "The Spanish-American Comanche Dance." *Journal of the Folklore Institute* 3(2):116–32.

Isaacs, Tony. 1991. Interview with author, Arroyo Seco, N.Mex., May 20.

Jameson, Frederick. 1981. *The Political Unconscious: Narrative As a Socially Symbolic Act.* Ithaca: Cornell University Press.

Jaramillo, Cleofas Martínez. 1980[1941]. *Shadows of the Past (Sombras del Pasado).* Reprint, Santa Fe, N.Mex.: Ancient City Press.

John, Elizabeth A. H. 1975. *Storms Brewed in Other Men's Worlds: The Confrontation of Indians, Spanish, and French in the Southwest, 1540–1795.* College Station: Texas A & M University Press.

Kanellos, Nicolás, ed. 1984. *Hispanic Theatre in the United States.* Houston: Arte Público Press.

Kapferer, Bruce. 1986. "Performance and the Structuring of Meaning." In *The Anthropology of Experience.* Edited by Victor Turner and Edward Bruner, 188–206. Urbana: University of Illinois Press.

Kavanagh, Thomas W. N.d. "Comanches: Comments on the Historical Context of a New Mexico Folk Drama." Unpublished manuscript. Lamadrid archive.

———. 1996. *Comanche Political History: An Ethnohistorical Perspective, 1706–1875.* Lincoln : University of Nebraska Press:.

Kenner, Charles L. 1966. *A History of New Mexico-Plains Indians Relations.* Norman: University of Oklahoma Press.

Kessell, John. 1987. *Kiva, Cross, and Crown: The Pecos Indians and New Mexico, 1540–1840.* Tucson, Ariz.: Southwest Parks and Monuments Association.

King, Scottie. 1979. "Los Comanches de la Serna." *New Mexico Magazine* (January):26–27, 42.

Kohlberg, Walter L., trans. 1973. *Letters of Ernst Kohlberg, 1875–1877.* Southwest Studies Monograph no. 38. El Paso: University of Texas.

Kurath, Gertrude P., and Antonio García. 1970. *Music and Dance of the Tewa Pueblos.* Museum of New Mexico Research Records, No. 8. Santa Fe: Museum of New Mexico Press.

Kurin, Richard. 2001. Interview with author, Washington, D.C., March 20.

Lafaye, Jacques. 1976. *Quetzalcoatl and Guadalupe: The Formation of a Mexican National Consciousness, 1531–1813.* Trans. Benjamin Keen. Chicago: University of Chicago Press.

Lamadrid, Enrique R. 1992a. "The Indo-Hispano Legacy of New Mexico." *1992 Festival of American Folklife,* 30–32. Washington, D.C.: Smithsonian Institution and National Park Service.

———. 1992b. "Los Comanches: The Celebration of Cultural Otherness in New Mexican Winter Feasts." (46 pp. report, 8 audio tapes and transcripts, 1 video tape, 39 transparencies.)

Washington, D.C.: New Mexico Festival of American Folklife Archive, Smithsonian Center for Folklife and Cultural Studies.

———. 1992c. "Ig/noble Savages of New Mexico's Silent Cinema, 1912–1914." *Spectator* 13(1):12–23.

———. 1993. "Entre Cíbolos Criado: Images of Native Americans in the Popular Culture of Colonial New Mexico." In *Reconstructing a Chicano/a Literary Heritage: Hispanic Colonial Literature of the Southwest.* Edited by María Herrera-Sobek. Tucson: University of Arizona Press.

———. 2000. "'Los Comanches': Text, Performance, and Transculturation in an 18th Century New Mexican Folk Drama." In *Recovering the U.S. Hispanic Literary Heritage,* 3:173–88. Houston: Arte Público Press.

———. 2002. "History, Faith, and Intercultural Relations in Two New Mexican Inditas: Plácida Romero and San Luis Gonzaga." In *Nuevomexicano Cultural Legacy: Forms, Agencies, and Discourse.* Edited by Francisco Lomelí and Genaro Padilla, 164–84. Albuquerque: University of New Mexico Press.

Lamadrid, Enrique R., and Jack Loeffler. 1994. *Tesoros del Espíritu: A Portrait in Sound of Hispanic New Mexico.* Albuquerque: Academia/El Norte Publications.

Levine, Frances. 1991. *Farmers, Hunters, and Colonists: Interaction between the Southwest and the Southern Plains.* Tucson: University of Arizona Press.

Leyva, Macario. 1980. "Indio Comanche." In *Hispanic Folk Music of New Mexico and the Southwest: A Self-Portrait of a People.* By John Donald Robb, 599–602. Norman: University of Oklahoma Press.

Loeffler, Jack, Katherine Loeffler, and Enrique R. Lamadrid. 1999. *La Música de los Viejitos: Hispano Folk Music of the Río Grande del Norte.* Albuquerque: University of New Mexico Press.

Lucero-White Lea, Aurora. 1953. *Literary Folklore of the Hispanic Southwest.* San Antonio, Tex.: Naylor Company.

Luján, Josie Espinoza de. 1992. *Los Moros y Cristianos: A Spectacular Historic Drama.* Chimayó, N.Mex.: J. Espinoza de Luján.

Lummis, Charles. 1912. *A New Mexico David and Other Stories and Sketches of the Southwest.* New York: C. Scribner's Sons. (Originally published 1981.).

Márez, Curtis. 2001. "Signifying Spain, Becoming Comanche, Making Mexicans: Indian Captivity and the History of Chicana/o Popular Performance." *American Quarterly* 53(2):267–307.

———. 2002. "The Rough Ride through Empire: 'Los Comanches' after 1898." In *Recovering the U.S. Hispanic Literary Heritage,* vol. 3. Houston: Arte Público Press.

Martínez, Antonio "Galento." 1983. Interview with author, Alcalde, N.Mex., December 27.

Martínez, María C. 2001. "Antoine Leroux fue trampero, guía y primo." *El Crepúsculo/Taos News,* Thursday, April 26, 2001:B9.

Martínez, Paul G. N.d. "*Los Comanches,* a Play Celebrated Yearly." (Typescript.) In W.P.A. Files, File 5, Drawer 5, Folder 45. Santa Fe: New Mexico Historical Library.

Martínez, Roberto. 1985. Interview with author, Albuquerque, N.Mex., September 6.

Mauldin, Barbara. 2002. Interview with author, Santa Fe, N.Mex., February 14.

McWilliams, Carey. 1990. *North from Mexico : The Spanish-speaking People of the United States.* New York: Greenwood Press.

Medrano de Luna, Gabriel. 1999. "Danza de indios de Mesillas, Tepezalá, Aguascalientes." Aguascalientes, Mexico: Colegio de Michoacán, Centro de Estudios de las Tradiciones/Instituto Cultural de Aguascalientes.

Meléndez, A. Gabriel. 1997. *So All Is Not Lost: The Poetics of Print in Nuevomexicano Communities, 1834–1958.* Albuquerque: University of New Mexico Press.

Mendoza, Vicente T., and Virginia R. R. de Mendoza. 1986. *Estudio y clasificación de la música tradicional hispánica de Nuevo México.* México: Universidad Nacional Autónoma de México.

Montoya, Alfredo. 1993. Interview with author, Alcalde, N.Mex., December 27.

Mora, Andy. 1991. Interview with author, Bernalillo, N.Mex., February 12.

Nieto-Phillips, John. 2000. "Spanish American Ethnic Identity and New Mexico's Statehood Struggle." In *The Contested Homeland: A Chicano History of New Mexico*. Edited by Erlinda Gonzales-Berry and David R. Maciel, 97–142. Albuquerque: University of New Mexico Press:.

Noyes, Stanley. 1993. *Los Comanches: The Horse People, 1751–1845*. Albuquerque: University of New Mexico Press.

Ong, Walter. 1982. *Orality and Literacy: The Technologizing of the Word*. New York: Routledge.

Ortiz y Pino Family Papers. N.d. "Los Comanches: A Historical Drama from New Mexico's Colonial Period." Center for Southwest Research, University of New Mexico, MSS 336, BC Box 1.

Ortiz, Alfonso. 1991. Interview with author, Albuquerque, N.Mex., September 23.

Ortiz, Alfonso, ed. 1972. *New Perspectives on the Pueblos*. Albuquerque: University of New Mexico Press.

Ortiz, Fernando. 1978. *Contrapunto Cubano*. Caracas: Biblioteca Ayacucho.

Padilla, Genaro. 1993. "Discontinuous Continuities: Remapping the Terrain of Spanish Colonial Narrative." In *Reconstructing a Chicano/a Literary Heritage*, ed. María Herrera-Sobek, 24–36. Tucson: University of Arizona Press:.

Padilla, Jerry A. 1998. "El Comanche." *La Herencia del Norte* 19:31–32.

———. 2001. Interview with author, Taos, N.Mex., May 31.

Paredes, Américo. 1994[1958]. *With his Pistol in his Hand: A Border Ballad and its Hero*. Austin: University of Texas Press.

Parker, Diana. 2001. Interview with author, Washington, D.C., March 19.

Parkhill, Forbes. 1965. *The Blazed Trail of Antoine Leroux*. Los Angeles: Westernlore Press.

Peña, Abe M. 1994. "Los Comanches." *La Herencia del Norte* 4:19.

———. 1997. "Los Comanches." In *Memories of Cíbola: Stories from New Mexico Villages*, 51–52. Albuquerque: University of New Mexico Press:.

Pettit, Arthur G. 1980. *Images of the Mexican American in Fiction and Film*. College Station: Texas A & M Press.

Pino, Pedro Baptista. 1995[1812]. *Exposición sucinta y sencilla de la provincia del Nuevo México*. Trans. and ed. Adrian Bustamante and Marc Simmons. Albuquerque: University of New Mexico Press.

Powers, William K. 1987. "The Vocable: An Evolutionary Perspective." In *Beyond the Vision: Essays on American Indian Culture*, 7–36. Norman: University of Oklahoma Press.

Pratt, Mary Louise. 1992. *Imperial Eyes: Travel Writing and Transculturation*. London: Routledge.

Price, Richard, and Sally Price. 1994. *On the Mall: Presenting Tradition Bearers at the 1992 Festival of American Folklife*. Bloomington, Indiana: Special Publications of the Folklore Institute, No. 4.

Punzo, José Luis. 2002. Interview with author, Casas Grandes, Chihuahua, Mexico, December 10.

Rael y Gálvez, Estevan. 2000. "Mal-criando Entre-metidos: Identifying Captivity and Capturing Identity in New Mexico and Colorado's Narratives of Indigenous Slavery and Peonage." Paper delivered at Zimmerman Library, University of New Mexico, July 18.

Rafaelita Salazar Baca, Eufemia Salazar Trujillo, Vangie Salazar Armijo, and Ida Salazar Segura. 1997. "'Inditas' from Los Comanches, San Mateo, New Mexico." Lamadrid archive.

Raines, Lester. 1936. "Los Comanches." (Typescript.) In W.P.A. Files, File 5, Drawer 5, Folder 45. Santa Fe: New Mexico Historical Library.

Rama, Angel. 1982. *Transculturación narrativa en América Latina*. México: Siglo Veintiuno.

Rebolledo, Tey Diana, and María Teresa Márquez. 2000. *Women's Tales from the New Mexico WPA: La Diabla a Pie*. Houston: Arte Público Press.

Rebolledo, Tey Diana, ed.; associate eds. Erlinda Gonzales-Berry and Millie Santillanes. 1992. *Nuestras Mujeres: Hispanas of New Mexico: Their Images and Their Lives, 1582–1992*. Albuquerque: El Norte/Academia Publications.

Redfield, Robert. 1930. *Tepoztlán, A Mexican Village: A Study of Folk Life*. Chicago: University of Chicago Press.

Revista Popular de Nuevo México 28(38) (miércoles 25 de septiembre de 1929).

Richardson, Rupert N. 1933. *The Comanche Barrier to South Plains Settlement; A Century and a Half of Savage Resistance to the Advancing White Frontier.* Glendale, Calif.: Arthur H. Clark.

Rivera, José. 1987. Interview with author, Albuquerque, N.Mex., October 3.

Robb, John Donald. 1980. *Hispanic Folk Music of New Mexico and the Southwest: A Self-Portrait of a People.* Norman: University of Oklahoma Press.

Rodríguez, Sylvia. 1994. *The Taos Fiesta: Invented Tradition and the Infrapolitics of Symbolic Reclamation.* Albuquerque: Southwest Hispanic Research Institute, University of New Mexico.

———. 1996. *The Matachines Dance: Ritual Symbolism and Interethnic Relations in the Upper Río Grande Valley.* Albuquerque: University of New Mexico Press.

Roeder, Beatrice A. 1976. "Los Comanches: A Bicentennial Folk Play." *Bilingual Review* 3:213–20.

Romero, Brenda M. 1991. "The Matachines of Alcalde, New Mexico." Ph.D. diss., University of California at Los Angeles.

———. 2002. "The Indita Genre of New Mexico: Gender and Cultural Identification." In *Chicana Traditions: Continuity and Change,* ed. Norma E. Cantú and Olga Nájera-Ramirez, 62–80. Champaign: University of Illinois Press.

Rosaldo, Renato. 1989. *Culture and Truth: The Remaking of Social Analysis.* Boston: Beacon Press.

Roybal, José Alvarado. N.d. "Los Comanches." (Manuscript.) From El Rancho, 1930s, directed by his father, Martín. Recovered by Alfonso R. Sánchez, in Las Cruces. (Lamadrid archive, 2001).

Salazar Armijo, Vangie. 2003. Interview with author, Bernalillo, N.Mex., May 9.

Salazar Baca, Rafaelita, Eufemia Salazar Trujillo, Vangie Salazar Armijo, and Ida Salazar Segura. 1997. "'Inditas' from Los Comanches, San Mateo, New Mexico." Lamadrid archive.

Salazar Segura, Ida. 1997. Interview with author, Los Griegos, N.Mex., January 5.

Sánchez, Tomás. 1992. Interview with author, Alcalde, N.Mex., May 7.

Sando, Joseph. 1998. Interview with author, Albuquerque, N.Mex., September 16.

Sedillo, Mela. 1945. *Mexican and New Mexican Folkdances.* Albuquerque: University of New Mexico Press.

Simmons, Marc. 1961. "On the Trail of the Comancheros." *New Mexico Magazine* 39:30–33, 39.

———. 1973. *The Little Lion of the Southwest: A Life of Manuel Antonio Chaves.* Chicago: Sage Books/Swallow Press.

———. 1988. *New Mexico: An Interpretive History.* Albuquerque: University of New Mexico Press.

Singer, Beverly. 2001. Interview with author, Albuquerque, N.Mex., September 16.

Sklar, Deidre. 2001. *Dancing with the Virgin: Body and Faith in the Fiesta of Tortugas, New Mexico.* Berkeley: University of California Press.

Smithsonian-Folkways. 1992. *Music of New Mexico: Hispanic Traditions* (CD SF 40409). Washington, D.C.: Smithsonian-Folkways.

Spicer, Edward H. 1954. "Spanish-Indian Acculturation in the Southwest." *American Anthropologist* 56:663–78.

———. 1958. "Social Structure and the Acculturation Process." *American Anthropologist* 60:433–41.

———. 1962. *Cycles of Conquest; The Impact of Spain, Mexico, and the United States on the Indians of the Southwest, 1533-1960.* Tucson: University of Arizona Press.

———. 1972. *Plural Society in the Southwest.* New York: Weatherhead Foundation.

Steiner, Stan, and Luis Valdez, eds. 1972. *Aztlan: An Anthology of Mexican American Literature.* New York: Vintage Books.

Sweet, Jill D. 1978. "Ritual Play, Role Reversal, and Humor: Symbolic Elements of a Tewa Pueblo Navajo Dance." *Dance Research Annual* 9 (New York: Congress on Research in Dance).

———. 1983. "Ritual and Theatre in Tewa Ceremonial Performances." *Journal of the Society for Ethnomusicology* 27(2):253–69.

———. 1985. *Dances of the Tewa Pueblo Indians: Expressions of New Life.* Santa Fe, N.Mex.: School of American Research.

———. 1999. "Dance: Folk and Ritual Drama." In *A Dictionary of Folklore,* ed. David Pickering. New York: Facts on File.

Tafoya, Cristino. N.d. "'Inditas' from *Los Comanches*, Cochití and Peña Blanca, New Mexico." Lamadrid archive.

Taos Valley News. 1929a. "A Play Most Spectacular." September 26, 1929:1.

———. 1929b. "Los Comanches." October 3, 1929:1.

Taussig, Michael. 1987. *Shamanism, Colonialism, and the Wild Man: A Study in Terror and Healing*. Chicago: University of Chicago Press.

Taylor, Ralph C. 1963. *Colorado, South of the Border*. Denver: Sage Books: 286.

Thomas, Alfred Barnaby. 1932. *Forgotten Frontiers: A Study of the Spanish Indian Policy of Don Juan Bautista de Anza, Governor of New Mexico, 1777–1787*. Norman: University of Oklahoma Press.

Torres, Larry, trans. and illustrator. 1999. *Six Nuevomexicano Folk Dramas for Advent Season*. Albuquerque: University of New Mexico Press.

———, trans. 2002. "Los Comanches." In *Herencia: The Anthology of Hispanic Literature of the United States*, by Nicolás Kanellos, Kenya Dworkin y Méndez, et al., 70–86. Oxford: Oxford University Press:.

Trujillo, Floyd. 1992. Interview with author, Washington, D.C., June 30.

Trujillo, Rosa. 1985. Interview with author, Grants, N.Mex., November 6.

Turner, Victor. 1974. *Dramas, Fields, and Metaphors; Symbolic Action in Human Society*. Ithaca, N.Y.: Cornell University Press.

Valerio, Ivan, Jr., and Ivan Valerio, Sr. 2002. Interview with author, Ranchos de Taos, N.Mex., August 25.

Van Stone, Mary R., record. and ed. 1933. *Los Pastores: Excerpts from an Old Christmas Play of the Southwest as Given Annually by the Griegos Family of Santa Fe, New Mexico*. Cleveland: Gates Press.

Vásquez, Dora Ortiz. 1975. *Enchanted Temples of Taos: My Story of Rosario*. Santa Fe: Rydal Press.

Vennum, Thomas. 2001. Interview with author, Washington, D.C., April 8.

Vialpando Lara, Roberto. 1992. Interview with author, Alcalde, N.Mex., January 1.

Vialpando, Roberto. 1963. "Antiguo juego dramático del folklore Nuevo Mexicano: Los comanches." (Typescript) Acto de Preservación, 1963. Lamadrid archive, 1979.

Vigil, Cleofes. 1992[1976]. "Himno a la nacioncita de la sangre de Cristo." In *Music of New Mexico, Hispanic Traditions* (CD SF 40409). Washington, D.C.: Smithsonian-Folkways.

Vigil, Michael. 1991. Interview with author, Tesuque, N.Mex., February 2.

Villagrá, Gaspar Pérez de. 1992. *Historia de la Nueva Mexico, 1610*. Trans. and ed. Miguel Encinias, Alfred Rodríguez, and Joseph P. Sánchez. Albuquerque: University of New Mexico Press.

Wallace, Ernest, and E. Adamson Hoebel. 1952. *The Comanches: Lords of the South Plains*. Civilization of the American Indian Series, vol. 34. Norman: University of Oklahoma Press.

Wapp, Edward. 1998. Interview with author, Santa Fe, N.Mex., March 30.

West, John O., ed. 1988. *Mexican-American Folklore: Legends, Songs, Festivals, Proverbs, Crafts, Tales of Saints, of Revolutionaries, and More*. Little Rock: August House.

Williams, María. 2000. Interview with author, Albuquerque, N.Mex., October 4.

Wilson, Chris. 1997. *The Myth of Santa Fe: Creating a Modern Regional Tradition*. Albuquerque: University of New Mexico Press.

Woodward, Arthur, ed. 1956. *Journal of Lieutenant Thomas W. Sweeney*. Los Angeles: Westernlore Press.

WPA. 1989. *The WPA Guide to 1930's New Mexico: Compiled by the Workers of the Writers' Program of the Works Projects Administration in the State of New Mexico*. Foreword by Marc Simmons. Tucson: University of Arizona Press.

Wroth, Will. 1983 *"La Sangre de Cristo:* History and Symbolism." In *Hispanic Arts and Ethnohistory in the Southwest: New Papers Inspired by the Work of E. Boyd*, ed. Marta Weigle, 283–92. Santa Fe: Ancient City:.

Young, Robert J. C. 1995. Colonial Desire: Hybridity in Theory, Culture and Race. London: Routledge.

Index

love lyrics, 149–50
Lucero, Rafael, 69, 242n. 3
Luhan, Mabel Dodge, 182
lullabies and laments, 92–101
Lummis, Charles, 184, 185, 242n. 5

Malinche (spirit guide), **2**, 74
Mansos, 83
Manueles Fiesta, 7, 141
Márez, Curtis, 53, 66, 242n.7, 245n. 4
Márquez, José, 6
Martín, Sebastián, 68, 183
Martínez, Alfredo, 158
Martínez, Antonio José, 176
Martínez, Galento, 75
Martínez, Jesús Armando, 126
Martínez, Noé, 73
Martínez, Roberto, 101
Martínez, Rosario "Ma-ya-yo", 176
Martínez, Tony "Galento", 6
Matachines dance (*Los Matachines*), 1, 15, 25, 72–75, 88, 127, 197
mayordomos, 73, 112
McWilliams, Carey, 241n. 7
Mendinueta, Pedro Fermín de, 53, 66, 67
mestizaje, 9, 13
mestizos, xi, xii, 177, 190–91, 193, 202; disregarding culture of, 9; growing interest in traditions of, 192; roots of discourse, 13
Mexican-American War, 27
Mexico, 13, 15, 82, 83, 86, 152, 190
Michoacán, Mexico, 152
Miera y Pacheco, Bernardo: map by, 29, 30
mock combat, 21
Moctezuma, **2**
Monclova, Mexico, 83
Montoya, Alfredo, 75
Mora, Andrés, 120
Mora, NM, 101, 158
Moros y cristianos (folk drama), 20–26, 51, 66, 69, 89, 197; assimilation rather than annihilation in, 25; enactment at Chimayó, **23**, **24**; excerpt of script from Chimayó performance, 21–24; hidden transcripts in, 21; and intimidation of Pueblo Indians, **24**
multiple border zones, 14
music, xii, 1, 15, 153, 178, **194**, 202. *See also* song scores with lyrics; songs

Nanillé music, **194**
National Hispanic Cultural Center, 202
nationalism, 179, 184
Native culture: idealization of, 191

Navajos, 15, 43, 79, 81, 82, 91, 104, 105, 133, 137, 149, 152, 168, 176, 177, 185; and music, 178, 202
Ndeh, 82
nepantla, 15
New Mexico: complex cultural diversity of, 9; cultural history of, 193; Indo-Hispano communities in, 85(map); statehood, 182, 191
New Mexico Folklore Society, 184
New Mexico Magazine, 102
New Mexico Writers' Project, 184, 185
newspapers, 182
Nuevo Mexicanos, xi, 31; defined, 240n. 1
Nuevo México Cuarto Centenario, 195, 197
Numunuh, 1, 10, 11, 15, 28, 56, 79, 83, 104, 105, 135, 141, 152, 168, 177, 180, 181, 183–84, 186, 202, 203; and adoption of captives, 154; annual pilgrimage to New Mexico, 38; and assimilation of other groups, 81; combat with Apaches, 147; and ethnonymic designations, 241n. 1; first appearance in historical documents, 136; history of, 30–38; little contemporary social contact with, 203; most formidable foe in New Mexico, 51; and music, 178, 202; scalp dance song, 153; seasonal visits to Río Grande Valley, 181

Ojo Caliente, NM, 33, 34, 73
Ojo Sarco, NM, 73
Oklahoma, 38, 105, 136, 146, 154, 177, 180
Old Ciénega Museum, 188
Onacama (Numunuh chief), 186, 187
Oñate, Juan de, 21, 27, 197; human rights record of, 195
Oñate Cultural Center: and removal of foot from statue, 195
oral history, 41, 136, 181, 185, 186
oral tradition, 43, 69, 135, 185, 186, 187
Orejas del Conejo, 55; massacre at, 62, 67
Ortiz, Alfonso, 9, 17
Ortiz, Emilio, **103**
Ortiz, Fernando, 14
Ortiz, Toribio (folk drama character), 53, 76
Oso Pardo (folk drama character), 61, 63
Otero, Rosanna, 89
Otos, 31

Padilla, Genero, 52
Padilla, Jerry, 188
padrinos, 91
Palace of the Governors, 28, 36
Palo Duro Canyon, 38